Vāstu, Astrology and Architecture

Vāstu, Astrology and Architecture

(Papers presented at the First All India Symposium on Vāstu, Bangalore, held on June 3-4, 1995)

GAYATRI DEVI VASUDEV

MOTILAL BANARSIDASS PUBLISHERS
PRIVATE LIMITED • DELHI

4th Reprint: Delhi, 2015
First Edition: Delhi, 1998

ISBN: 978-81-208-1605-3 (Cloth)
ISBN: 978-81-208-1606-0 (Paper)

MOTILAL BANARSIDASS
41 U.A. Bungalow Road, Jawahar Nagar, Delhi 110 007
8 Mahalaxmi Chamber, 22 Bhulabhai Desai Road, Mumbai 400 026
203 Royapettah High Road, Mylapore, Chennai 600 004
236, 9th Main III Block, Jayanagar, Bengaluru 560 011
Sanas Plaza, 1302 Baji Rao Road, Pune 411 002
8 Camac Street, Kolkata 700 017
Ashok Rajpath, Patna 800 004
Chowk, Varanasi 221 001

Printed in India
by RP Jain at NAB Printing Unit,
A-44, Naraina Industrial Area, Phase I, New Delhi–110028
and published by JP Jain for Motilal Banarsidass Publishers (P) Ltd,
41 U.A. Bungalow Road, Jawahar Nagar, Delhi-110007

Editor's Note

We are happy to bring out this collection of papers read at the First All India Symposium on *Vāstu* held on June 3 and 4, 1995, at the Banquet Hall of the Vidhana Saudha, Bangalore. The Symposium was organised by Raman Rajeswari Research Foundation, Bangalore.

Vāstu Śāstra, an important limb of *Jyotiṣa* or astrology, is the science and study of ancient architecture and engineering. *Vāstu* rules have been followed meticulously in temple and town construction of ancient times. Many temples, such as the Tirupati Sri Venkatesvara Temple and the Ramesvaram Temple are standing monuments to the profundity and correctness of *Vāstu* principles.

As a result of political convulsions in India, the science of *Jyotiṣa* which includes *Vāstu*, was neglected for a long time. Thanks to untiring efforts of Dr. B.V. Raman, Editor, *The Astrological Magazine*, *Jyotiṣa* or astrology is being revived with great interest in the country.

The principles of *Vāstu* are now being explored and applied with excellent results in the construction of residential buildings, including official quarters, commercial complexes, hotels, amusement centres, business premises, public buildings such as schools and hospitals as also industries. In fact, renovation and reconstruction of sick units in accordance with principles of *Vāstu* have led to greater prosperity.

The goals of this Symposium were:

1. To bring before discerning public and intelligentsia the lost glory of *Vāstu* and its relevance to modern times.
2. To present research findings by *Vāstu* scholars which validate ancient *Vāstu* principles.
3. To promote free exchange of ideas on *Vāstu* between scholars of *Vāstu* and modern architects and engineers.

4. To revive and promote a study of *Vāstu* in its application to house construction, public buildings, commercial complexes and construction of temples, gurudwaras and other places of worship.

The fact that the Symposium was held under our banner and was able to bring together for the first time best men in the field on a national level, was a matter of great gratification for all interested in an ancient Vedic culture, especially *Jyotiṣa* and its various aspects including *Vāstu Vidyā.*

Many of the papers presented by galaxy of speakers on different aspects of science and technology of *Vāstu* at the Symposium could not be included in the Souvenir released on the occasion and have been included in this volume. A few of the papers have already appeared in the Symposium Souvenir, but since only a limited number of copies were brought out for the occasion, they have also been included in this volume. We believe these papers will stimulate greater interest in *Vāstu* amongst modern architects and engineers and impress upon academic bodies the need to include this Vedic science in the engineering course as part of curriculum. We thank all those who presented the papers included in this volume.

The papers have been divided into three Sections—"Vāstu and Its Relevance to Modern Times" (Section I); "Vāstu and Jyotiṣa" (Section II) and "Vāstu and Temple Architecture" (Section III). However, it has not been possible to rigidly compartmentalise the papers in terms of content into these three sections and some overlapping has been unavoidable.

Thanks are due to Prof. N.M. Kansaria for his commendable assistance in thorough revision of the Sanskrit quotations and his transliteration of Sanskrit Ślokas and terms into the Roman script.

We are thankful to Mr. J.P. Jain of Motilal Banarsidass for having come forward to bring out all papers in a book form.

4.9.1995 GAYATRI DEVI VASUDEV

Contents

Section I

VĀSTU AND ITS RELEVANCE TO MODERN TIMES

Relevance of *Vāstu*

*Dr. B.V. Raman**

A study of ancient literature bearing on *Jyotiṣa*, medicine, *Vāstu*, etc., will reveal that the vision of ancient sages was far more deeply based on, and intimately correlated to the realities and values of life than dreamt of in modern times.

A careful examination of Hindu methodology which is necessary for a right understanding of Hindu attainments in *Vāstu Śāstra* reveals that the whole movement was genuinely and positively scientific, the ultimate goal being spiritual; and it was arrested at an important stage due to political convulsions.

Though perception, observation and experiment were the main criteria of truth, institutional wisdom, now neglected in the name of scientific temper, was mainly responsible for development of disciplines like *Jyotiṣa*, *Vāstu*, etc.

Today we are surrounded by fanatical advocates of the one and only method and that is the so-called scientific method. Any one who honestly stresses the limits of this scientific method is dubbed as an obscurantist. As Whitehead says: "Today it is our scientists who, entrenched in their orthodoxy, are refusing to look at every evidence falling outside the purview of their own blinkered methodology."

Ever since Galileo, Descartes and Newton, Western scientific culture, confused in India as modern, has been obsessed with the so-called rational knowledge, objectivity and quantification, that intuition and subjective knowledge are completely ignored.

Many English-educated Indians, while showing a high level of intellectual ability, are generally alienated from their own scientific and spiritual heritage, of which *Vāstu*

* Editor, *The Astrological Magazine*, "Sri Rajeswari", 115/1, New Extension, Sheshadripuram, Bangalore-560 020.

forms an important part.

Many of them are not aware because they are not taught, or they have not learnt, of the original contributions made in ancient India to the cause of knowledge in general and science in particular, independent of Western influence.

Whenever reference is made to the importance of *Jyotiṣa*, *Vāstu*, *Praśna*, etc., flippant and derogatory views are aired in the name of scientific temper, rationalism, etc. Paradoxically, many of the critics themselves make full use of *Jyotiṣa* or *Vāstu* when their own interests are involved. This schism between logical and analytical on the one hand, and intuitive and cognitive on the other, never characterised ancient Indian thought.

We must understand that the frame-work designed by the scientist to bring in any knowledge within the purview of laws known to it is as brittle as the frame-work of the scientists of 16th century when science in Europe was dominated by Church. Galileo was persecuted because he expressed views not acceptable to the scientists of those times.

Luckily there is no fear of our meeting with the same fate when claims of some of the scientists are questioned. We live in a land where even two thousands years ago the *Cārvākas* (materialists and atheists) along with *Ācāryas* lived together indulging in intellectual battles which ultimately resulted in the rout of the Cārvāka mischief.

Therefore, it behoves all patriotic Indians to study, understand and take pride in their ancient scientific heritage and not dismiss it as of no relevance to modern times or modern India.

An essential difference between the approach of Rishes and modern science is that the former is comprehensive, integral, holistic and spiritual; while the latter is mostly adhoc, fragmentary, reductionist and mechanistic.

According to Indian tradition, eighteen sages, such as Bhṛgu, Atri, Vaśiṣṭha, Viśvakarma, Maya, etc., have established the science of *Vāstu*. Amongst the more important works we have *Viśvakarma-Vāstu-śastra*, *Samarāṅgaṇa-sūtradhāra*, *Maṇḍana-sūtradhāra*, *Rājasiṁha-Vāstu*,

Dīpārṇava, *Śilparatna* and *Mayamata*. There are other works which are generally based on one or the other of the classics. *Vāstu* is also dealt with in the Āgamas, such as the *Karṇikāgama*, *Suprabhedāgama*, *Vaikhānasāgama*, etc., and works on Tantra, such as the *Hayaśīrṣa-tantra*, *Kiraṇas-tantra*, and Purāṇas such as the *Agnipurāṇa*, *Matsyapurāṇa* and *viṣṇudharmottara-purāṇa*, etc.

It is interesting to note that Dr. Robert Pinotti II, an Italian scientist, observed at the World Space Conference that in the text of the great classical work on *Vāstu*, *Samarāṅgaṇa-sūtradhāra*, there were 230 stanzas devoted to the principles of constructing Vimānas and their use in peace and war. Dr. Pinotti says that it will be better to examine the Hindu texts instead of dismissing the traditions as myths.

Vāstu principles are more or less common all over India, living from times immemorial as a cultural entity. *Vāstu* has retained its traditions for thousands of years and it is as relevant today as it was when first propounded. There are also *Vāstu* texts for Jainism and Buddhism, such as, the *Gautamīyam*, *Bauddhamatam* and *Caitya*. The *Vāstu* Śilpa traditions is purely Indian in its fundamental concepts and currency.

There is a belief that the text of the *Bṛhat-saṁhitā*, has as its source the work *Mānasāra*, though there are some differences of opinion regarding this. Mānasāra is a comprehensive treatise on architecture and iconography. According to Mr. P.K. Acharya, the editor of the work, it is considered to be a "source of all presentations of architecture in Purāṇa and Āgama as well as in more specialised texts such as the *Brihat Samhita* and *Mayamata*. In fact this treatise is identified as a *Vāstu Śāstra*, the first *Vāstu* being the earth".

Mānasāra represents the universality of *Vāstu* tradition and contains also the iconography of Jain and Buddhist images. This work is universally consulted all over India.

The literature on *Vāstu* can be roughly classified as *Śilpa Śāstra* and *Gṛha Vāstu* or *Devaśilpa* and *Mānavaśilpa*. It is said that the Saivite and Vaiṣṇavite Āgamas of various persuasions as well as the *Gṛhya Sūtras* and the *Arthaśāstra* contain abundant material on *Vāstu*, but somewhat scattered.

Of all the various treatises on *Vāstu*, the *Mayamata* is said to occupy a very important place. It is a general treatise on *Vāstu Śāstra*, written in Sanskrit, but originating from South India. It is said to be part of Śaivite Āgamic literature free from sectarianism and it might have been authored during the Choḷa period when architecture, it describes, had reached the peak of its maturity. In fact many *Vāstu* experts and Sthapatis feel that the *Mayamata* is the best known amongst Sanskrit treatises dealing with architecture and iconography. The work is coherent. It defines *Vāstu* as anywhere wherein immortals or mortals live.

Maya was not only an expert in *Vāstu* but also in *Jyotiṣa*. Whoever be this Maya, the *Mayamata* confers on the architect the task of putting into practice what is prescribed. Inspite of the constraints, an architect has also considerable latitude at his disposal. Sectarianism is completely absent. Maya has been described as a divine architect and an expert as Viśvakarman. He is also author of the famous astronomical treatise, the *Sūrya-siddhānta*, a source book for all Pañcāṅga calculations. It is possible that both these treatises were authored by the same Maya.

The uses of *Vāstu* have been well described in the *Samarāṅgaṇa-sūtradhara*. What is *Vāstu*? The word *Vāstu* is derived from the word *vasu*, or the earth. The earth is the principal *Vāstu* and all the buildings, situated on the earth are also *Vāstu*. Apart from this, whatever is created from *Vāstu* or objects of the earth are also *Vāstu*:

भूरेव मुख्यं वस्तु स्यात् तत्र जातानि यानि हि।
प्रासादादीनि वस्तूनि वस्तुत्वात् वस्तुसंश्रयात्॥

bhūr eva mukhyaṁ vastu syāt tatra Jātāni yāni hi /
prāsādādīni vastūni vastutvāt vastu-saṁśrayat //

Modern engineers and architects may be interested to know that valuable information is also available even in respect of materials to be used. For instance, according to Hiraṇyagarbha, there are different kinds of houses based on the materials used for construction. Built by stones is *Mandira*; of baked bricks *Vāstu*; of raw bricks *Sumanta*; of mud *Sudhara*; of wooden logs or bamboos *Nandaka*; of varieties of straw *Kelina*.

Vāstu Śāstra cannot be divorced from Jyotiṣa. It is worthwhile studying by a team of scientists - of course. Today many of them are indifferent to most of the great disciplines of ancient India. It looks as if in *Vāstu* much importance is given to the Sun's movements in the heavens in placing the construction of a house in such a manner that more open space is left and more windows and doors are provided towards east and north than towards west and south so that a house is exposed to maximum influence of solar energy.

To suggest that ancient sages were not aware of the existence and operation of various forms of energy coming from the Sun is not correct. It is possible that, though not said in so many words but explained in a language commonly understood, they were aware of different forms of energies radiating from the Sun and planets and various field-forces in different seasons.

Modern engineers, house builders and architects will be surprised to know how our *Vāstu* experts devised simple methods and most inexpensive contrivancies for examining a site, measuring and taking possession of it, orientation, etc. They are advised to study carefully what is called *Ayādivarga*. This is said to enable one to find out the fitness of the structure and ensure well-being of both the builder and owner. Terms like *Dhvajāva*, *Siṁhāya*, *Vṛṣabhāya*, *Gajāya*, etc., are said to be auspicious; while those like *Dhūmāya*, *Śvānāya*, *Kharāya*, etc., are inauspicious.

According to the *Samarāṅgaṇa sūtradhāra*, the *ayas* have to do with measurements of a building. These *ayas* are obtained by a certain manipulation of numbers:

e.g. (area × 9)/8 - while the remainder indicates the *aya*. There are also clear indications as to the flaws to be avoided in construction of a house to ensure a long life to a building and happiness to the owner. For example, the *Samarānganaṇasūtradhāra* cautions a house-builder in the following terms:

एवंविधं दोषकरं गृहं स्याद् भर्तुश्च कर्तुश्च यतस्तुदेते ।
ज्ञेयाः सदा शिल्पिभिरप्रमत्तैस्त्याज्याश्च दोषाः शुभकीर्तिकामैः ॥
evaṁvidhaṁ doṣakaraṁ gṛhaṁ syād Bhartuś ca kartuś ca yatas tudete /
jñeyāḥ sadā śilpibhir apramattaiṣ Tyājyāś ca doṣāḥ śubhakīrtikāmaiḥ //

'A house constructed with any *doṣas* will result in suffering to the builder and the owner. Those desiring happiness and fame are advised to construct a house without any *doṣas*.'

According to the *Viśvakarma-prakāśikā*, sixteen *doṣas* are possible and these should be avoided:

अन्धकं रूधिरं चैव कुब्जं काणं बधीरकम् ।
दिग्वक्त्रं चिपिटं चैव व्यङ्गजं मरणं तदा ॥
कुटिलं कुब्जकं चैवं सुप्तं च शङ्खपालकम् ।
विघटं च कथारकं कैङ्करं षोडशं स्मृतम् ॥
andhakaṁ rudhiraṁ caiva kubjaṁ kāṇaṁ badhīrakam /
digvaktraṁ cipiṭaṁ caiva vyaṅgajaṁ maraṇam tathā//
kuṭilaṁ kubjakaṁ caiva suptaṁ ca Śaṅkhapālakam /
vighaṭaṁ ca kathārakaṁ kainkaraṁ ṣodaśaṁ smṛtam//

They are: *Andhaka, Rudhira, Kubja, Kāṇa, Badhīraka, Digvaktra, Cipiṭa, Vyaṅgaja, Maraṇa, Kuṭila, Kubjaka, Supta, Śaṅkhapālaka, Vighaṭa, Kathāraka,* and *Kaiṅkara*. To mention a few: *Andhaka* having no windows; *Rudhira* having disproportionate doors; *Kubja* having small doors, *Digvaktra* having disproportionate windows; *Śaṅkhapālika* without pillars, *Badhiraka* having doors without lintels, etc.

Then there are also ten types of *Vedha-doṣas*:

अन्धके रोगमतुलं रूधिरेऽतिसारजं भयम् ।
कुब्जे कुष्ठादिरोगः स्यात् काणेऽन्धत्वं प्रजायते ॥
पृथ्विद्वारे सर्वदुःखं मरणं वा प्रजायते।
दिग्वक्त्रे गर्भनाशः स्याच्चिपिटे नीचसङ्गतिः॥
andhake rogam atulaṁ rudhire 'tisārajaṁ bhayam /

kubje kuṣṭhādirogaḥ syāt kāne 'ndhatvaṁ prajāyate //
pṛthvi-dvāre sarva-duḥkhaṁ maraṇam vā prajāyate /
digvaktre garbhanāśaḥ syac cipiṭe nīca-saṅgatiḥ //

Each *vedha* or obstruction would result in some unfortunate happenings. For instance, *Andhaka-vedha* denotes frequent illness to the family. *Kubja-vedha* denotes Karmic diseases like leprosy; *Kāṇa-vedha* indicates blindness to the owner, etc. It is cautioned that a literal interpretation of the results is not called for.

All these can be studied by modern architects. No house of the shape of a triangle should be built as it is said to cause early death to the owner and to remain unused for a long time: त्रिकोणे निधनं शीघ्रं गृहं दीर्घं निरर्थकम्। (*Trikoṇe nidhanaṁ śīghraṁ gṛhaṁ dīrghaṁ nirarthakam*). These details are given so that one can have an idea of their depth of the study of this problem.

Other important rules are given for the construction of public buildings. According to the *Gupta-Vāstu*, when constructing schools and other teaching places, walls in the East and North must be constructed first. The Southern and Western walls are to be constructed next. It is also not advisable to have a common wall for two buildings. There are other helpful hints. For instance, if an old house is to be reconstructed only new wood should be used. Nor should one use old wood for a new construction. There is no aspect of human habitat - homes, factories, offices, etc., which cannot find a place in the *Vāstu* scheme.

After acquiring possession of a site, the first thing is to test the soil: पूर्वं भूमिं परीक्षते पश्चाल्लक्षण मुच्यताम्। (*Pūrvam bhumiṁ parīkṣeta pasicāl lakṣanam ucyatām*). Ancient masters have divided the soil into three categories based on its quality, viz., the best (*uttama*), the middle one (*madhyama*), and ordinary (*adhama*). The soil should be examined with reference to its taste (*rasa*), colour (*varṇa*), touch (*sparśa*), smell (*gandha*), etc.

Architects and engineers will do well to study *Vāstu Śāstra* in details so that they can appreciate the ancient masters, in the words of Michael Jamsen, who was in India sometimes ago, after researching in Chinese architecture and who said: "The Hindu people of the past made full use of the Sun's radiance from Jaipur in the North to Kancheepuram in the South."

Look at the temples built in our country more than one thousand years ago. Most of them are still intact because they were constructed according to *Vāstu Śāstra* which takes into consideration the effects of planetary movements, earth's atmosphere, the magnetic and gravitational fields and other forces. It is because of these considerations that important functions are always done when the Sun is in the northern hemisphere or Uttarāyaṇa, recognising these factors and also the importance of the magnetic field. Every object in nature radiates energy in some form or the other, which today is said to be amenable to Kirlian photography. In Gṛha-*Vāstu*, the materials collected for building a structure itself, involve the influx and interaction of a series of invisible forces that the time selected should be capable of screening off the destructive forces and calling into action the constructive ones.

Then we have the marvellous conception of *Vāstu Puruṣa* or Space Personified, just as Jyotiṣa considers *Kāla Puruṣa* or Time Personified. Concepts about Space and Time were not new to our ancient sages. They had established a scientific concept of not only space and time, but also space-time based on their intuitive wisdom. According to Sage Vyāsa, Time does not exist independently; but it has a relative material existence.

That Time has a form of existence of matter is a concept established in modern times by Einstein. The universe is a space-time continuum. But, according to sage Vyāsa, the universe is comprehensible only by conceiving it as annihilation (*śūnya*) of the distinction (*bheda*) between space (*digdesa*) and time (*kāla*).

Vāstu Puruṣa is an important factor in constructing buildings. The location of the different parts of a house must conform to the position of *Vāstu Puruṣa* during different months. Astrologically, the beginning of the construction of a building during certain months leads to misfortunes, such as financial losses, ill-health, etc., while during other months the acquisition of wealth and general happiness are indicated. *Vāstu* Puruṣa is said to sleep on his left with his head to the East during the months of Bhādrapada, Āśvina and Kārtika (August to October); with his head to the South during Mārgaśīrṣa, Pauṣa and Māgha (November to February); with his head to the West during Phālguna, Caitra and Vaiśākha (February to May) and with his head to the North during Jyeṣṭha, Āṣāḍha and Śrāvaṇa (May to August). No building should be erected on the ground covered by his head, his legs, his hands and his back, as it is said to prove fatal to the father, wife and children, respectively, and cause fear of thieves. The most suitable section would be the ground covered by the stomach of *Vāstu* Puruṣa, as it is said to give rise to plenty and prosperity.

There are quite a number of other astrological factors which should be considered for fixing the door-frames, digging wells and finally for *Gṛha-praveśa* or entering a new house; this is most important. The importance given to *Jyotiṣa* by the author of the *Mayamata* becomes evident when he says: A house is to be entered at an auspicious time which accords with the owner's horoscope, after doing the propitiatory rites.

Today, scarcity of housing, especially in urban areas is so pronounced that it may not be possible to strictly follow all the rules of *Vāstu*. Hence experts, learned in its various aspects, scientists, engineers, astrological savants and architects should debate and decide the *Vāstu* rules that can be adapted to suit modern conditions. The importance of *Vāstu* in city or town planning and development for the welfare of the public cannot be underrated. While forming new layouts, town planners should consult engineers and architects well-versed both in modern architecture and *Vāstu* discipline. Otherwise, many buildings including government buildings mostly constructed on some grounds may develop cracks in the walls and may even collapse. I invite our esteemed Chief Ministers to give due importance to *Vāstu* in the planning of suburbs. The timing of the foundations, etc., of many of the public buildings should be based on *Vāstu* and astrological factors if the structures have to last long. It is hoped that these observations will receive attention of powers that be.

Summing up: *Vāstu* is a science of Time and Space, just as *Jyotiṣa* is also a science of Time. While the approach of *Vāstu Śāstra* is scientific, the goal is always spiritual.

Vāstu-Vidyā*

*Prof. S.K. Ramachandra Rao***

(I)

The word '*Vāstu*' etymologically means 'the place where people dwell' (*vasanti prāṇino 'tra*) from the root '*vas*' 'to dwell' (*nivāse*). The place may either be the ground or land on which people reside, or the house and other buildings people build for their use. The word '*vāstu*' refers both to the site on which buildings are raised and to the buildings themselves (*vases tunn agare ṇic ca*, as per the *Uṇādi-sūtra* 1.75).

The early Vedic references (e.g., *Ṛgveda* 10.107.10; 10.146.3) suggest that the buildings, especially houses, were more important than the land on which they stood. The Vedic word for 'house' is '*veśma*' meaning 'that in which people enter' (*viśanti iti*); it could be decorated, consecrated and rendered charming and beneficient, like the abode of the gods (RV.10.107.10: *veśma pariṣkṛtaṁ devamāneva citram*). The *Atharvaveda* (5.17.13) even speaks of the spirit that chooses to dwell in the houses thus build (*na vikarṇaḥ pṛthu-śiras tasmin veśmani jāyate*). The *Amarakośa* gives the word '*vāstu*' as synonymous with the site on which houses are built (*veśmabhūr vāstur astriyām* / 2.2.19).

The word "*vāstoṣpati*" (the lord of Vāstu) occurs in the *Ṛgveda* 7.54.1) and Sāyaṇa explains that this is the spirit that protects the house (*vāstoṣpate gṛhasya pālayitar deva*). This spirit is identified with Indra by Devarāja-yajvan in his commentary on the *Nighṇṭu*. He takes *vāstu* as signifying mid-region (*vāstu antarikṣam)* and *'vāstoṣpati'* as protector of this region by virtue of his pervading it. In the Vedic context, the mid-region (*antarikṣa*) signifies the starry

* Keynote Address delivered at The First All India Symposium on Vāstu.

** 305, 6th Cross, I Block, Jaynagar, Bangalore-560 011.

vault (*antaḥ madhye ṛkṣāni nakṣatrāṇi yasya tat*), and the gods in this sphere include Indra the chief of the gods, *vāyu* the god of winds, *parjanya* the god of rains, Rudra the god of thundering clouds, and the *Marud-devatās* the gods presiding over breezes and currents. In later literature, the gods of this realm were personified as *Dik-pālas* the guardians of the eight directions, even as the lord of the heavenly region *Śūrya* got structured into the nine *Grahas*.

Vāstoṣpati as the protector of house (*gṛha*) or site on which the house rests (*gṛha-kṣetra*) is intimately related to stars and planets above and guardian deities around. The association of Vāstu with Jyotiṣa (astrology) dates back to early Vedic period. More significantly, the expression '*Vāstu*' is associated with the Vedic god Rudra, who is described as '*vāstavya*' in the *Śatapatha-brāhmaṇa* (1.7.3.7.) and the *Taittirīya-brāhmaṇa* (1.7.8.15; 3.7.9.7) and the *Āpastamba-śrauta-sūtra* (13.20.1) speak of *Vāstoṣpati* as the lord of house (*gṛha-devatā*) as also of the site on which it stands (*gṛha-kṣetra-devatā*). A house was where the four values of life (*puruṣārthas*) were accomplished. In the *Samarāṅgaṇa-sūtradhāra*, we read: धर्मार्थकाम मोक्षाणां यदेकमिह कारणम्। (*Dharmārtha-kāma-mokṣāṇām yad ēkam iha kāraṇam*).

The *Smṛti* texts and the Puranas extended the scope of Vastu to include not only residential buildings but all constructions for private and public utility. The *Garuḍa-purāṇa*, for instance, takes the word *vāstu* in the sense of building houses, hamlets and mansions, formation of townships, laying out of parks and gardens, construction of commercial streets, forts, temples and monasteries (46.2-3):

आवास वासवे श्मादौ पुरे ग्रामे वणिक्पथे ।
प्रासादारामदुर्गेषु देवालयमठेषु च ॥
āvāsa-vāsma-veśmādau pure grāme vaṇikpathe /
prāsādārāma-durgeṣu devālaya-meṭheṣu ca //

The *Arthaśāstra* (65.1) adds to this list the building of dams and digging of tanks: गृहक्षेत्र मारामः सेतुबन्ध स्तडाक माधारो वा वास्तुः। (*gṛhakṣetram ārāmaḥ setubandhas taḍākam ādhāro vā vāstuḥ*). Both these sources include the land on which the buildings and gardens are raised in the definition of Vāstu.

The references in the *Purāṇas* and in the texts like the *Arthaśāstra* (Ch. 45) and the *Śukranīti* (4.3) suggest the existence of the art or the science of building houses, palaces, bridges, canals, forts, dams, tanks, roads and parks. This was known as *Vāstu-vidyā* or *Vāstu-karma* or *Vāstu-śāstra*. Occasionally, this discipline was called just *Vāstu*, as in the *Garuḍa-purāṇa* (46.1: वास्तु संक्षेपतो वक्ष्ये गृहादौ विघ्ननाशनम् ॥—*Vāstu saṁkṣepato vakṣye gṛhādau vighnanāśanam*). And, there are references to this art or science having been assiduously cultivated by a long line of wise sages and expert-engineers. The *Matsya-purāṇa* (Ch. 226), for instance, provides a long list of eighteen experts who handed down this art in a traditional manner. They are: Bhṛgu, Atri, Vasiṣṭha, Viśvakarma, Yama, Nārada, Nagnajit, Viśālākṣa, Aniruddha, Śukra and Bṛhaspati. The text further says that Viṣṇu in his first incarnation as Matsya delivered in brief this discipline to the first of mortals, Manu संक्षेपेणोपदिष्टं यन्मनवे मत्स्यरूपिणा। तदिदानीं प्रवक्ष्यामि वास्तु शास्त्रमनुत्तमम् (*Saṁkṣepeṇopadiṣṭaṁ yan manave matsyarūpiṇā/ Tad idānīṁ pravakṣyāmi vāstu-śastram anuttamam*).

(II)

Whatever the origin of this art or science, of architecture, known later as *Sthāpatyaveda*, of sculpture in its own right, and whatever the historicity of the personages mentioned above, it is certain that there is a vast literature concerning *Vāstu* in Sanskrit. Among the Purāṇas, *Agni* (Ch. 104, concerning mansions and palaces; Ch. 105, concerning houses), *Garuḍa* (Ch. 46, about building houses, gardens, forts, temples and monasteries), *Brahmāṇḍa* (Ch. 7, about building houses), *Bhaviṣya* (Ch. 130, about building mansions), *Matsya* (Ch. 225, about pillars; Ch. 257, about selection of wood for construction; Ch. 258, about measurements; Ch. 269, about houses and palaces) and *Skanda* contain interesting material for architects.

The *Maya-mata*, or *Maya-vāstu-śāstra* includes sections on measurements for houses, on the four types of houses, and on the rituals for occupation of the built house. The

Manuṣyālaya-candrikā (in 65 verses), the *Viśvakarma-vāstu-śāstra* (in 81 chapters), the *Maya-vāstu* (in 4 chapters), the *Kaśyapa-śilpa* (in 88 patalas), the *Samarāṅgaṇa-sūtradhāra* (in 83 chapters), the *Aparājita-pṛcchā* (in 239 sutras), the *Mānasāra* (in 70 chapters), the *Arthaśāstra*, the *Vāstu-kuṇḍali*, the *Yukti-kalpatara*, the *Vāstu-tattva* (by Ganapati-śiṣya), the *Vāstu-yoga-tattva* (by Raghunandana Bhattācārya), the *Mānasollāsa* (by Cālukya Someśvara), the Vāstuvidyā (dealing with doors, walls and roofs of houses), the *Viśvakarma-prakāśa* (Ch. 7, about selection of sites; Ch. 8, about proper time to commence construction of houses; Ch. 10, about āyavyayādi calculations; Ch. 12, about types of houses; Ch. 13, about doors and their measurements; Ch. 14, about pillars; Ch. 15, about divisions and apartments, etc.) and *Sanatkumāra-vāstu-śāstra* (dealing with examination of the site, etc.) are the most noteworthy works on *Vāstu Śastra*. And, there are also works which concern themselves with astrological considerations in building a house. The last work mentioned above deals with proper constellation (Ch. 2, *Nakṣatra-graha-yoga-vidhi*), planetary positions favourable to the house (Ch. 3, *gṛha-lagna-vidhi*), and suitable period for occupations of the house (Ch. 8, *gṛha-praveśa*). Śrīpati's *Ratnamālā* is another manual of house-building mainly on astrological considerations (Ch. 17, *vāstu-prakaraṇa*). The *Laghu-śilpa-jyotisāra* of Śivarāma is meant to explain briefly elaborate the astrological background for the science of architecture, especially construction of houses:

आयराशिश्च नक्षत्रं व्ययस्तारांशकस्तथा।
गृहमैत्री राशिमैत्री नातिवेदगणेन्दवः॥
आधिपत्यं वारलग्ने तिथ्युत्पत्तिस्तथैव च ।
आधिपत्यं वर्गवैरं तथैव योनिवैरकम् ॥
ऋक्षवैरं स्थितिर्नाशो लक्षणान्येक विंशतिः ।
कथितानि मुनिश्रेष्ठ शिल्प विद्भिर्गृहादिषु ॥

āyaraśiś ca nakṣatraṁ vyayas tārāṁ śakas tathā /
grahamaitrī rāśimaitrī nātivedagaṇen davaḥ //
ādhipatyaṁ vāralagne tithyutpattis tahaiva ca /
ādhipatyaṁ vargavaīrnaṁ tathaiva yonivairakam //

Ṛkṣavaisaṁ sthitir nāśo lakṣaṇāny ekaviṁsatiḥ /
Kathitani muniśrestha silpividbhir gṛhādiṣu //

Vāstu as art or science of architecture comes in for elaborate treatment in the Āgamas and Śilpa-śāstra texts. Among topics discussed in great detail is the *Vāstu-puruṣa* as unified personification of forces and spirits that dwell in the site divided into a number of cells (padas). The conception of Vāstu-puruṣa is well-known. It suffices to remember that Vāstu-puruṣa is essentially an abstraction based entirely on the site-plan (*pada-vinyāsa*) and that the Vāstu-deities of plan-cells must properly be propitiated before construction of the site commences (*vāstu-śamana*). We see here a recurrence of Vedic mythology about the everlasting fight between Indra as chief of the gods and Vṛtra the demon of drought. Vṛtra is here the *asura* (*Vāstu-puruṣa*) that signifies birth and all that it contains. And Indra as Vāstoṣpati has to hold him in check. Vāstu is aggression against *antarikṣa*, as any construction on earth, in fact, is. This is corrected by a ritual known as *Vāstu-praśamana*. It must also be noted that the god of earth in the Vedic context is Agni, even as *Indra* or *Vāsu* is the god of the mid-region (*antarikṣasthāna*) and Sūrya of the heavens (*dyusthāna*). *Agni* located in a house is *gārha-patyāgni*, a representative of *Sūrya* or *Indra*. The propitiation of *Agni* everyday in the ritual of *Agnihotra* is to counteract the power of *āsura*, *Vāstu*. Propitiation of *Vāstu-puruṣa* is indicated not only while building a house, but also while effecting repairs, renovating an old construction, and making additions to an already built house. And, care must be taken not to violate *marma-sthānas*, *sandhis*, rajjus and nāḍis of the site-plan for they are all vital in their influences on the inhabitants:

जीर्णोद्धारे तथोद्याने तथा गृहनिवेशने ।
द्वाराभिवर्धने तद्वत् प्रासादेषु गृहेषु च ।
वास्तुपशमनं कुर्यात् . . . ॥

jirṇoddhāre tathodyāne tathā gṛhaniveśane /
dvārābhivardhane tadvat prāsādeṣu gṛheṣu ca /
vāstupaśamaṁ kuryāt //

Broadly in the *Matsya-purāṇa* (Ch. 228), architectural considerations are divided into two areas: construction of temples (*ālaya-vāstu*) and building of houses (*gṛha-vāstu*). The latter division includes building of palaces (*prāsāda*), forts (*durga*) and ordinary houses (*gṛha*), digging step-wells, wells and tanks (*vāpī-kūpa-taḍāka*) and laying out parks and gardens (*udyāna*). However, much of the attention is devoted to the residences of kings (*rājā*), princes (*yuvarāja*), commanders (*senāpati*), counsellors (*mantrī*), feudal chieftains (*sāmanta*) and officials (*dūta-karmāntika*). Details of a plan depend upon the measurement of central area of the site, which is also called *brahmā* (*hṛdaye sa tu pūjyate*). The principle followed is this: गर्भमानेन मानं तु सर्ववास्तुषु शस्यते। (*garbhamānena mānaṁ tu sarvavāstuṣu śasyate*).

The texts mentioned above also prescribe where different functional apartments of a house (like kitchen, bath-room, store, etc.) must be located, what the advantages and disadvantages are with regard to particular orientation of the house (*diṅ-mukha*), the type of the house (*sarvatobhadra, nandyāvarta, svastika, etc.*), the placement and number of doors (*dvāra*) and pillars (*stambha*), the trees and plants that must be grown around a house (*vṛksa*), and so on. Accounts contained in these books would surely be interesting to a student of religious as well as secular architecture.

But our present interest lies in certain basic ideas governing construction of houses. It may be noted that plans and measurements of buildings originated in the *Śulba-sūtras*, which were supplementary treatises to the *Kalpasūtras*. The Śulba-sūtras pertain mainly to measurements and constructions of different kinds of altars (*citi, vedi*). In the Vedic ideology, sacrificial altar is the representation in miniature of the entire universe; and is, therefore, extremely important. It must be properly planned, accurately measured and suitable located. Different sacrifices have their own appropriate altars (like *samiki-vedi, paitṛki-vedi*, etc.). Baudhāyana and Āpastamba enumerate several altars constructed out of bricks. The *Taittirīya Saṁhitā* (5.5.-11) mentions that altars are of diverse shapes. The *Śulba-śutras* provide general rules for construction of these altars as abodes of sacred fire. They are in two main divisions: *Mānava Śulba-sūtras* and *Maitrāyaṇīya Śulba-sūtras*.

All Indian architecture has grown out to these Śulba-sūtras. To apply the principles enunciated in these aphoristic texts to buildings for religious and secular use, they had to make relevant changes, with ommissions, additions and alternations. The *Kāmikāgama* (41.57) suggests that buildings must be constructed with rational planning and taste, making necessary changes in scriptural prescriptions:

The expression '*ūha-pratyūha*' is interesting. '*Ūha*' is conjecture or hypothetical reasoning for appropriate additions, functionally relevant and structurally viable; *pratyūha* (or *apoha*) relates to omissions. The former refers to built area while the latter to unfilled spaces. The *Mānasāra* (20.105-106) insists that whatever the scriptural injunctions, clever architect must use his intelligence and discretion to make the building useful and delightful. The counsel of expert architect is of greater importance than canonical principles:

पूज्यं व्ययं सममेव तत्र दोषो न विद्यते ।
आयाधिकं व्ययं हीनं सर्वसम्पत्करं तथा ।
आयहीनं व्ययाधिक्यं सर्वदोषकरं भवेत् ॥
pujyaṁ vyayaṁ samam eva tatra doṣo na vidyāte /
āyādhikaṁ vyayaṁ hīnaṁ sarva-sampatkaraṁ tathā /
āyahīnaṁ vyayādhikyaṁ sarvadoṣakaraṁ bhavet //

The *Yukti-kalpataru* (section on *Rāja-gṛha-yukti*) suggests that the rules provided in Vāstu texts are only broad guidelines (*niyama*); the actual principles to be followed while building a house are to be pragmatic and rational; and the architect is a best judge:

However, the Vāstu principles are inalienably linked with astrological considerations, for a building is not only to serve practical and immediate purposes, but to make for gain, happiness, longevity and prosperity of the inhabitants of the house. The several inherent and occasional defects of a house (*gṛha-doṣa*) resulting in loss, poverty, misfortune and so on are also to be avoided or undone. The architect must, therefore, understand the relevant astrological particulars. In his *Bṛhat-saṁhitā* (53.1) Varāhamihira sets about to explain the art and science of architecture, which has been handed down in a long line of sages for the edifications of clever and trusted astrologers:

वास्तुज्ञानमथातः कमलभवने मुनिपरम्परायातम् ।
क्रियतेऽधुना मयदें विदग्धसंवत्सर प्रीत्यै ॥

vāstujñānamathātaḥ kamalabhavane muniparaṁparā-yātam /
kriyate'dhunā mayedaṁ vidagdha saṁvatsara prītyai//

There are considerations like *āyādi-ṣadvarga*, i.e., a set of formulae concerning six main proportions (viz., *āya, vyaya, ṛksa, yoni, vāra, tithi,* together with *aṁśa* relevant for the sancita type of buildings), to conform to the six main architectural limbs (viz., base, column, entablature, wings, roof and dome). These formulae involve astrological details with numerical correspondences (*āya* 12, *vyaya* 10, *ṛksa* 27, *yoni* 8, *vāra* 7, *tithi* 30 and *aṁśa* 9). The measurements pertaining to breadth (*vistara*) by formulae under *vyaya* and *yoni*, and those pertaining to height (*ucchrāya*) by formulae under *vāra* and *tithi*. The calculations are meant to predict gain or loss by the principles like those quoted above in the verse "*Pūjayaṁ*" etc.

These considerations, relevant as they are architecturally, also suggest measurements for the buildings which are of practical importance. When for instance, the height of the building (*utsedha*) is equal to the breadth in *ganya-māna* units, it is called 'pacific' (*śāntika*); if it is one-fourth (1/4) of the breadth, it is 'nourishing' (*pauṣṭika*); the inhabitants will be strong, celebrated and wealthy. If the height is one-half (1/2) of the breadth, it is 'victory-giving' (*jayada*); the inhabitants will find happiness, and the building will be charming. If it is three-fourth (3/4), it is 'wealth-giving' (*dhanada*), also called *sārva-kāmika*; it is excellent in all respects. If the height is twice the breadth, it is marvellous (*adbhuta*); the building will be lofty, eminent and awe-inspiring.

Determination of the direction in which a building is

oriented is an important consideration. Known as *dig-vidik-saṁsthāna* it consists of an ascertainment of the cardinal points. The *Yukti-kalapataru* has a section on the divisions of the house-site (*vāstu-bhāga*) in terms of death (*mṛtyu*), fear (*bhaya*), firmness (*sthira*), force (*caṇḍa*), wealth (*dhana*), prosperity (*vibhava*), valour (*vīra*) and hot (*tāpa*), corresponding to the directions, South, South-West, West, North-West, North, North-East, East and South-East, respectively:

मृत्युर्भयः स्थिरश्चण्डो धनं विभव एव च ।
वीरस्तापश्च इत्यष्टौ वास्तुभागा यथाक्रमम् ॥
यमनैर्ऋततोयशे वायु यक्षेश शङ्कराः ।
इन्द्रो वह्निरिति प्रोक्ता विभागानामधीश्वराः ॥
mṛtyur bhayaḥ sthiraś caṇḍo dhanaṁ vibhava eva ca /
viras tāpaś ca ity aṣṭau vāstubhāgā yathā kramam //
yamanaiṛrtatoyeśavāyuya kṣeśa śaṁkarāḥ /
indro vahnir iti proktā vibhāgānām adhiśvarāḥ //

These divisions are meant to locate the apartments of a place or mansion.

The second consideration of significance is the determination of direction which a building should face (*vāstu-sthāna-nirṇaya*). If a house faces the West, it is called banner (*dhvaja*), and it secures prosperity for the inhabitant; if it faces the North-West, it is called smoke (*dhūma*) and spells disaster for the residents; if it faces the North, it is lion (*siṁha*) and foretells enjoyment; if it faces the North-East, it is dog (*śvā*) and forebodes total loss; if it faces the East, it is bull (*vṛṣa*) and forecasts happiness; if it faces the South-East, it is donkey (*gardabha*) and spells ruin; if it faces the South, it is elephant (*gaja*) and the outcome is wealth; and if it faces the South-West, it is crow (*kāka*) and predicts death and disaster:

ध्वजो धूमस्तथा सिंहः श्वा वृषो गर्दभो गजः ।
काक इत्येष गदितो वास्तुस्थानस्य निर्णयः ॥
ध्वजे विभूतिर्विपदश्च धूमे सिंहे विभोगाः शुनि सर्वनाशः ।
वृषे सुखं गर्दभतो विनाशो गजे धनं काकपदे च मृत्युः ॥
dhvajo dhūmastathā siṁhaḥ śvā vṛṣo gardabho gajaḥ /

kāka ityeṣa gadito vāstusthānarsya nirṇayaḥ //
dhvaje vibhutirvipadaśca dhūme siṁhe vibhogāḥ śuni sarvanāśaḥ /
vṛṣe sukhaṁ gardabhato vināśo gaje dhanaṁ kākapade ca mṛtyuḥ //

It may be noted that houses facing the four main directions are beneficient, while those facing the corner points forebode evil.

Further, the planning of a house with regard to corner lines (*koṇarekhā*) and pole-lengths (*daṇḍa*) with different directional orientations become relevant. For instance, if the pole-length runs East-West, it is called *Udaya-daṇḍa*, and it augurs well; if, on the other hand, the pole length is South-North in orientation, it is called *yama-daṇḍa*, and it forebodes destruction of the family. The architect must plan in such a way that the evils of pole-lengths are avoided:

पूर्वपश्चिमतो दण्ड उदयाख्यः सुखावहः ।
दक्षिणोत्तरतो दण्डो वंशहा यमदण्डक ॥
pūrvapaścimato daṇḍah udayākhyaḥ sukhāvahaḥ /
dakṣiṇottarato daṇḍo vaṁśahā yamadaṇḍakaḥ //

There are many defects that one must avoid in building a house; defects pertaining to site-cells (*padaghāta*), defects in the moat-area of the site-plan (*parikhāghāta*), defects in the forcelines in the plan (*pathaghāta*), defects concerning the availability of water (*jaladoṣa*), defects emanating from the plants and trees around a house (*vṛksa-doṣa*). These defects are said to forebode loss of children, wealth, health and happiness.

These are also rules pertaining to location, number and nature of the doors. The *Bṛhat-saṁhitā* (53.72-80) speaks of defective planning of doors leading to distress and disaster (*dvāra-doṣa*). Doors must be planned in the four major directions, and not in the corners, according to the *Agni-purāṇa* (104.24): दिक्षु द्वाराणि कार्याणि, न विदिक्षु कदाचन। (*Dikṣu dvāraṇi kāryāṇi na vidikṣu kadācana*). However, entering a house by door in the southern directions is commended by the

Matsya-purāṇa (255.29). The main door must be shaped like a plough (*Mānasāra*, 9.360: महाद्वारं लांगलाकारसंनिभम् (*Mahādvāraṁ laṅgalākārasaṁnibhaṁ*) and must be in two panels (कपारटद्वयसंयुक्तम्).

Wood to be chosen for the doors of a house is also specified; the rear door must be in the east and made of *plakṣa*-wood, the door on the southern side must be the main door and made of *plakṣa*-wood, the door on the southern side must be the main door and made in *udumdara*-wood; the door on the west should be in *aśvattha*-wood, and the door on the northern side in *nyagrodha*-wood (*Matsyapurāṇa*, 264.5.15).

Likewise, the texts like *Suprabhedāgama* (31.4, etc.) and the *Mānasāra* (9.360) provide regulations about the walls and their measurements (*bhittimāna*).

The Vāstu texts also provide prescriptions about directions which are suitable for several apartments necessary in a household. The prescriptions are by no means uniform. There is a fair degree of agreement as to the main apartments like kitchen, room of worship, bed-room and so on.

North-East, the direction over which *Iśāna* presides, is suitable for a room for the household gods (*devatāgāra*), according to all texts. The *Kāmikāgama* (35.177-191), however would have the kitchen (*pacana-sthāna*) also in this direction.

East is Indra's direction. The *Kāmikāgama* prescribes dining hall (*bhojana-sthāna*) to be located here. The *Vāstu-tattva* would have a common room (*sarva-vastu-gṛha*) as well as bath room (*snāna-gṛha*) in this direction (cf. also *Vāstu-prabandha*, 2.25-26).

South-East is the direction where Agni, the fire-god, is the deity. Kitchen (*pacanālaya*) is to be located here, according to most of the texts. The *Vastu-prabandha* calls the kitchen 'pacanālaya', while the *Śilpaśāstra-saṁgraha* (9.24-28) calls it '*pāka-sadana*'.

South is Yama's direction. The *Kāmilkāgama*, the *Vāstu-tattva* and the *Vāstu-prabandha* prescribe that bed-room (*śayanāgāra / śayana-sthāna*) should find its place here.

South-West, presided by Nirṛti, is the direction in which all things required for running the household (*gṛhasyopaskaraṁ sarvam*) according to the *Matsyapurāṇa*, 264.33-36) are stored; it is also the direction in which armoury (*śastragṛha/āyudhālaya*), according to the *Vāstu-tattva* and the *Kāmikāgama*, and library (*śāstra-mandira*), according to the *Vāstu-prabandha*, are also to be located. According to the *Matsyapurāṇa*, bath-room should be located outside the house in this direction.

The *Śilpaśāstra-sāra-saṁgraha* (9.24-28) suggests that toilet (*purīṣa-tyāga-mandira*) be located between the South and South-West (*yāmya-nairṛtyayor madhye*); the text would have the delivery-room (*sūtikā-geha*) in the South-Westerly direction.

West is the quarter of Varuṇa. The *Kāmikāgama* wants water-storage (*udkālaya*) here; the *Vāstu-tattva* would have dining room (*bhojanā-gāra*) here, as well as study-room (*vidyābhyāsa-gṛha*).

North-West is presided over by Vāyu. Here must be located cattleshed (*goṣatthāgāra*), according to the Kāmikāgama, and store-room for grains (*dhānya-gṛha*) according to the *Vāstu-prabandha*, and store-room for wealth as well as grains, according to the *Matsyapurāṇa*. Outside the house, in this direction, must be work-house (*karma-śālā*), according to the *Matsyapurāṇa*.

The *Śilpaśāstra-sāra-saṁgraha* suggests that the apartment for enjoyment (*rati-geha*) be located in between the North-West and North. The *Vāstu-prabandha* would place cattle-shed (*paśu-mandira*) here.

North is Kubera's quarter. It is, therefore proper that treasury (*dhanālaya/bhaṇḍāra/kośa/dravyālaya*) should find its place here. All the texts prescribe this.

The *Śilpaśāstra-sāra-saṁgraha* suggests that medicines and herbs (*auṣadhārtha*) be stored in between North and North-East.

It may be noticed that above prescriptions are based on the supposed personality and functions of the guardians of eight directions, as crystallized in the Purāṇas, Epics and Smṛti texts. They together represent the space or the universe, of which a house is but a representation. The lord of a house (*gṛha-devatā*) is attended by these guardian-spirits, who must occupy their proper positions within the site-plan. *Vāstu*, in fact, refers to a place where human beings reside with immortal spirits, according to the *Mayamata* (2.1).

It remains to be mentioned that Vāstu-vidyā has not only a great antiquity but considerable literature. It is regrettable that despite a phenomenal increase of interest in Vāstu of late, the study of the extant literature on the subject is sadly neglected, thus occasioning a rich harvest of charlatans. It is not often realized that Vāstu-vidyā is a comprehensive discipline, and all aspects thereof must be taken into account, before suggestions for Vāstu alterations and planning are made. In fact Vāstu is a collective expression:

> वास्तुसामूहिको नाम दीप्यते सर्वतस्तु यः ।
> *vāstusamūhiko nāma dīpyate sarvatas tu yaḥ /*

The *Mānasāra* (7.268-269) says that mere speculations with regard to alterations of a house should not be entertained, for a house when completed and constructed is an organic whole and must not be mutilated on any account:

> अज्ञानादङ्गहीनं च कर्ता विनश्यति ।
> तस्मात्तु शिल्पिभिः प्राज्ञै रूहापेक्षोट्टान्न योजयेत् ॥
> *ajñanād aṅgahīnaṁ ca kartā vinaśyati /*
> *tasmāttu śilpibhiḥ prājñair uhapekṣoṭṭān na yojayet//*

Should, by necessity, an alteration needs to be effected, then the textual prescription must be followed meticulously. A comprehensive acquaintance with Vāstu-śāstra is, therefore, a sine qua non for a practitioner or Vāstu, who is competent to suggest wholesome changes in an already built house. It must also be recognized that much of the Vastu provisions relate to the site (*gṛha-kṣetra*) on which a house is built, and the planning (*pada-vinyāsa*) that is done prior to construction. The initial and preparatory pacification of the deities in the site-cells (*vāstūpaśamana*) is insisted upon in all the *Vāstu* texts as indispensable.

The *Mayamata* (2.2) which speaks of four kinds of *Vāstu*,

viz., the site, building, mode of conveyance and furniture, says that the site is the most important *Vāstu*, for all others depend upon it; it is the first among *Vāstus* chronologically and provides a foundation for the world:

भूमिप्रासादयानानि शयनं च चतुर्विधम् ।
भूरेव मुख्यवास्तु स्यात्तत्र च जातान्यन्यानि हि ।
भूतानामादि भूतत्वादाधारत्वाज्जगत्स्थितेः ॥

bhūmi prāsādayānanani śayanaṁ ca caturvidham /
bhur eva mukhyavāstu syāt tatra ca jātānya nyāni hi /
bhūtānam ādibhūtatvād ādhāratvaj jagatsthiteḥ //

The *Agnipurāṇa* (106.1) even mentions that the area of the town or village in which a house is built must also be taken into account (*nagarādika vāstu*). The character or personality of a house varies with where it is located. According to the *Mānasāra* (36.1-96), a house may be built in a village, a town, a settlement, a suburb, a grove, a hermitage, near a hill or river. The architect should plan a house in accordance with these details. And whatever man makes is secondary (*gauṇa*) *Vāstu*, while the site is the principle one, according to the *Mayamata* (2.6). The natural lay of a land is the principle *Vāstu*.

The house is not to be regarded as an isolated phenomena; its plan should be in reasonable consonance with the surroundings; and of course, the owner's personal details ascertained by astrological considerations, and also his tastes must be taken into account. The owner should spend his honestly earned wealth and build the house, and furnish it with his own efforts. He will then be happy in the house, even as a planet in its own habitat. Thus, we read in the *Yukti-kalpataru*: what the books say about the king applied to anyone who builds a house.

REFERENCES AND NOTES

Besides the works on Vāstu mentioned earlier in the text, there are several manuscripts dealing with the subject in the oriental libraries like the one in Mysore, Baroda, Trivandrum and Chennai. A list of manuscripts consulted by me is given below:

1. *Vāstu maṇḍana;*
2. *Gṛha-vāstu-sāra ;*
3. *Nirdoṣa-vāstu;*
4. *Vāstu-cakra* (Vikṣācārya);
5. *Vāstu-śastra* (of Bhojadeva);
6. *Vāstu-mañjarī;*
7. *Vāstu-vadhikāra;*
8. *Vāstu-ratnāvalī;*
9. *Vāstu-vidhi;*
10. *Vāstu-paddhati;*
11. *Vāstu-tilaka* (of Keśava);
12. *Vāstu-vidyāpati* (of Vāsudeva);
13. *Vāstu-sāṅkhya* (of Todarananda);
14. *Āyādi-lakṣaṇa;*
15. *Kumāra-vāstu;*
16. *Prāsada-nirṇaya;*
17. *Viśvambhara-vāstu;* and
18. *Mana-vijñāna.*

The Status and Relevance of Vāstu in the Contemporary Context

V. Ganapati Sthapati

According to a report of W.H.O. that appeared in the *New York Times*, the scientists of USA have declared 2000 buildings as sick. The sickness is attributed to the disorderly arrangement of spaces within the built environment. They say that such residential buildings are found to be the sources of mental and physical disorders.

At the time when the *Vāstu* conscience has started wielding its sway all over the world, the organisation of a symposium of this kind on *Vāstu* by Dr. B.V. Raman, an international authority on *Jyotiṣa*, is most welcome. This symposium will strengthen the hands of the *Vāstu* tradition and add another dimension to the contemporary architecture. On behalf of the *Śilpīs*, I thank the doyen astrologer whose admirers take delight in equating his services with those of Varāhamihira of historic fame.

The individual and independent role of the *Vāstu* tradition in providing not only physical or material welfare but also spiritual well being is justified in the erstwhile existence of 32 *śāstras*, followed by *Śilpī* guilds of Bharat. The *Śilpīs* were essentially advains, possessing a rare Veda called the Praṇava Veda, traditionally said to have existed independently of the four *Vedas* by some, or one as a part of the *Atharva Veda* by some other. That the designer-builder-sculptor, known as '*Śthapati*' was well versed in the *Vedas* is clearly stated in all the *Vāstu Śāstras*. The *Mayamatam*, the most ancient authoritative work on *vāstu* says:

स्थानाधिपतिः यस्मात् तस्मात् स्थपतिरुच्यते ।
स्थपतिः सर्वशास्त्रज्ञो वेदविच्छास्त्र पारगः ॥

Sthānādhipatiḥ yasmāt tasmāt sthapatir ucyate /
Sthapatiḥ sarvaśāstrajño vedavic chāstra pāragaḥ //

Even the markers, carvers and joiners working under the *Sthapatis* were Vedic scholars, says the *Mānasāra*:

श्रुतज्ञः सूत्रग्राही च रेखाज्ञः शास्त्रवित्तम) ।
विचारज्ञः श्रुतज्ञश्च चित्रकर्मज्ञः वर्धकी ।
तक्षकः श्रुतिशास्त्रज्ञः सर्वलक्षणसंपन्न ।
śrutajñaḥ sūtragrāhī ca rekhājñaḥ śāstravittamaḥ /
vicārajñaḥ śrutajñaś ca citrakarmajña vardhakī /
takṣakaḥ śrutiśāstrajñaḥ sarvalakṣaṇasampannaḥ /

It will not be an exaggeration to say that the *Vāstu Śilpa* tradition was mostly responsible for the culture and civilization which we feel proud of even today. I am happy to say, to highlight this aspect of Indian culture, an academy called 'Vishakarma Sahitya Academy' is established in Madras with eminent scholars in Vedic lore and Sanskrit literature, drawn mostly from Karnataka, Andhra and Kerala as resource persons. The aim of the academy is to collect all technical material on *Vāstu* found scattered in *Vedas*, *Āgamas*, *Itihāsas*, *Purāṇas*, *Kāvyas*, *Saṅgīta* and *Nāṭya Śāstras*, and present them to the contemporary community of architects and Sthapatis for their professional enrichment.

This symposium on *Vāstu*, according to Raman and Rajeswari Research Foundation, and according to what I feel, is to identify the role of *Jyotiṣa* in *Vāstu* and that of *Vāstu* in *Jyotiṣa*. In the primary note circulated among the delegates, by the organisers of this meet, the *Vāstu* is stated to be a limb of *Jyotiṣa*. Though at one context of experiencing with the built space, certain astronomical and astrological aspects are taken into consideration, *Vāstu* has an identity of its own, in as much as *Jyotiṣa* has its own identity. This is because the house building is designed to be a living organism with capacity to pulsate from within, like a human being, and resonate with the pulsation of the individual or family members occupying the built-space. The master of the house is actually wedded to the house, by a set of rare astronomical formulae called *Āyādi-sūtra* just as we do calculations for a boy to be married to a girl.

Jyotiṣa is a discipline belonging to the six *Vedāṅgas*, viz., *Śikṣā* or the science of proper articulation, *Chandas* or the science of prosody, *Vyākaraṇa* or grammar, *Nirukta* or etymological explanation of difficult Vedic words, *Jyotiṣa* or astronomy, and *Kalpa* or ritual or ceremonial.

In the cultural domain of the Vedas there is another group of five disciplines, called *Upavedas*, viz., *Nāṭyaveda* or Dance attached to the *Atharvaveda*, *Gandharvaveda* or Music attached to the *Sāmaveda*, *Dhanurveda* or Military attached to the *Yajurveda*, *Āyurveda* or Medicine attached to the *Atharvaveda*, and *Sthāpatyaveda* or Art and Architecture attached to the *Atharvaveda*.

But the *Śilpis* of South Indian also refer to another set of five *Upavedas*, viz., *Śabdaveda* or poetry, *Gandharvaveda* or music, *Nāṭyaveda* or dance, *Vāstuveda* or Architecture, and *Śilpaveda* or Sculpture. The last two, viz., *Vāstu* and *Śilpa* are collectively called *Sthāpatyaveda*. There are other names also, such as *Vāstuveda*, *Arthaveda* and *Vāstu-vidyā*, juxtaposed to *Śabdaveda* or *Vāgveda*.

If one examines these five *Upavedas*, one would find them falling under two distinct categories of Universes, the former three classified under *Śabda-prapañca* (universe of articulated sound forms, i.e., words) and the other two under *Artha-prapañca* (the universe of material forms, i.e., visual objects). We all know that the *Sabda-prapañca* is rooted in OM sound or *Nāda-brahman*. If this is so, is it not logical to ask whether the *Artha-prapañca* is rooted in any other *Brahman* ? Yes. The technical tradition says that it is rooted in a subtle matter called **Light**. And this substance called **Light** is rooted in *Artha-brahman* or *Vāstu-brahman*. So, the technical tradition has identified and confirmed the existence of another OM called **OM-light**. This is the unique discovery of the *Vāstu-vedins*

I would like to quote a verse from the *Tejo-bindu-upaniṣad* of Atharva-vedic origin, in support of this discovery and discussion:

द्वे ब्रह्मणी वेदितव्ये शब्दब्रह्म परं च यत् ।
शब्दब्रह्मणि निष्णातः परं ब्रह्माधिगच्छति ॥

dve brahmaṇī veditavye śabdabrahma paraṁ ca yat /
śabdabrahmaṇi niṣṇātaḥ paraṁ brahmādhigacchati //

It says that there are two *Brahmans*, one is *Śabda-brahman* and the other is *Para-brahman*, which according to the technical tradition *is Artha-brahman* or *Vāstu-brahman*. It also says that he who is able to understand the dynamics of the *Śabda-brahman* will alone be able to appreciate the existence and dynamics of the *Para-brahman* or the *Artha-brahman*. This concept is further simplified, abridged and implied in the epithets like *Vāgartha* and *Padārtha*.

This phenomena would lead us to the conclusion that we must have had two distinct *Vedas*—one as *Vāgveda* and the other as *Vāstuveda*; they look like the two sides of a coin, as word and form, both being inseparable. In fact, the visual forms and the aural forms point to one entity which is denoted by the word *Parabrahman* in the foregoing verse. The *Śiplis* regard this *Parabrahman* as *Paravāstu*.

As a corrolary, it may be stated that in as much as there is grammar for sound forms (language) called *Vyākaraṇa*, it is logical to say that there should be a similar *Vyākaraṇa* for visual forms. And this grammar of visual forms is called *Vāstu Śāstra*, applicable to two levels of expression, one at subtle or inner level and the other at gross or outer level. This can be interpreted that sound technology and *Vāstu* technology are but two streams of expression with a common base—technological and scientific.

Architecture, whether ancient or modern, is concerned with spaces and configuration of spaces. On that account, architecture is defined as a science of spaces. The *Śabda-prapañca* and the *Artha-prapañca* are spaces and objects of the universe are also spaces. Even the universe wherein we are all suspended is also a space. These are all existential spaces.

There is one concept which we have to appreciate before we speak of space and spatial forms. Spaces, be they subtle of gross, should have three dimensions, viz., length, breath and depth, if they are to exist. Two dimensional things do not or cannot exist in this universe. For instance, a sheet of paper with length and breadth looking two dimensional, cannot exist if there is no thickness, which is the third dimension. So, when we speak of spaces, we have to assume that they are all Tri-dimensional. This would apply to music and dance as to sculpture and architecture, because sound is as much a matter as light is also a matter, though subtle. So, *Vāstu Śāstra* is very much concerned with spaces, i.e. Tri-dimensional spaces.

When we speak of spaces, we have to introduce you the existence of spaces at three levels, viz., the universal spaces that surrounds all objects of nature, our inner space which is a part of the outer space, and finally the earthly space which has erupted out of the outer celestial space. All these spaces have the innate capacity of going into experience and vibrating the experience into spatial forms. This is *Vāstu Veda*, a core science on which the whole corpus of *Vāstu* is anchored.

Now, let me say a few words on the origin and quality of space, both at subtle and gross levels and show how they are incorporated in the technology of Vāstu for raising buildings and preparing the layout of towns and villages.

As referred to earlier, the *Vāstu* principles are founded on a unique science of space with its origin in the primordial energy called *Brahman*. According to the *Taittirīya Upaniṣad*, from *Brahman* evolved the space, first. And from the space came forth air, fire, water and earth:

तस्माद् वा एतस्मादात्म आकाशः संभूतः । आकाशाद् वायुः । वायोरग्निः । अग्नेरापः । अद्भ्यः पृथिवी । पृथिव्या ओषधयः ।

tasmād vā etasmād ātmaṇah ākāśaḥ saṁbhutaḥ/ ākāśād vāyuḥ / Vāyor agniḥ /
agner āpaḥ/ Adbhyaḥ pṛthivī /Pṛthivyā oṣadhayaḥ //

The primordial energy, according to technical tradition, is called *Vāstu* and the elemental substances that issued forth thereafter are all called manifest energies. The word *Vāstu* is derived from the root '*vas*' to dwell or to exist. That substance which is subtle and eternal is called *Para Vāstu*. So, *Vāstu* is a common term denoting both gross and subtle substances. Therefore, the manifest energies or material energies are technically called *Vāstus*. What is very significant in this context is that in each of the space, air, water, fire and earth, the primordial energy dwells without which these *Vāstus* cannot function. The particle of energy dwelling in all the above-said substances as also in all the objects of the Universe is, therefore, called *Vāstu Puruṣa, Puruṣa* meaning energy. Therefore, we are all *Vāstus* and the energy dwelling in us is *Vāstu Puruṣa*. The word *Vāstu Puruṣa* can be interpreted as embodied energy or material energy. In fine, it must be clear that *Vāstu* is 'energy with matter' and *Vāstu* is 'matter with energy'. If we look at the whole phenomenon of Brahman evolving into material form, namely, earth and abstract it into a maxim it would sound that it is 'the subtle that turns into gross'. This phenomenon, stated technically, would run into a fact of science, viz., that it is '*vastu*' that turns into *Vāstu*'. Hence, the sūtra '*Vastu* is *Vāstu*'.

This space that has been referred to above is the space filled with energy. A part of the energetic space, we all know, lives in our physical body whereby we call it inner space. by which we are all called living beings. It is this free space that turns into or metamorphoses into Earth. From this the technical tradition has evolved a unique scientific theory about space and spatial forms. To restate that theory briefly in thiṣ When a part of the free space is isolated and enclosed by a four walled structure called building, it becomes a living organism and pulsates like a human being. The building is, therefore, an embodied energy, and has come to be called technically '*Prāsāda-puruṣa*', *prāsāda* meaning building, just like the energy contained in the earth is called '*Bhūmi-puruṣa*' or '*Vāstu puruṣa*'.

Primarily, the outer space (*bahirākāśa*) has a unique quality of experiencing and vibrating its experience into spatial forms, in an order, in as much as our inner space has the quality of experiencing and vibrating its experiences into spatial forms inwardly first and replicating them into material forms later, outwardly. In the same way, the earth, being a living organism, is capable of experiencing and sending forth waves of energy through its vibrations.

What is that phenomenon which looks common for all the three spaces? They all invariably pulsate and gush forth waves of energy, on account of which there occurs material growth of the living beings. And these energy waves, at the primary level of experience, is recognised to be a pattern of concentric squares, emanating from the centre, which centre is designated as centre of consciousness. This centre is denoted by the term '*Brahma-bindu*' in Vāstu and in the Āgamic scriptures, and '*Tejo-bindu*' in the *Vedānta.*

The concentric square pattern referred to above is a common and constant pattern emerging, at the primary level of experience, in terms of forms, irrespective of the space being the outer one, or the inner one or the earthly space. This framework of concentric squares is technically called *Vāstu-puruṣa-maṇḍala.* This means 'a pattern of material energy'! In modern parlance this is called 'energy grid'. In this process of evolution there occurs an explosion in the space by which the space splits itself into a grid of sixty-four small squares, each square being called '*Pada*'. The flowering of the '*Binḍu*' into sixty-four squares is called *Pada-vinyāsa.* In this process of expansion there is an orderly sequence of 1, 4, 16, 64, which is technically called *Pada-vibhāga* or *Pada-vinyāsa*, meaning division of spaces. And all such fractional spaces, starting from 1 to 4 and from 4 to 16 and finally from 16 to 64, are all perfect squares, thereby expressing the innate sense of order of the universal space. This order is called rhythm in respect of time and space. There are still more subtle points, which we shall not go into at this point.

There is one more aspect of the science of space, which would be of greater interest to all of us. This is with respect to another element emanating from the dormant primordial energy and which is responsible for the phenomenal explosion, and subsequent split into fractional spaces and ordering of the fractional spaces into a grid of perfect squares. That element which causes this phenomenon is called *Kāla* or Time which is actually the effortive force of energy exhibiting in terms of vibrations. For all the spaces into spatial form, this *Kala* is the root cause. The time-vibration emanating from the inner space continues to vibrate in a living body right from the birth till death. This *Kāla* is recognised as absolute and hence the saying that absolute time creates life, sustains life and causes its death.

In this connection, I would like to quote a śloka from the Skanda-purāṇa:

कालः सृजति भूतानि कालः संहरति प्रजाः ।
सर्वे कालस्य वशगाः स कालोऽस्य वशे स्थितः ॥
kālaḥ sṛjati bhūtani kālaḥ saṁharati prajāḥ /
sarve kālasya vaśagāḥ sa kālo'sya vaśe sthitaḥ //

Let me, at this juncture, elaborate a little on the concept of Absolute Time and explain briefly how the time-vibration causes the emanation of forms. To help understand it, let us bring into discussion the sound and sound spaces and how they are turned into sound forms and finally into pleasing musical forms.

The vibrations turning into sound forms can be understood easily if we look at the vibrations of a stringed instrument causing the emergence of sound spaces. If a discipline is imposed on the frequency of vibration it would be realised that they turn into variety of sound forms. The order imposed on the vibration is called rhythm or *Tālam*. It would be interesting to note that rhythm-bound sound spaces turn into sweet musical structures or forms. This is in brief the dynamics of sound and sound spaces.

The *Vāstu* technology is concerned with material spaces. The same unit of time or rhythm is extended to evolution of material spaces into spatial forms such as residential buildings, temple buildings, town and village layouts and extended even to imagic forms, furniture and household utensils. They are all, according to *Vāstu* technology, rhythm-bound material forms. It is in this process that the *Vāstu-puruṣa-maṇḍala* plays an important role.

This rhythm is the rhythm of the universal space which actually branches off into luminous material space and sound material space, with their source in light OM and sound OM, respectively. For these to function and take visual form, the emergence of *Kāla Brahman* turning into energy-grid is of paramount importance and significance, in the domain of *Vastu* and *Vāstu.*

And, lastly, I would also like to focus your attention on the aspect of evolution of energy waves from out of the inner space, outer space and earthly space. So far as the outer and earthly spaces are concerned, they maintain one and the same frequency of vibration or rhythm. But the wave pattern of human beings vary from individual to individual. Similarly, the wave patterns emanating from the enclosed space (building) vary from building to building. By a mathematical calculation, the building waves are made to resonate or harmonize with that of the individual's frequency of vibration. This is how man is prepared by *Vāstu* to live in harmony with the spirit of the earth and of the universe. This kind of harmonious life leads to spiritual well-being and material prosperity. This is achieved by what is called *Āyādi-gaṇana,* taking into calculation the birth star (*nakṣatra*) of the occupant and orientation of building called *Yoni.* Thereby, the peripheral measure of the building, derived from the *Vāstu-puruṣa-maṇḍala,* is arrived at.

Then comes the preparation of layout for a building, positioning of various living spaces within the building space, placements of doors and windows, etc.

The subject is so vast that it cannot be exhausted within the time-frame offered by the organisers of this symposium. I have been able to give you only some glimpses of the science underlying the technological operations in the domain of *Vāstu.*

The Concept of Vāstu-Puruṣa-Maṇḍala

*H.A. Savarkar**

Deho devālayaḥ proktaḥ sa jīvaḥ kevalaḥ śivaḥ /

The body is the temple of God and the Soul is God Absolute.

—*Skandopaniṣad,* 10ab

From the time immemorial, man has been striving to live his life in a painfree state. The very motive of experiments and inventions in all branches of science is to achieve pleasure, spiritual or mundane. It appears that through this process man has come to the present stage. The learned of the past have thought over the motive of man's endeavour and adopted certain rules which now have become customs. It is unfortunate that modern man has ignored the scientific principles underlying these rules.

Let us examine *Vāstu-puruṣa-maṇḍala* to find out the secrets about the health of a construction or a building.

It has been found that the buildings built in accordance with the rules of the *Vāstu-puruṣa-maṇḍala* have proved conducive to the 'health' of a building. In other words, the health of the inmates of a house is safeguarded. *Vāstu-puruṣa* means in the present context a site-plan or a location plan.

Mr. V. Ganapati, the well-known *Sthapati* from Madras has said that *Vāstu* is a living organism. While examining the statement, I have observed the following: The movable and immovable earth and its atmosphere consist of five basic elements of Earth (*pṛthvī*), Water (*āpa*), Light (*tejas*), Air (*vāyu*) and Ether (*ākāśa*). It is said that what obtains in a molecule obtains in the universe too: *Yathā piṇḍe tathā brahmāṇḍe* (see Fig. 1).

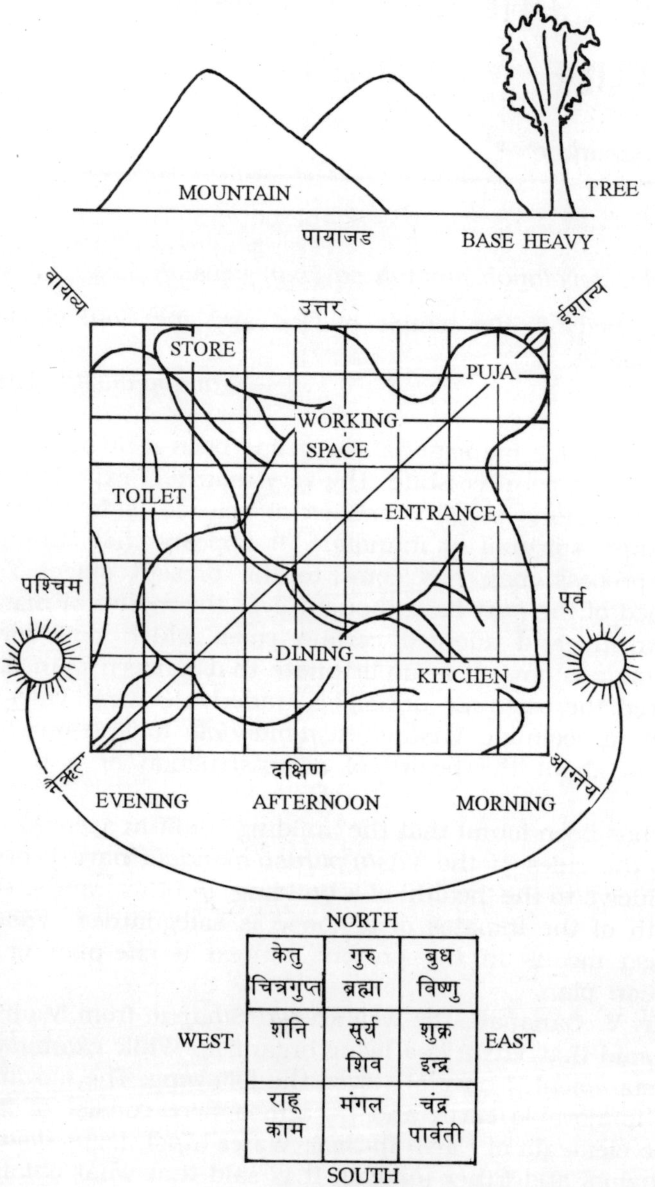

मत्स्यपुराण

MATSYAPURĀṆA

Fig. 1

We can concur with the statement for the following reasons:

1. The *Vāstu-puruṣa* is said to be lying with his face and stomach touching the ground. His head is at the North-East (*Aiśānya*) and legs at South-West (*nairṛtya*). The pressure point, i.e., the *Mulādhāra Cakra* in our body is at the bottom. The Mulādhāra Cakra denotes earth (*pṛthvī*) element. The base (*adhiṣṭhāna*) for the *Mulādhāra Cakra* should be stable. As per the position in the plan of *Vāstu Puruṣa* the direction is South-West (*nairṛtya*). Accordingly, it has been prescribed that the South-West portion of a building should be built in such a way as to be able to bear heavier weight. Even according to atmospheric circle, South-West (*nairṛtya*) portion receives more heat. Accordingly, it has been suggested that the walls in that direction should be made thicker.
2. The *Svādhiṣṭhāna Cakra* in the body is in lower stomach, near two kidneys. It is connected with water (*āpa*) element. According to *Vāstu-Puruṣa-Maṇḍala*, the position of this *Cakra* is to the South and West. Therefore, it has been prescribed that wet areas, like bathroom, etc., should be constructed in that direction. It is for sewerage (*utsarjana*).
3. The *Maṇipura Cakra* is at the navel. This *Cakra* is related to energy/fire (*tejas*). While in the womb of a mother, a foetus is fed with the essence of food and energy through umbilical cord connected with its navel. The *Vāstu Puruṣa Maṇḍala* shows *Brahmā* at the place of navel. The Lotus is the base (*āsana* or *adhiṣṭhāna*) of *Brahmā*. Thus, it is navel that connects *Brahman* with *Jīva* or *Piṇḍa* or life. It has, therefore, been prescribed to keep this particular place unoccupied or vacant. Therefore, the central square within a building is to be kept open to the skies. It is believed that *Vāstu Puruṣa* breathes through this open area (see Fig. 1).
4. *Anāhata Cakra* is near the heart. It is related to atmosphere or air (*vāyu*). The air is regulated by

lungs in the body.

5. *Viśuddha Cakra* is said to be in the throat. The hollowness in a throat denotes the ether (*ākāśa*) element. The word 'Om' is uttered through throat. The echo of an utterance exists in the hollow of the bone-box of head and the space in brain. The head of *Vāstu Puruṣa* is at the North-East (*aiśānya*). This direction is related to space (*ākāśa*). Atmospherically, this portion is cooler. It has, therefore, been suggested to construct a *Pūja* room (*devagṛha*) in this direction (see Fig. 2).

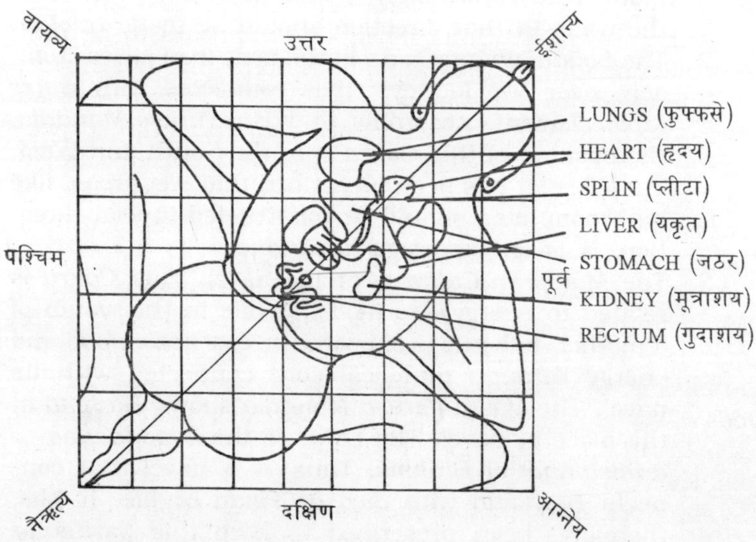

Fig. 2

The limbs, other than the above, of *Vāstu Puruṣa* are also connected with construction of a building. Liver (*yakṛt*) is an important organ for digestion. Liver is towards the South-West in the body. The *Sthapatis*, therefore, suggest to place cooking room or kitchen towards that direction, because it is related to *Agni*. Rays of the Sun first reach this direction. Pollution collected through a night is swept away by rays of the Sun. It is, therefore, possible that the suggestion of locating kitchen towards the South-East is due to this aspect.

The North-West (*vāyavyā*) is said to be the field presided by air (*vāyu*). Organs like stomach, spleen and rectum of the *Vāstu Puruṣa* fall on that portion. The store-room has been suggested towards that direction. A spleen, according to the science of medicine, does the work of storing and restoring blood in a body. Herbs of medicine are recommended to be planted towards the North-West. The suggestion through this recommendation appears to be that a dweller should get the fragrance of herbs through the air.

According to the *Matsya Purāṇa*, the Vāstu *Puruṣa Maṇḍala* has particular deities of *Vāstu Puruṣa* in respective places. The North-East (*aiśānya*) is said to be occupied by Mercury (*budha*) and Viṣṇu. Accordingly, the place of conducting mental work and the worship chamber in a house is to be situated in that direction.

The South-East (*agneyī*) is said to be occupied by the Moon and Pārvatī. The Moon is said to be the controller of mind and *Pārvatī* is the symbol of mother, of mind. Frailty is the nature of mind. If *Pārvatī* becomes the possessor of the house-hold, her place like that a housewife is in that direction. Cooking room is to be in the South-East.

The North-East (*Aiśānyā*) is said to be occupied by *Ketu* and *Citragupta*. So it is recommended that treasury accounts and store should be on that side.

The South-West (*nairṛtya*) is said to be controlled by *Rāhu* and *Kāma* or cupid. So a bedroom should be situated in that direction. *Rāhu* is said to be incomplete. Therefore, in order to bring completeness to life, this side must have been chosen for the purpose of marital life.

As stated before, the *Vāstu Puruṣa* lies with his back up. The concept may be that the burden is carried on the back. It is a rule that pillars are not to be raised on the sensitive points of *Vāstu Puruṣa.* The sensitive points according to the science of physics are inlets and outlets. It is presumed that the *Vāstu Puruṣa* would suffocate if inlets and outlets are blocked with pillars. The sensitive points exist also on the folds of the arms and legs. Pillars, if erected on those points, would not find enough base and support. Therefore, those points are to be avoided for pillars.

As stated before the South-West (*nairṛtya*) should be heavier and the North-East (*aiśānya*) should no be so. *Aisānya* is a place of *ākāśa-tattva* and, therefore, a place of deities. It is in consistence with Nature that the base should be heavier and the head should not be burdened. The hills and mountains and the trees too indicate so. Nature has given us five organs. The main organs are the eyes for vision, the ears for hearing, the nose to smell and the mouth to taste. They all are, geographically speaking, in the head portion of a body. The head of the *Vāstu Puruṣa* is at the *Aiśānya.* The head should be secure. It appears, therefore, that the North-East is to be kept free from heavy structures like pillars, etc. (see Fig. 3).

Our health is maintained, if we follow the rules of diet consistent with the rules of Nature. In the same manner, the health of a building or *Vāstu* can be maintained if the construction is made giving due regard to the principles of Nature. The limbs in a body should invariably be in their proper places. So much so, the rooms in a house should be designed in their proper places. That will keep the house healthy and thereby the inmates too happy. If one's eyes are placed at the shoulder, it would be abnormal. So is the case with a building.

The rule of the Universe is that the Sun is at the central place and the Earth and the other planets move around the Sun. *Vāstu Śāstra* appears to observe the same rule. The household duties such as deity-worship, study, or cooking are to be performed towards the East and the adjoining directions, i.e. the North-East and the South-East. The sun is in the mid-sky at noon, and so the middle

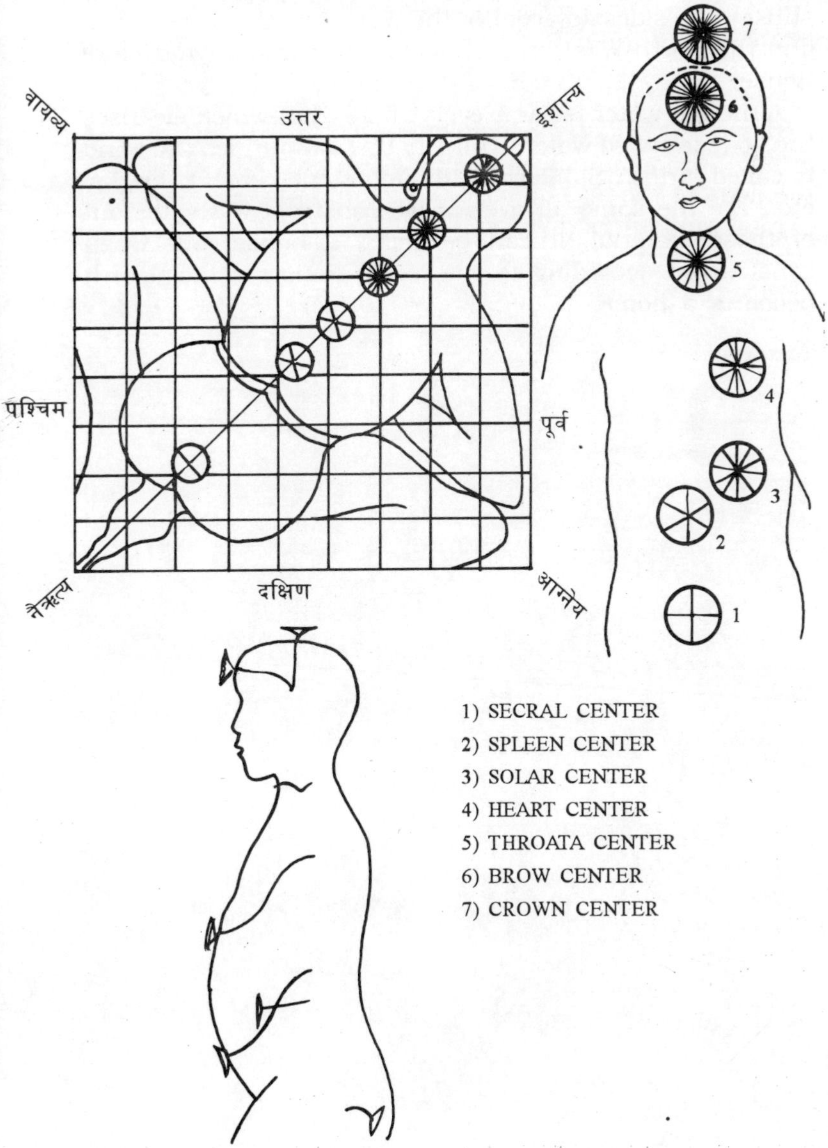
वायव्य
उत्तर
ईशान्य
पश्चिम
पूर्व
नैऋत्य
दक्षिण
आग्नेय
7
6
5
4
3
2
1
1) SECRAL CENTER
2) SPLEEN CENTER
3) SOLAR CENTER
4) HEART CENTER
5) THROATA CENTER
6) BROW CENTER
7) CROWN CENTER

Fig. 3

house is the dining hall and working place. After the sunset, the skies adjacent to the West, i.e., the South-West and the North-West are covered with bedrooms and store house.

Although water is same everywhere, that which cleanses the body is called water, while that which purifies the mind is called '*tīrtha*'. Similarly, although stone cement, bricks, etc., are the same all over, if we construct a shelter out of these material, it can be called a house, but when constructed according to the *Vāstu Puruṣa* principles, it becomes a home.

The Vāstu Puruṣa

*M.S. Thirumalachar**

There are many stories regarding *Vāstu Puruṣa*. As per the Hindu Mythology, in a war between Devas and Asuras, a demon appeared and started torturing the Devas. Ultimately the Devas pushed him down and sat over him. The demon appealed to Lord Brahmā for help. Lord Brahmā named him *Vāstu Puruṣa* and blessed him with the words: "All works on the earth will have to be commenced and concluded only after propitiating you." In essence, without *Vāstu Puruṣa* nothing will happen on the earth. The Vedas also give similar ideas to *Viśvakarman* or *Vāstu Puruṣa*. The *Ṛgveda* (10.81.3) says:

> विश्वतश्चक्षुरूत विश्ववतोमुखो विश्ववतोबाहुरुत विश्ववतस्पात्।
> सं बाहुभ्यां धमति सं पतत्रैर्द्यावाभूमी जनयन् देव एकः॥
> *viśvataścakṣur uta viśvatomukho viśvatobahur uta viśvataspāt /*
> *saṁ bāhubhyāṁ dhamati saṁ patatrair Dyāvābhumī janayan deva ekaḥ //*

'He who has eyes on all sides, mouth, arms and feet on all sides, and he who creates Heaven and Earth, wields them together with his arms as wings pervading the entire Universe.'

People think that construction of a house or abode is nothing but construction with bricks and mortar as per the plan. There are various aspects to be considered and consulted before and during construction. Even the position of doors (especially front door) and windows and the direction in which an entrance to the house is fixed, have

*99, Postal Colony, I Stage, Sanjaynagar, Bangalore-560 094.

a lot of significance in the well-being of owner and residents. The position of Vāstu Puruṣa and the direction of natural elements are shown in the diagram below. It shows all the Five Elements created by the Creator, Lord Brahmā, in this Universe.

The Divine Architect
(Vāstu Puruṣa)

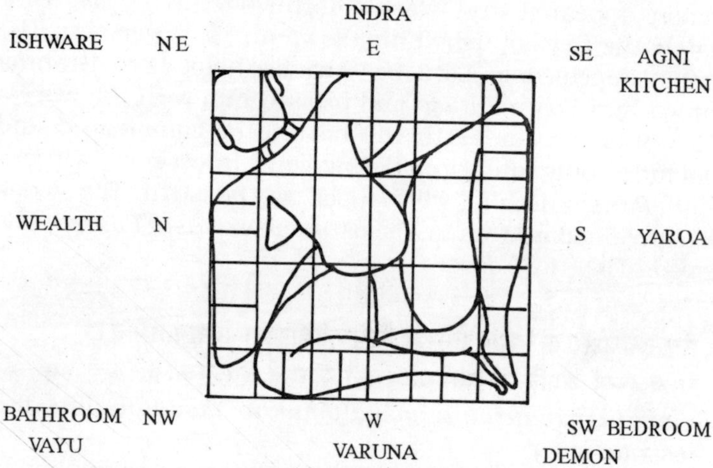

Vāstu Puruṣa Maṇḍala

The *Vāstu Maṇḍala* diagram showing the position where various utility services like kitchen, bedroom, bathroom, etc., should be situated in a house is also furnished. The sages have given beautiful and elaborate ideas for the construction of houses, temples, dams, towns, etc., according to *Vāstu Vidya* principles so that one can be happy without any trouble in life. Before starting construction of a house, according to the birth star and the *Lagna* of the owner of the house, the following are to be determined : the auspicious day, the direction in which (whether South, North, East or West) the entrance should be made, where the kitchen, bedroom, etc., are to be located. All these details are available in the Pañcāṅga.

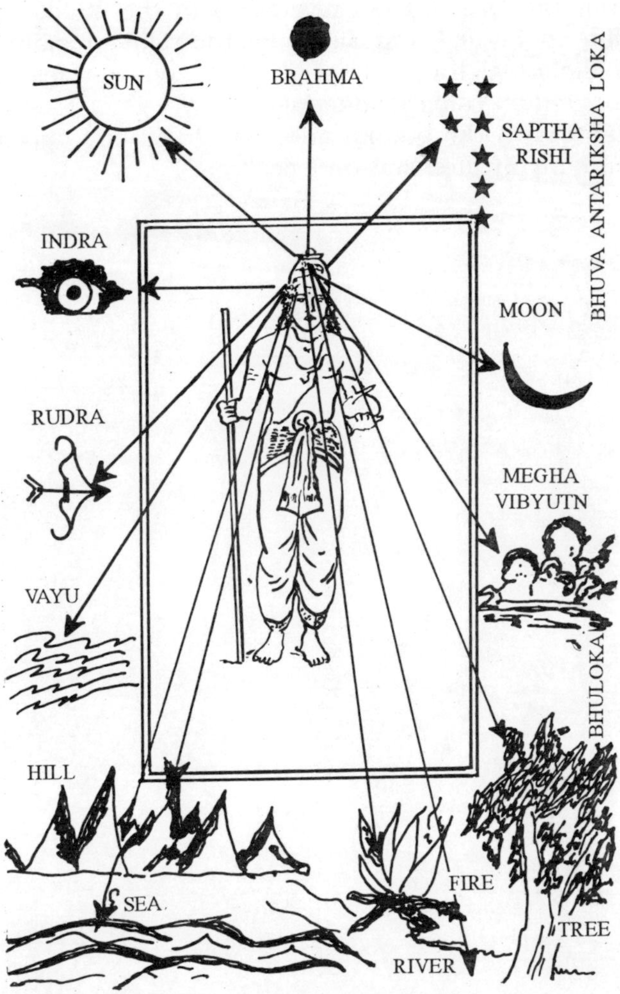

According to the Upaniṣads, Brahmā created the world out of Five. Elements, namely Air, Fire, Water, Earth and Atmosphere (*akasa*). Ravi, Candra, Sáni, Guru, Kuja (or *Aṅgāraka*) represent the five elements which make the Universe. Besides the above five, Dhanañjaya (the sixth Element) and Śukra (the seventh Element) are responsible for the life of all living beings on the earth and their happiness.

Sun, the lord of the Universe, is in the middle having Budha on his left and Śukra on the right presiding over and dictating the course of other planets (elements): *Brahmāṇḍaṁ caiva piṇḍāṇḍam.*

Rāhu is at the bottom and Ketu is exactly opposite to *Rāhu* both in direction and position.

Vāstu for Multi-Storeyed Residential Buildings

Dr. S.P. Sabharathnam, Ph.D., F.I.S.E.

Being the perfect and immaculate science of existence and energy, *Vāstu Vidyā* lays down rules for congenial and compact constructions that enhance harmony, longevity and beatitude in those dwelling in them. When each bit of the construction—be it a temple or residential building, sculpture or idol, vehicle or bedstead—becomes charged with harmony and beauty effected by relevant proportions, it harmonises not only with the other parts of the construction, but also with the people living there. This theory of *Vāstu* science is aimed at accomplishing an integrated, harmonious, sweet and bliss-oriented life. In setting forth the concept of mutual sweetness, the *Madhu Brāhmaṇa* of the *Bṛhadāraṇyaka Upaniṣad* (2.5.1) states:

> "This earth is honey to all beings; and all beings are honey to this earth. This shining immortal person who is in this earth (i.e. *Vāstu Puruṣa*) is honey to all beings and all beings are honey to this person. This shining immortal person who dwells as spirit in the body is honey to all beings and all beings are honey to this person. The Self is none other than this. This is the immortal; this is Brahman; this is all."

The exact meaning and significance of this mantra can be understood only against the background of *Vāstu* Vedic principles. At this juncture, it would be relevant to state that most of the Vedic mantras still remain to be explained. I understood and experienced them from the standpoint of the *Vāstu* Vedic principles. Without the application of *Vāstu* science, the exact purport of the Vedic and Āgamic passages could not be brought out.[1]

Vāstu Śāstras frequently emphasise the truth that there is no lifeless energy—less or soulless substance in the world. The dichotomy of insentient and sentient or that of inertness and consciousness may hold good in philosophical discussions but not in the science of the *Āgamas* and *Vāstu Veda*, according to which there is nothing in the universe bereft of animation and vibrancy. They view the entire world and worldly things as invested with breathing life, as invested with soul having proportionate dimensions. The undeniable common factor existing in both the beings and substances is what is known as proportion. "Proportions in things give pleasure to the mind because the same proportions are in the soul."[2] All things are suffused with breath and soul. That is why the *Vāstu Vedas* and the *Āgamas* speak of the classification as male, female and neuter to be observed in stones, trees, plants, lands, buildings and so on.

Buildings are essentially living organisms; breathing and living frames. Not only this. They have *movement* in their own static existence. They have *music* in their own structure. Mayan, in his work called the '*Aintiram*' goes to the extent of saying that each static substance is moving within itself and as such there is no substance which could be stated as absolutely static. Each static substance is associated with proportionate dynamism. So all the buildings are dynamic structures and all of them are musical and melodious,—if at all they have been constructed according to the *Vāstu Vedic* directions.

Even though there are innumerable injunctions to be followed for the construction of perfect buildings, there are some principles which need immediate attention and observation, and which should not be neglected or violated, especially in the case of multi-storeyed buildings. They are the rules related to the central square or central space (*brahma-sthāna*) and the plinths, rules related to the height of the building and to the height of each floor or storey and the principles concerned with the final or top construction. These are briefly discussed here.

Central Space and Plinth

In the construction of a temple or residential or other civic building, the central square, technically known as *Brahman-sthāna* and decided by an appropriate *Vāstu-maṇḍala*, is the main factor for the longevity of the building. In the temple, usually this central square becomes the main shrine (*garbha-gṛha*). In a house it becomes the central and unoccupied open space for homely functions and ritualistic activities. The rule that no construction should be laid on the *Brahma-sthāna* is not strictly adhered to in modern days. Since this rule is the most scientific, it should not be neglected.

Architectural constructions are, as stated earlier, living organisms and they behave like human beings. Like the living beings, they vibrate and pulsate; they breathe. For such breathing structures, the central space serves as the lungs. If the lungs are filled with substances other than air, what would happen?

The central space should be set aside or left free for the confluence of cosmic and elemental energies. It should be free of structural elements and it is meant to effect breathing power to the enclosed space. It is considered to be the spiritual centre and when it is maintained in perfect order and harmony, those dwelling in it could experience well-being and sweetness. The central space could be used as a hall or open courtyard meant for celebrations and weddings. It is prohibited for daily household activities. The daily activities, such as bathing, eating, sleeping and others are restricted to the rings known as *Manuṣya-pada* and *Paiśāca-pada*. No construction is laid down either in *Brahma-pada* or in *Daiva-pada*.[3]

Rules related to the plinth (*upāna and Adhiṣṭhāna*) are also to be essentially followed. The height of the plinth should be determined based on the height of the whole structure, which height is ascertained from the width of the building. For the building which is akin to the human form. Upana, the lower level of the basement and *Adhiṣṭhāna*, the upper level serve as the footrest and foot respectively. On the importance of plinth, G.K. Pillai writes: "The *Śilpis* used to pay great attention to plinth, which the present builders avoid as much as possible probably based on a false idea of economy. The height of the plinth should be proportionate to the height of the columns or to the height of the walls. A high plinth not only presents a goods elevation but it makes the verandahs useable when the rain falls. The secondary plinths not only covers the building, but it covers the yards all around or the '*bāhyāṅgaṇa*'. This remedies a great deal, the trouble from insects and creeping abominations that are abundant in a climate like that of India.[4]

More specifically, the rules governing the central space and the plinth should be meticulously observed in the case of multi-storeyed buildings.

Height of the Multi-storeyed Buildings

As set forth in the *Mānasāra*, there are six types of building-designs and they are: *Daṇḍaka*, *Svastika*, *Maulika*, *Caturmukha*, *Sarvatobhadra* and *Vardhamāna*. For all designs of the buildings, the width is considered to be the fundamental dimension.[5] All other dimensions are derived only from the width. Whether the architectural structure is a temple or residential or official building, the width remains as the primal measure.[6] The width is further divided into smaller units known as modules to facilitate the calculation of the dimensions of minor members of the structure. The modern architects, who are not well-rooted in the science of *Vāstu*, do not consider the exact 'dimension' of the width dimension. By according disproportionate length and height, they disturb the harmony of the building, distort the energy balance and displace its central axis, the main conduit for the inflow of cosmic forces.

According to the Vāstu Śāstra, the length of the building is ascertained in the following proportions, based on its width:

Width	:	Length	Width	:	Length	Width	:	Length
1	:	1¼	1	:	2	1	:	2¾
1	:	1½	1	:	2¼	*1*	*:*	*3*
1	:	1¾	1	:	2½			

(Maximum length allowed is three times the width.)

The proportion 1 : 2 is considered to be most suitable and favourite, because this proportion is capable of effecting an octave note. Again, this recommendation strengthens the concept that a building is essentially a musical structure.

The height of a building is the distant between the basement and the top (*Upānādi stupi-paryantam; janmādi stupi-paryantam*). This height dimension is also determined on the basis of the width. There are five kinds of height, each bearing a significant name:

1. Height in proportion to width as 1:1 is called *Śāntika*;
2. Height in proportion to width as 1:1¼ is called *Pauṣṭika*;
3. Height in proportion to width as 1:1½ is called *Jayada*;
4. Height in proportion to width as 1:1¾ is called *Dhanada*;
5. Height in proportion to width as 2 is called *Adbhuta*.

(The proportions $1{:}1^{3}/_{7}$, 1:1½ , 1:¾; 1:2, $1{:}2^{1}/_{8}$ are applicable to temples only.)

If the width is 20 feet, we can have five different heights as 20, 25, 30, 35 and 40 feet.

Different heights may be derived from the process known as *Patti-māna* or *Patti-bheda*, which means modular division of the width. Based on the width of the ground floor, the height of the ground floor is first ascertained. The height of the ground floor should be divided into six modular units and leaving the dimension of one unit, the dimension of five units should be taken as the height of the first floor:

Height of the first floor=of the height of the ground floor;
Height of the second floor=of the height of the first floor;
Height of the third floor=of the height of the second floor;
Height of the fourth floor=of the height of the third floor;

and so on. But this rhythmic method of the proportions determining the heights of the upper storeys is not followed by modern builders; they accord equal height to all the storeys. In the non-traditional method of providing equal height to the storeys, what happens is the imbalance of the enclosed space, and the impediment to the equal and uniform distribution of energy throughout the whole structure. In short, the harmony and melody of the building are vitiated.

There should be a gradual and rhythmic reduction in the

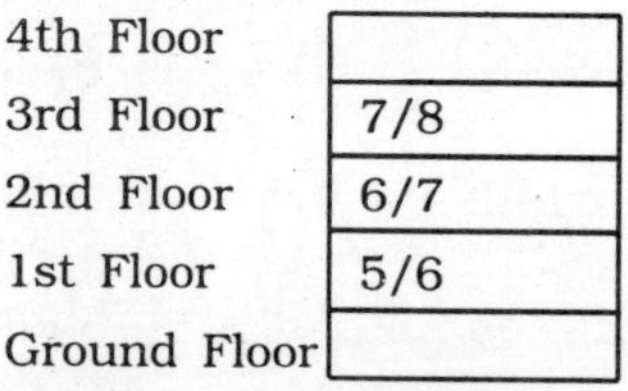

Recommended height for multistoreyed buildings according to *Vāstu Śāstra*.

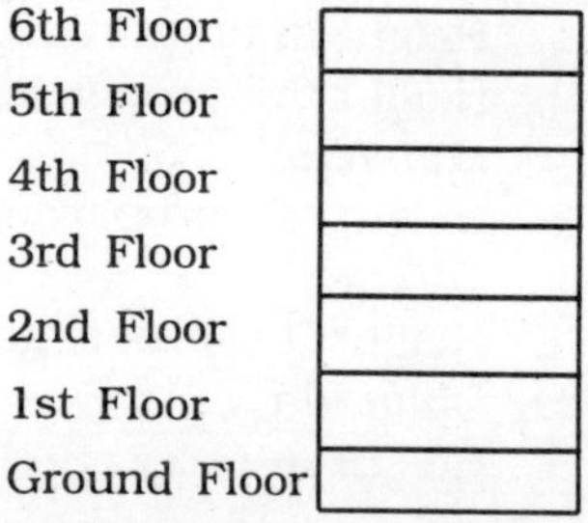

Equal heights for the floors not recommended nor desirable.

height of each succeeding storey:

There is another method of determining the proportionate heights of the storeys as prescribed in the *Mānasāra*. The total height of the whole building should first be determined based on the width. The dimension of height should be divided into convenient number of modular units and these units should be distributed from the plinth to the top. For example, if the total height of a six-storeyed building is divided into fifty-seven equal parts,

Plinth : 4½ parts	pillar : 5 parts	Entablature: 1 ½ parts
Pillar : 7 "	Entablature: 2½ "	Vedika : 1 "
Entablature : 3½ "	Pillar : 4½ "	Neck : 4 "
Pillar : 6 "	Entablature: 2 "	Sherical roof 4 "
Entablature : 3 "	Pillar : 4½ "	Finial : 4 "

Total: 57 parts.

the distribution of these parts would be as follows:

This scheme also shows the gradual and rhythmic reduction in the height of the succeeding upper storeys. (Note: With all the reverence and appreciation to P. K. Acharya whose service in the field of traditional *Vāstu* should be cherished and acknowledged, I beg to state that his English translated of the *Mānasāra* needs revision and re-editing. He translates ślokas 27 and 28 of Chapter 35 thus: "Of the five proportions, the height, from the base to the top of the upper storeys, should be less than the height of the lower storeys by one-sixth, one-seventh, one-eight, one-ninth and one-tenth, respectively (i.e. for *Śāntika*, *Pauṣṭika*, *Jayaka*, *Dhanada* and *Adbhuta*)". This is not the exact sense of the ślokas referred to. This should be understood as one-sixth for the first floor, one-seventh for the second floor, and so on.)

It may well be observed that the multi-storeyed building whose floors are according to the prescribed height-dimensions, would exactly fit in into the shaft of *Vīṇā* instrument. In the shaft of the *Vīṇā* from the left to the right, the distance between the two consecutive rods is gradually reduced. They are closer on the side of the resonating spherical frame. If this reduction is not rendered, we cannot hear pleasant and sweet music, according to the *Svaras*. In the like manner, the multi-storeyed building, being essentially a musical structure, has its floors with gradual reduction of height. This is because the measure used both in the building and in the musical instrument *Vīṇā* is the Time-measure.[7]

"Wherever there is harmony or an apt numerical relationship, there is music, and thus, there is music everywhere in the world."[8] The aestheticians assert that the essence of music is proportion and number. Music of sound is only one form of music. Movement is also one of the multi-varied forms of music. Since the building is brought into existence with proportion and number, and since it is invested with movement from top to bottom, it emits musical notes on par with a musical instrument.

Ganapathy Sthapati, in his recent work entitled 'Temples

of Space-science' succinctly reiterates the view that buildings are musical structures and that both the human body and the building are in the modified form of the *Vīṇā.*[9]

According to the science of *Vāstu*, the top of the uppermost floor should not be vacant, giving a truncated appearance. The roof should be rendered with head and tuft (*śikhara* and *stūpi*) beautified by architectural ornamentations. With regard to the human form, the head with an uptied tuft would seen more pleasant than the cropped or shaven head. Similarly, the roof endowed with *Śikhara* and *Stūpi* would be more pleasant than the flat and empty roof. In the multi-storeyed building which is akin to the shaft of the Vina, the space surrounding the *Śikhara* and *Stūpi* serves as the resonating spherical frame of the *Vīṇā* instrument. Only the elements related to the finial give pleasant effect to the whole building and produce cooling effect in the floor below. The space rendered by *Śikhara* and *Stūpi* is considered to be a logical completion bereft of truncation and unevenness. Perfect order and harmony are maintained only by the *Śikhara*, *Stūpi* and other finial members.

With regard to the proportion, the scriptures on Vastu state that the height of the roof (*prastara*) should be 1½ times the modular unit of the last storey. Above the *Prastara*, the *Vedikā* should be half the number of times the modular unit of the last storey. Above the *Vedikā* is *Kaṇṭha*, whose height should be twice the height of *Vedikā*. Then comes *Śikhara* whose height is twice the height of the *Kaṇṭha*. The remainder part would be the height of the *Stūpi*.

* * *

Vitruvious lists out six important characteristics of a building—order, arrangement, economy, symmetria, eurhythmy and suitability. Of these, eurhythmy is the most important. Eurhythmy is that pleasantness which depends on the beautiful shape of the building and on the proper appearance achieved by the arrangement of its individual parts. The science of Vāstu renders all these essential characteristics to the building by means of proportionate dimensions and proper allocation of parts. The *Vāstu* tradition provides simple techniques to effect everlasting harmony between the outer space, the built space and the inner space of the inhabitant. The trinity of music comprises music in the universe, music in man and music in the work of man. Likewise, the trinity of space comprises the universal space, the individual or inner space and the enclosed space. When all the three spaces are in harmony or in identical proportions, then it is possible for the inhabitants to experience peace, contentment and bliss.

It is said that the true musician is one who understands the harmony of being. The true architect is one who understands the harmony of being and the harmony of structure. It is the hope of the traditional architects that the modern builders would take into consideration the basic tenets laid down in the *Vāstu Śāstra* for the construction of multi-storeyed buildings.

REFERENCES AND NOTES

1. I invite the kind attention of the Vedic scholars to the significant explanation for the *Rgvedic Mantra*: '*Sa bhūmiṁ viśvato vṛtvā*" given by Ganapathy Sthapati based on the science of *Vāstu*.
2. *History of Aesthetics* by Wladyslaw Tatarkiewicz, Vol. II, p. 75.
3. Only this pada theory is valid and applicable. There is another process known as Vithi-mana which does not suit the concept of Pada-mana.
4. G.K. Pillai, *The Way of the Silpis*, pp. 240-241.
5. Even in some western traditions, width is considered to be basic. This was the case with the Gothic architects. See the *History of Aesthetics*, Vol. II, p. 160.
6. See Mayan's *Aintiram*.
7. "Space unit = Time unit. This is the Time-measure that is being used by the traditional architects to produce three dimensional building forms." - "*The Scale*" by Ganapathi Sthapati.
8. *History of Aesthetics*, Vol. II, p. 126.
9. *Temple of Space Science*, p. 61; p. 66.

Vāstu and Modern Engineering

Dr. Bangalore Sureshwara

The *Vedas* and the *Vedāṅgas* include vast information related to various disciplines of science and technology, including *Vāstu Śāstra. Vāstu* or *Vāstu Śāstra* is a treasure-house of knowledge relating to dwellings of all sorts. The traditional knowledge of *Vāstu* is primarily related to various phases encompassing dwellings covering houses of God and humans. The word *Śāstra* clearly implies that it is a science that evolved over a period of time extending to thousands of years. When a subject such as *Vāstu* develops over such an extended time period, it is expected that the various masters must have carefully and cautiously observed and documented the correlation between certain input and the corresponding output. It is a straightforward but not a simple correlation. The input is represented by the architectural, construction and engineering components defined by *Vāstu.* The output is the effect and influences of *Vāstu* on the humans. The output is essentially represented by the emotional, physical and material aspects experienced by the individuals and society at large. A particular individual or Yajamana is usually identified with a dwelling. Thus, an instant equation or a relationship is established between the horoscope of the individual and the physical dwelling. Thus *Grahacāra* and *Gṛhacāra* (effects related to or influenced by dwelling) are the two components of the Vedic equation. These two components are inter-related, inter-dependent and inter-twined. Therefore, it is necessary to recognize that the best of constructions based on *Vāstu* alone will not be a magic wand that will minimize

*463, Surryse Road, Lake Zurich, Illinois-60047, U.S.A.

or eliminate all the problems, related to mental, physical and material components of one's life. Only if the horoscope has non-negative indications, can one expect the effects of *Vāstu* to smoothen many bumpy aspects of life into tolerable ones. Thus *Gṛhacāra* of *Vāstu* will complement *Grahacāra* to relatively enhance or improve the quality of one's life.

As an engineer who is experienced with both low-tech and high-tech engineering, I like to share with you primarily some aspects relating to the strength and construction characteristics that are contained in the great treasure house of knowledge that is wrapped in *Vāstu Śāstra*.

The modern knowledge identified with civil and structural engineering covers the construction and strength characteristics of a dwelling. The size, location and orientation characteristics of the dwelling and its components are viewed usually from the angle of *Vāstu*. It is important to note that certain overlapping as well as conflicting requirements are possible when one wants to achieve the best of the two worlds by integrating the modern discipline with the Vedic treasure-house of information and knowledge.

Until now only the tip of the knowledge available from Vāstu has been recognized. It appears the emphasis is to look at the *Vāstu* from only the angle of location, size and orientation of the structure. Such an emphasis is not complete, because it does not take into account the information that it contains related to the construction materials and strength characteristics. At this time there is not enough evidence to show that the information related to material strength characteristics has been explored to the point that certain comfortable conclusions can be made. There is vast ocean of knowledge available in *Vāstu* that has to be discovered by students and researchers. The available literature on Vāstu already indicates that it also contains some applied structural engineering too.

Some of the ancient architectural masters were Viśvakarmā, Maya, Kāma and Hiraṇyagarbha. Palaces or mansions of many storeys have been mentioned in the *Vāstu* literature. Obviously, high-rise buildings of modern times are not the exclusive innovation or invention of the modern man. The existence of sophisticated construction technology is indicated by the reference to various construction materials : *Mandira* (stone), *Vāstu* (backed bricks), *Sudhara* (mud), *Manasya* (woodlogs), *Nandana* (bamboos), *Vijaya* (canvas), *Kalima* (straw). The resistance to or transfer of external loads (wind, hail, snow, or other dead or live loads) in any structure (dwelling) can be considered as a simple mechanism consisting of tensile (stretch), compression (shrink) and/or combination loads. All the Vedic construction materials identified above possess strength characteristics relative to either compression or tensile load.

We can observe that the ancient masters have used generic names for the construction materials. For example, *Manasya* or wood logs, could be wood beams or columns of circular or other geometric shapes. These wood structural elements could be of any specie, size or geometric shape. In fact, it is very common to see in many Western countries, such as the United States and Canada, the extensive use of wood as structural or load carrying members.

What is *Kalima* or straw? No one will believe for a moment that the architects of yesterday generations were talking of the common straw that one obtains from green grass of similar materials. The straw is a generic identification of a structural member that supports load primarily by tension or stretch characteristics.

The simple but a significant structural member identified as straw by Vedic architects is identified to-day by the high-tech engineering as cable. Straw signifies stretch by tension. Cable also signifies stretch by tension. Neither straw nor cable are utilized for taking any compression loads. What is *Nandana* or canvas? Canvas is a thin membrane material of certain strength or structural characteristics. It easily bends but it supports structural load by stretching, which generates pure and simple tension or tensile stresses. Another way to define a canvas is to consider it as a series of straws that are integrated. Further, the ancient architects were familiar not only with structural engineering but also with the construction technology related to building materials. In fact bricks were categorized as old, new, raw, and backed bricks. When we see such a close correlation between the materials used in the Vedic period to the materials used today, we may be inclined to express an opinion that may be all said and done, we may after all somewhat be reinventing the wheel that existed in the Vedic period!

Chapter 53 of Varāhamihira's *Bṛhatsaṁhitā* covers *Vāstu-vidyā* or house building. Śloka 23 indicates that the walls of house made of burnt-bricks should be one-sixteenth part of their breadth. It can be inferred that the recommendation regarding the thickness of the brick is based on certain analytical engineering principles. It is well known that the load distribution characteristics is through compressive or bearing load. Its tensile strength is virtually negligible. In typical house construction, every civil and construction engineer is aware that the load transfer from the roof to the brick wall is primarily through compression.

The question is not only whether the thickness of the wall should be atleast one-sixteenth part of the breadth, but more importantly, why? While avoiding a detailed discussion on the strength characteristics of the various bricks, one needs to remember that all bricks need not necessarily have same or similar strengths. Therefore, the thickness of the wall depends upon the strength of the type of brick used in a particular construction.

Another recommendation or requirement in Vāstu, as indicated in Śloka 11, Chapter 53 of the *Bṛhatsaṁhitā* is that it is auspicious if the height and the breadth of the house should be the same.

The word "auspicious" must be taken in the context of the time. A number of questions arise in the mind of the architect or the engineer regarding the 1:1 ration relating to the height and breadth of the house. Was the ratio prescribed for aesthetic purposes ? Does the ratio relate to proper and optimum distribution of loads acting on the walls ? Do certain openings in the wall present ventilation and light based on the ration value ? These and other questions need to be reviewed after careful study of the texts. There is a lot of information that is not obvious at the first review of the text. But one thing is clear that *Vāstu* encompasses vitality beyond the size, location and orientation of the building.

We all have noticed that in some of the sophisticated buildings one thing that makes it look majestic is the massive supporting columns or pillars. Great historical buildings are brought to life by those magnificent pillars. Therefore, no doubt, our ancients had also given great importance to pillars, the important structural component of a building. Ślokas 28, 29 and 30 pertain to architectural and structural aspects related to pillars and beams. Śloka 30 explicitly indicates that the thickness of the chief or primary beam is equal to that of the pillar. When the chief beam is supported by the pillar, the load distribution from the beam to the pillar is through two interfaces located at the junction of the two structures. As the bearing surface areas are equal, the stresses occurring at the interface are equal. Although, this is elementary engineering analysis, it is yet another reminder that the strength aspect is a vital part of *Vāstu.* There is mention of "beams and minor beams". This correlates to the secondary and tertiary beams that are used in modern day structures, such as portal-frames. Śloka 30 also indicates that the thickness of beams and minor beams "is lessened by a quarter of the immediately preceding one". This statement clearly establishes that the inclusion of structural design guidelines in Vāstu reflects the design guidelines of many portal structures of today.

Here, it is upto us now to carefully study the implications of the various structural characteristics indicated in the *Vāstu Vedas*, relative to the requirements covered under today's engineering criterae. Any comparison or correlation between the requirements indicated in *Vāstu Śāstra* and modern engineering is possible only when we fully understand or comprehend the classical equations or relationships furnished by our seers and sages. However, ignoring any criteria because of possible oversight or unfamiliarity with either the terminology or implied meaning or message is to be avoided.

One of our objectives today is to understand the intrinsic value or utility of *Vāstu Śāstra* as an applied science and technology related to the construction of a building. Its use will result in enhancing the quality material and spiritual—of life in today's troubled world. As the results of the application of *Vāstu Śāstra* spread around our environment, it will remind us that the Vedic science and technology are not time related subjects but eternal. While we are enthused about the intended benefits of *Vāstu Śāstra*, we need to be equally aware that further study and research are vital to fully comprehend the subtle information contained in the texts authored by our sages and seers. While we need not rush to judgments in our understanding of the material, it is necessary to devote and dedicate sufficient time and effort so that we can play a vital role in guiding and helping the coming generations.

Importance of Vāstu*

Madhura Krishnamurthy Sastry

Vāstu is of paramount significance in Indian culture and it has a rich heritage. There are many works on *Vāstu*. Of these the most important are: the *Mayamata*, the *Samarāṅgaṇa-sūtradhāra*, the *Mānasāra*, the *Aparājitapṛcchā*, etc. Right from the selection of a site, every single detail of architecture and living is analysed with reference to both the body and mind, matter and energy.

Land is the most important criterian in *Vāstu*. Regarding this, the *Mayamata* says:

> *bhūr eva mukhyaṁ vāstu syāt tatra jātāni yāni hi /*
> *prāsādādīni vastūni vastutvāt vāstu-saṁśrayāt /*
> *vastuṁ evā 'vanīm eva prāptaṁ yasmin purātanaiḥ //*

Vāstu is also classified into different categories on the basis of Jāti and Varṇa. In Jāti we have the Devatā, Mānava and Rākṣasa. In Varṇa we have Brahma, Kṣatra, Vaiśya and Sūdra.

The *Samarāṅgaṇa-sūtradhāra* widely discusses these various types of lands based on geographical and climatic conditions. Accordingly, we have three main types: Jāṅgala, Anūja and Sādhāraṇa. Of these, Jāṅgala is a site full of forests. Anūja is marshy land, while Sādhāraṇa refers to the common. However, some authors add a fourth type, namely the Ūṣara (the desert). Bhoja again classifies these three main types into sixteen sub-divisions. However, these sixteen types are based on the nature of the possessor also. *Sthala* is a technical term given to the static constructions and they also bear the name *Sthala-vāstu*. The fundamental patterns of *Sthala-vāstu* are myriad. However, Bhoja

* Translated into English from Telugu by S. Ranganath and R. Ganesan.

considers only twelve. They include the Sanene, rectangle, triangle, circle, trapezim, rhombus, semi-circle, elliptical, wide opened, parabolic and odd. Of these Bhoja prefers only the first two.

Vāstu, though mainly akin to the earth, is also concerned with other *Mahābhūtas*. Hence, based on the pronounced effect of different Bhūtas, lands can also be classified.

The classification of *Vāstu* according to the parameter *Jāti* principally has to do with structural elegance and material management. The classification of *Vāstu* in accordance with *Varṇa* mainly has a professional view and cultural needs.

The foremost step to be taken while erecting a *Vāstu* is the test of a site (*bhū-pariśodhana*). This has a Vedic significance also. Here, inauspicious omens and the like, and deposits in the land will be checked and finally the land will be ploughed and set in grit. Here, we have different ways of *bhū-pariśodhana* as expounded in methods like *Catuṣṣaṣṭipadā Vāstu*, *Ekāśitipadā Vāstu*, *Śatapadā Vāstu*, *Padavinyāsa Paddhati*, etc. Among these, the last is very useful as it considers all the aspects of *Vāstu* implications. It is also lamented that modern civil and architectural engineering methods are unaware of these subtleties.

Now coming to general construction of a common residence, we have chapters like *Gṛhotpatti*, *Ālaya-nirmāṇa-vidhi*, *Manuṣyalenya-candrikā*, etc. The concept of *Sthla* is very significant in Indian *Vāstu*. *Sthala* generally refers to a covering and depending upon the numbers, we have *Ekasthala*, *Dvisthala*, *Tristhala*, and *Catuḥsthala*. There are several other types of houses like *Chandogṛha* and *Miśragṛha*. As the names themselves indicate, they are constructed freely and with combinations. Classical works, like the *Mānasāra* and the *Samarāṅgaṇa-sūtradhāra*, subdivide the *Sthalagṛhas* into several hundred ways and even add the concepts of *Vaneha-sthala*, *Ṣaṭsthala*, *Śapta-sthala*, *Aṣṭa-sthala*, *Nava-sthala* and *Daśa-sthala*. Thus, the *Aparājita-pṛcchā* finally discusses a total number of 10,48,576 types of *Gṛhas*. This itself is a striking evidence of the constructional wisdom of our ancients. The *Samarāṅgaṇa-sūtradhāra* is unique when it says:

मूषासंस्थान भेदेन भिन्नानां वेश्मनां पुनः।
जायन्ते कोटिशो भेदा यस्मान्नोक्तानि तान्यतः॥

(*Sam. Sū* 25,163)

mūṣa-saṁsthāna-bhedena bhinnānaṁ vesmanāṁ punaḥ/
jāyante kotiśo bhedā yasmān noktāni tāny ataḥ //

Depending upon the status of people residing in the structures, we have a set of different classification, like the *Sāmānyajana-nivāsa-gṛha* (common man's residence), *Prabhu-nivāsa-gṛha* (residence of lords), *Devatā-gṛha* (abode of gods) and *Prajopayukta-nirmāṇa* (structure of public utility).

The *Śilpa-Śāstra* prescribes a minimum of eight sections in a common residence. They are: *Snāna-gṛha* (bath-room), *Alaṅkāra-gṛha* (dressing room), *Dravya-sthāpana-gṛha* (store room), *Pacana-gṛha* (kitchen), *Pūjā-gṛha* (place of worship, *Bhojana-gṛha* (dining room), *Śayana-gṛha* (bed-room) and *Dhanagṛha* (treasury).

Residences of rich and high officials may have many more facilities ranging upto fortytwo classes. Additional rooms like *Vāsa-gṛha* (living room), *Kūja* (well), *Gṛhiṇī-gṛha* (mistress room), *Āyudha-gṛha* (arms cell), *Vasanālaya* (common room), *Homakarma-gṛha* (place of sacred fire), *Cākara-gṛha* (place of servants), Sūtikālaya (maternity home), *Dāsālaya* (servants' place), *Saṁmelana-gṛha* (friends' room), *Gośālā* (cattle shed), *Vahanaśālā* (vehicles shed), *Bālālokana-maṇḍapa* (children's play house), *Vivāha-maṇḍapa* (marriage place), *Vastrācchādana-gṛha* (dressing room), *Kanyārtālaya* (maiden room), *Bāla-gṛha* (boys' room), *Vidyābhyāsa-maṇḍapa* (learning place), *Tailābhyṅga-maṇḍapa* (place of oil-bath), *Āsthāna-maṇḍapa* (formal court), *vilāsa-vilāsinī-maṇḍapa* (amusement room for gents and ladies), *Atithi-gṛha* (guest house), *Rakṣākāra-gṛha* (body-guards' house), *Parivāra-gṛha* (attendant room), *Yojya-gṛha* (solders' place), *Yuvarāja-gṛha* (prince's place), *Amātya-sandhāna-gṛha* (commanding room), *Sopāna-maṇḍapa* (staircase), *Nāṭyamaṇḍapa* (dance hall), etc.

Now coming to an important aspect of *Vāstu-guṇa-doṣa-viveka*, we have some salient points:

1. The spot should preferably be savana or rectangular in shape.
2. The plot should not slope in the eastern and northern directions.
3. Entry should be provided from the North-Western and North-Eastern directions for a house which has roads by Eastern and Northern directions.
4. North-Western, North-Eastern and South-Eastern entries can be provided for residences where roads pass by the Southern direction.
5. The roads should be constructed in such a way that the streets which run from South to North should be much wider than those which run from East to West.
6. In the case of multi-storeyed buildings, the walls of the lower floors should be comparatively thicker than those of the higher ones.
7. Regarding the steps and staircases, not much restriction is imposed. However, in the *Mānasāra*, preference is given for quadrangular steps.
8. A rule is also provided as not to construct the main entrances of the opposite houses in one line.
9. A quadrangle and the corridor of the house should preferable lead to the main entrance in clockwise direction.
10. Gates, pillars, beams, doors and windows should be even in number.
11. The length and breadth of the residences should be in even proportion with the height of pillars.

The *Narada-mata* gives a few hints regarding directional location of some of the residential features. Accordingly, always a bath-room should be provided in the Western direction. Kitchen, toilet, arms cell and dining halls can be accommodated in the South-Eastern direction. Southern side is preferred for bed-rooms. South-Eastern direction is good for granery, store house, treasury and ladies room.

North-Eastern direction is advisable for Dvara (shed for domestic animals like sheep, and hen).

By looking at these varieties we can very easily infer the life-styles of our ancient people. It is also stated that the common man's residence can have some of the above-mentioned features. A few Śāstrakāras add *Dadhimathana-gṛha* (curd-churning place), *Vaneno-gṛha* (toilet), *Gīta-gṛha* (music hall), *Vāda-gṛha* (debate room), etc.

A residence is divided into three wings: the front, the central and the dorsal. Of them, the front portion is named as *Brahma-bhāga* and here studies, official transactions, discussions and other study transactions may be carried out. The central portion named as *Gandharva-bhāga* consists of bed rooms, living rooms, treasuries, entertainment features, etc. The last portion named as *Manuṣya-bhāga* consists of kitchen, bath-room, toilet, shed, stable, etc. Here we can see a scientific classification based on use and ease.

Bath-rooms and water tanks, and dressing rooms are prescribed to be located in the North-Western direction. Thus, the classical medium of the *Vāstu Śāstra* not only caters to the needs of physical comforts of residents but also looks at the spiritual and psychological implications. In this way, it can very easily be preferred to other systems of uni-directional thought. In a word, *Vāstu* is a holistic approach towards happy living.

Vāstu for Revival of Sick Industries

B.N. Reddy, M.S. (U.S.A.)*

The Government of India, in order to improve the economy of the nation, has taken several steps recently. One important decision was to take a realistic view of the working of Public Undertakings all over the country. Most of the industries in the State and Central sectors have become sick and are not in a position to meet the salaries of lakhs of employees working in these units, thus incurring a loss of several thousand crores every year. Therefore, the Government has taken a good decision to close down some of these huge loss making units. But, where to absorb the employees is a big question that has remained unanswered till today.

The statistics for 1991 show that there were 29,487 sick industries in Andhra Pradesh alone, and 2,21,427 at the All India level in the small scale sector only. These industries have to pay heavy dues to the Financial Institutions amounting to the tune of Rs. 755 crores in Andhra Pradesh and Rs. 10,767 crores all over the country.

Out of 163 sick units referred to by the Andhra Pradesh State, B.I.F.R. recommended closure of 16 industries, whereas 64 industries were under their consideration and 19 were outside of their purview. Some of the State undertakings under B.I.F.R. consideration are Allwyn, A.P. Scooters, A.P. Steels, Republic Forge and Southern Transformers. And a "package" was recommended for the reconstruction of Singareni Colleries. Privatisation of some of these units as per recent Central Government policy was also under serious consideration of the State Government.

* Virgo, 6-1-1063/B/3, Ist Floor, Rajbhavan Road, Hyderabad-500 004

While the Government was trying to hand over Allwyn to some private Agency, no one was coming forward to take over A.P. Scooters. Consequently, B.I.F.R. recommended the closure of this unit.

Out of 57 industries started in the Joint sector with A.P.I.D.C. collaboration, about 40 were sick and 5 unable to pay their instalments. Thus, only 12 of them are doing well.

The reasons for these sick units, as given by the department, were deficit finances, poor managerial talent, raw material shortage, wrong location of plants, non-availability of good technical personnel, marketing and labour problems.

As per March 1993 records, there were 1145 industries with an investment of Rs. 18,522 crores, having 5,35,000 employees in major and medium sectors in Andhra Pradesh, whereas in small scale sector, there were 1,05,000 units with an investment of Rs. 1,400 crores, having about 9 lakh employees.

It is also noticed that while 25 to 30% of the units are sick in private sector, as many as 75% units are sick in the Government sector, whether State or Central, thus rendering colossal investment worthless. Needless to say that this is a mind-boggling drain on the wealth of the nation.

When the nation is passing through an untold economic crisis, and millions of employees are threatened with loss of jobs rendering their families without subsistence, why cannot a fair trial be given to effect Vāstu changes in these industries, methodically in some sample units on an experimental basis under the supervision of a panel of advisers and experts to carry out the corrections?

During the course of my research of *Vāstu*, for last twenty years, I have found out that this ancient science of Vāstu has a tremendous bearing on the running of business concerns and industrial units.

In the last five years, I have visited hundreds of business and industrial houses all over India and corrected them as per *Vāstu* which resulted in converting 90% of them into profit making units. In Andhra Pradesh, *Vāstu* is very popular, and several *Vāstu Paṇḍits* from here are going to other parts of the country to give Vāstu advice. I have visited not only several big industrial houses within the country, such as Orient Fans of Calcutta, Fedder Lloyds of Delhi, Unity Steels of Baroda, Saurashtra Chemicals and Digjam of Birlas, but have also travelled all the way to Thailand to advise a few Coir and Jute Industries in Bangkok. I have also visited New York (U.S.A.) in July, 1993 to present a paper on Vāstu at an international conference, sponsored by Harvard University, which was attended by several scholars from all over the world.

My anxiety is that time has come when we should try to put a stop to this drift and drain on the national exchequer by exploring new avenues to breathe life into these industries. One of them is an honest application of the age-old science of *Vāstu*. It may not be out of place to mention here that even a strong communist nation like China is following a similar science called *Feng-Shai*.

Therefore it is my earnest appeal to the Government of India in general and the State Governments in particular to give a serious thought to this new avenue to tackle the vexatious problem of industrial sickness with application of *Vāstu*. While we should continue to invite new industries to the State, we should not lose sight of the urgency of reviving old units as the lives of millions of employees are dependent on the health of these units.

For industries too, the selection of the site is very important. Besides the fact that sufficient water and electricity should be available, the *Vāstu* of the plot, such as the shape of the plot, the roads facing the plots and the ground levels inside and outside the site are very important points that are to be observed.

The various principles of *Vāstu* that did in setting up an industry are as follows:

1. Main roads towards the East, North or North-East are advisable with wide gates on two sides.
2. Gates in the North-East or the East or the North or the North-West are recommended.

3. The guard-room should be either on the North-West side of the North gate or the South-East side of the East gate.
4. Minimum space should be kept in the South and the West where big trees could be grown. More open space should be left in North and East where lawns and other greenery can be grown.
5. The floor levels in the South-West must be higher than other sides and the height of the building also must be higher than all the other corners. Care has to be taken to have the store-rooms in the South-West fully loaded with stocks to the extent possible. As and when the stocks are consumed, they should be replenished immediately.
6. Car parkings may be provided in the North-West if open area is available. For light vehicles, the North-East also could be used.
7. The administrative offices are to be located either in the North or the East, away from boundary walls with less height than the main factory. Here special care has to be taken in keeping the North-East corner open.
8. Staff quarters may be constructed in the South-East and the North-West. If quarters are multi-storeyed and if the height is more than that of the main factory, they should be constructed in the South-West without touching the main premises.
9. Toilets should be placed in the North-West or the South-Eastern part of the buildings, and not in the North-East or South-West.
10. Wells, bore-wells, water sumps and water ponds, etc., should be in the North-Eastern area.
11. Overhead tanks may be created in the West and nearby, duly maintaining the heights. The South-West and the North-East sides including the North and East should be avoided, for constructing overhead tanks. This is a bit controversial subject and hence one should be very careful in locating the overhead tanks and also the water tanks above the ground level.

12. Heavy machinery has to be installed in the South, the West or the South-West in the factory.
13. Raw material storage, whether inside the factory or sheds outside, should be in the South or the West or the South-West.
14. Products under process or unfinished goods may be kept in the West direction.
15. Finished products are to be kept in the North-West corner. It will help in quick movement of the stocks.
16. The weighing machine may be located near the gate either in the North or the East, because that area is not subjected to permanent weight.
17. Transformers, generators, motors, boilers, furnaces, oil engines, etc., should be kept in the South-East or close to the South-East.

Vāstu Śāstra: Its Importance

*K.V.R. Anjaneyulu, B.Sc., M.A., Ph.D. (Lit.)

What is Vāstu?

Vāstu syāt vastūni vastutvād vastu-saṁsrayād;
Vasa nivāse vastu iti vāstu śāstrataḥ.

'That which was *Vāstu* (earth as the basis) as well as those things (*vāstus* of earth) form, construction materials, the process of house construction—all these go under the name of *Vāstu-Śāstra*—the science of Architecture.'

The principles of *Vāstu* are abundantly available in the various Vedas and the Purāṇas. The modern historians Mr. James Ferguson, Dr. Havell and Sir Cunning Ham have come to the conclusion that the historic development of *Vāstu Śāstra* took place during the period 6000 B.C. to 3000 B.C.

The excavations of Mohenjodaro and Harappa, the Maya Sculptures of Central America, the architectural techniques of China, the Symbolic Monuments of Japan, the Civil Buildings of British Empire, the magnificent temples of South India, the charm of beauty of Italian structures, the Pyramids of Egypt, the Raj Bhavans of Travancore, Jaipur and Mysore, the Flucknames of Nizam, the Palaces of Akbar and Aurangzeb, the forts of Golkonda, Jodhpur, Lal Quilla, Agra and Doelatabad, the Makbaras of Mecca and Madeena and the Church of Velankini are standing examples of *Vāstu* techniques as revealed and as recorded in ancient *Vāstu* texts, viz., (1) the *Vāstu-vidyā*, (2) the *Manuṣyālaya-candrika*, (3) the *Mayamata*, (4) the *Śilpa-ratna*, (5) the *Samarāṅgaṇa-sūtradhāra*, (6) the *Viśvakarma-prakāśa*, (7) the *Śukra-nīti*, (8) the *Aparājita-pṛcchā*, (9) the *Mānasāra*; and the Saṁhitās of (10) Kāśyapa, (11) Garga,

* 49-39-22/1, Akkayyapalem, Vishakhapatnam-530 016, Andhra Pradesh.

(12) Nārada, (13) Vasiṣṭha, (14) Varāhamihira, (15) Viśvakarma, (16) Hara, and (17) Kaumāra.

About two lakh ślokas are available in manuscript form at different places throughout the world. In addition to the manuscript literature, the secrets, the traditional lore and practical guidance handed down from generation to generation in the families of scholars, masons architects, scattered throughout the world, is an asset to *Vāstu Śāstra*.

A dive deep into the unfathomable depths of the intellectual feat of the ancient masters into these manuscripts reveals to me beyond doubt that the principles recorded are geological, geometrical, geophysical, botanical and above all cosmological and celestial. To understand the mind of the Maharishis and how *Vāstu* discipline is designed, we have to bring to our mind the cosmogony of the Universe, the position of Earth and how the Earth is being influenced by the celestial spheres.

Apart from (1) the natural magnetic influx and gravitational power of Earth, (2) the reflected power of the Moon, and (3) the direct transmission power of the Sun, our Maharishis have visualized a constant magnetic gravitational power in space flowing from the North-East corner to South-West corner of the entire topography of the universe including Mother Earth.

The force has been allegorically depicted as *Vāstu Puruṣa* with head in the North-East and legs in the South-West and as personifying the dwelling place. He works with *Kāla Puruṣa* who personifies the Time. *Vāstu Puruṣa* and *Kāla Puruṣa* jointly influence the Earth and the working pattern is allegorically explained as wakeful state and dormant state.

All objects in Nature whether mineral, vegetable or animal are produced, protected and perish under the influence of the solar ray. The solar light is scientifically slit into three segments, first, a visible spectrum of coloured rays, ranging from the deepest blue to the deepest red with different wave lengths flanked by two invisible zones known as ultra-violet and infra-red.

Even though the ancient scholars of *Vāstu Śāstra* did not

possess the present day appliances of Western Science, ancient masters of *Vāstu* split the Solar White Light into visible middle spectrum and the invisible spectrum on either side and specified their names as (1) *Kāñcana Soma*, (2) *Sphāṭika Nirmala*, (3) *Indranīla*, (4) *Vaiḍūrya*, (5) *Padmarāga*, (6) *Vajra*, and (7) *Sūrya-ratna*; with their presiding deities as (1) *Parjanya*, (2) *Kaśyapa*, (3) *Mahendra*, (4) *Sūrya*, (5) *Vṛṣa*, (6) *Nāmaka*, the nomenclature of which indicate the nature, quality and character of each ray. Western science did not go beyond the seven colours *VIBGYOR*. The North-East corner of the spectrum is given the name *Aiśānya* which corresponds to the ultraviolet spectrum, which is oxygenic and hydrogenic, standing for purity, divinity and wisdom. The South-East corner of the spectrum is given the name *Āgneya* which corresponds to the infrared, the thermic spectrum, standing for heat, fire action and assimilation.

Man is essentially cosmic in character. The Earth is made up of cosmic materials and Nature radiates cosmic forces. The interplay of cosmic forces between the objects in Nature and man are fully reflected in the discipline and principles of *Gṛha-vāstu*, *Grāma-vāstu*, *Pattana-vāstu*, *Nagara-vāstu* and *Rāja-gṛha-vāstu*.

The principles of *Vāstu Śāstra* relate to: (1) the history of the plot; (2) selection of a site; (3) examination of a site; (4) shape of a site; (5) slopes of a site; (6) flow of water; (7) planning of a structure; (8) space around a structure; (9) utility of the different segments of a structure; (10) main door; (11) placement of other doors; (12) placement of almirahs; (13) windows; (14) utility of the space around a building; (15) sub-houses in a site; (16) direction of a building; (17) direction of a site (18) extension of a site by direction; (19) crushings of a site; (20) *Piśāca-sthāna-nirṇaya*; (21) *Ekasūtipada-vinyāsā*; (22) *Ṣaṣṭhi-pada*; (23) *Śata-pada*; (24) well; (25) septic tank; (26) steps; (27) trees in a site; (28) domestic animals; (29) pet animals; (30) birds; (31) placement of photos; (32) Vidhi-śūla; (33) materials selected for the building; (34) boundary walls; (35) measurement of the rooms; (36) master bed-room; (37) bedrooms of family members; (38) hall;

(39) attach bathrooms and toilets; (40) kitchen; (41) prayer room; (42) study room; (43) placement of cots; (44) placement of articles; (45) dining hall; (46) guest room; (47) *Muhūrtas* of *śaṅku-sthāpana*, digging of well, fixation of main door and *gṛha-praveśa*; (48) entry into a site and exit; (49) entry into a house. These principles when applied offer strength, safety and longevity of a structure, and peace, progress and prosperity of dwellers; and when adversely disposed they destroy the structure and create misery, unhappiness and distress to the dwellers.

The experience of many generations has proved that the planning of the village, towns, cities and capitals of ancient India was best and it gave health and happiness and also prosperity to the people.

The easterly axis of the *Rāja Vidhi* ensured that the principal streets were purified by rays of the morning Sun as also of the evening Sun, while the interaction of the streets running from South to North provided a perfect circulation of air and utmost benefits of a cool breeze.

But now the engineering authorities decide layout plots, roads, shopping complexes, parks, health centres, cremating grounds, etc., within cognisance of neither the magnetic direction nor the wind chart, nor the water table, buy purely based on commercial instinct as a result of which people are subjected to suffering and sickness.

It is true that there is no institution in our country or in the world, where students can get proper training, either in theoretical or practical Vāstu Śāstra. Civil engineers educated and trained in modern engineering institutions, owing to their deplorable ignorance of *Vāstu Śāstra*, failed to develop the Indian Science of Architecture. They can neither guarantee the strength and longevity of the structure, nor promise peace, progress and prosperity to the dwellers. Many of these constructions intended for the welfare of an individual or a community or the nation have caused ruin and brought about big historic disasters.

The following instances show the dangers of neglecting *Vāstu* principles:

1. A famous educational institution built up a number of constructions on all sides without consideration

of direction, shape or slop, but only with the commercial point of view in mind. This brought bad luck to the Chief Executive of the institution.

2. An ultra-modern seven-star hotel at New Delhi was completely destroyed within one hour of construction killing the several dignitaries.
3. A beautiful building constructed under the supervision of the best engineering personnel, brought ruin to all the family members in a split second.

It cannot be said that these constructions had no good engineering skills involved in them. Coordinated effort is the need of the day, as both the science of structural engineering and *Vāstu Śāstra* aim at providing comfort and joy to the dwellers.

Vāstu and Town Planning

*K. Marimuthu**

For a town, the site should be selected at the bank of a river, sea shore or lake. The site should be surrounded by milky trees, full of fruits and flowers. *Nimba* tree leaves are purifying and antimalarial in effect.

The Eastern side of the town should be lowered to get sun rays on the door fronts. The site should not be selected on the Western side of a mountain. The capital of the state should be selected at the centre of a town, classified as:

1. *Stanya* - Centre of 800 villages
2. *Droṇamukha* - Centre of 400 villages
3. *Kharviṭika* - Centre of 200 villages
4. *Saṁgrahaṇa* - Centre of 10 villages

Shapes of Town

Vāstu Śāstra recommends five shapes of towns: 1.*Chandura* (square); 2. *Agatara* (rectangle); 3. *Vṛtta* (circle); 4. *Kṛttta Vṛtta* (elliptical); and 5. *Gola Vṛtta* (full circle).

A city resembling *Vajra-sūci* or a diamond (octagonal) should be regarded as inauspicious. If the front part of the city is in the shape of a bow, it is very good and auspicious. The *Agni-purāṇa* recommends highly the semi- lunar shape of the town. The holy city of Banaras is situated on the convex side of the Gangetic belt and presents a semilunar phase. Nanjangud town near Mysore also is situated on the convex side of the river Kapila. The *Matsya-purāṇa* says that the semilunar shape of a town is not auspicious. The development of industrial factories at Nanjangud brings the shape of the town to a semilunar aspect. This is not auspicious. The factories may become sick.

* Scientific Astrologer, 24, II Cross Extension, Nanjangud-571801, Mysore,

India is situated to the North of the equator and North is the quarter of light, i.e., the area of the *Devas*, the shining ones. The South is the quarter of *Yama* or the god of Death. In a hot country like India, Southerly inclination would bring too much exposure to sun rays. The monsoon wind and rain in India are from South and West. Therefore, if the ground is sloped towards that direction, the houses there will be dangerously exposed to every storm.

The engineer should consider the weather records of the area for the past ten years in designing any building. From the weather records obtained from the meteorological centre of the region, we can understand the influence of the site affected by the weather. In the consideration of the weather data, such as wind velocity and its direction, rainfall, evaporation, humidity of the area, sunlight and maximum and minimum temperature, etc., if we design the building, it will satisfy most of the specifications of *Vāstu.*

Town Planning

Data: The plans showing the ancient shape of Town in 1845 and the shape of present development are shown below:

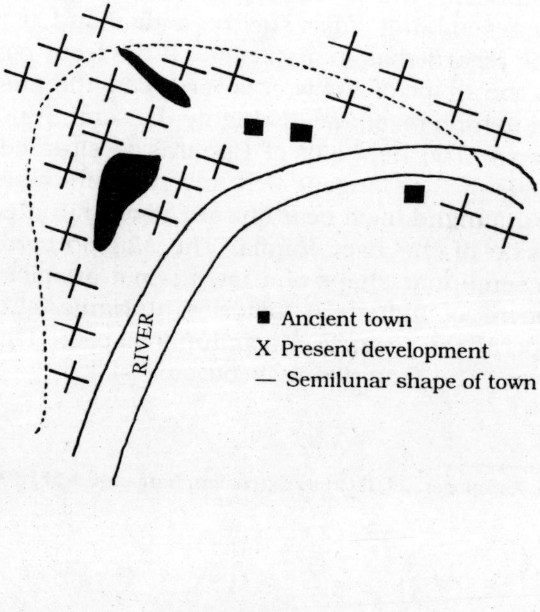

Report

Nanjangud town was square in shape in 1845 at the convex side of the river bend of Kapila bank.

Now the town is developed and many buildings have come up. The development brings the shape of the town to a semilunar shape.

The *Agnipurāṇa* says that the semilunar shape of the town is only useful for a riparian town, but not for a cosmopolitan city of the now developed Nanjangud.

The *Matsyapurāṇa* says that the semilunar shape of the town will have a weak defence. People will be too selfish and expect too much with too little effort. In general, the semilunar shaped town will face much difficulty in power, water supply, drainage, transport and communications. Nanjangud town has a semilunar shape at present. Most of the factories will become sick.

Relevance of Ancient Vāstu Technology to Modern Town Planning

*K.V. Raja Rao, B.Arch.**

Right from time immemorial *Vāstu* principles (Vedic Methods) have been applied in design and development of villages, towns and cities. The science of town planning during Vedic period was given paramount importance to an extent that Indo-Aryans perfectly shaped the human settlements into various categories depending upon the characteristics of the population. In the context of ancient Indian cities, the capital city was given due significance in defending it using all kinds of protectional avenues based on scientific and *Vāstu* imparted innovations. The important structures which were absolutely subjected to meticulous planning ideas using Vāstu technology were the military cantonments, market towns, ports of commercial significance, temples and palaces.

The *Vāstu* scripts have clearly defined the norms for the proper development of such civic constructions. These group of settlements actually played an important role even in the aspects and concepts of regional planning and is obvious in the enhancement of prosperity of the kingdom which in fact elevated the Indo-Aryan planners. In this direction the opinion of city architect was greatly valued in view of the fact that democratic functions of the city administration kept immense regards to *Vāstu* sciences.

Ancient Indian civilization gave more importance to the governing institutions of village communities from which

* Architect, Space Based Urban Planner, No. 1361, 25th Main, 24th Cross, BSK II Stage, Bangalore-560 070.

can be drawn concepts of design and planning of cities to act as work horses to today's planning concepts of cities in India.

Sage Bhṛgu has described in depth the science of town planning in his Saṁitā. These *Upaśāstras* running into ten volumes, further fragmented into thirty-two branches deal in application knowledge of branches of engineering, architecture and *Vāstu* sciences applicable in the design and development of cities.

The *Vāstu* science, traces the origin of town planning to Brahmā, the creator. Sage *Mānasāra* deduces mythological genealogy of the architect originated from the four faces of Brahmā, namely Viśvakarmā, Maya, Tvastṛ and Manu, and further linked to their four sons, viz., Sthapati, Sūtragrāhī, Vardhakī and Takṣaka. These four architects of the highest order holding divinity in their souls, seem to be apotheosized ancestors of the four classes of professionals, who took the reigns of execution power in building temples, cities, towns, villages and palaces in accordance with the principles of *Vāstu* technology.

Ancient Urban Evolution

Ancient cities were usually located on the banks of rivers, especially Ganges and their tributaries, essentially for ritualistic and sanitary purposes, including communications with other cities using water. This concept in fact helped to foster and encourage commerce which ultimately favoured establishment of townships, particularly on the right bank of rivers, which answers the reasons for today's geographical placement of temple cities across the country.

In fact the rivers of Punjab played a pivotal role in establishing terrestrial deities of the Vedic Aryans which are more often glorified in the sacred hymns available from the Vedas. These hymns establish the geography of the Aryan civilization which flourished here starting from 1500 B.C. It is evident in this context to ascribe the same period for composition of the *Ṛgveda*.* Accordingly, it highlights

* This theory of Max Müller is long out of date. The Vedic age goes for beyond 3000 B.C.—*Editor*.

the expounders of the Vedas as having had the remarkable knowledge of the science of habitation, i.e. *Vāstu-vidyā.* Mohenjodaro and Harappa, which are the only two* outstanding cities belonging to Indus Valley Civilization have resemblance to the planning concepts, of both the ancient and modern towns and cities of India.

Site Selection

Vāstu Śāstra has laid strong emphasis on the selection of a proper site for establishing a new village, town or a city. The sites or places on which cities are proposed are generally classified under three categories. Barren land used to be called as *Jāṅgala*, where wind is hotter and the soil is black. Secondly, *Anupama*, ascribing for a beautiful country, which is surrounded by rivers, where the climate is fresh and cool, with the soft characteristics being humid and cool. Thirdly, *Sādhāraṅa* category used to be given to average quality where huge stretches of land existed in useless conditions. The placement technology of towns and villages was essentially distributed all round the capital city holding equidistances and methodologies in controlling their physical sprawls coupled with human population and building densities.

Śukrācārya had the remarkable intelligence in saying that capital city should be placed in such a local geographical position where various kinds of trees, water bodies, rivers, plants, shrubs, green vegetation cover, including cattle should be present in great numbers. For example, the city of Pāṭaliputra was planned on a magnificent scale where existed the confluence of Soṇa and Ganges. The city had a long river front exceeding nine miles, coupled with beautiful embankments and harbours. It had timber walls alround defended with three successive brick-lined moats filled with water. In addition, it has sixty-four watch-towers placed over sixty-four gates. According to Kauṭilya, a fortress named *Sthānīya* encompassed eighty villages within

* This information of the author is also out of date; many other sites of this civilization have been excavated in Gujarat, since then.—*Editor*

its womb. So also *Droṇamukha* encompassed two hundred villages an lastly *Saṁgrahaṇa* encompassed ten villages. The *Mānasāra* describes that these sites for establishing a city used to be determined from its smell, taste, shape direction, sound and touch. The topography should have inclination towards East and North, coupled with higher ground levels in South-West, West and South. If a river adjoins the site it should run from left to right or West to East or South to North. Also the site should have water table at a depth equal to a man's height with his arms raised above his head. The site should also comply with moderate temperature during summers and winters. If these parameters were not met with, the land used to be rejected straight away.

Even meteorological data was used as a deciding factor. For example, wind direction in India predominantly prevails from South-West to North-East. If terrain of the land slopes in this direction, the buildings would be exposed to rough storms and rain beatings effecting even the local micro climate. The lands which are shaped similar to circles, semicircles, containing 3, 5, 7 angles on its sides, hind parts of fish, back of the elephant or a turtle or face of the cow or land filled with human skulls or stones, anthills, dilapidated wells, decayed woodyards, lime stone yards, such lands used to be rejected. Lands with huge trees in the four corners were declared as sterile. Even geological characteristics that prevailed in such lands were strictly examined and decided upon, coupled with topography, drainage patterns, vegetation covers, wild life pockets and climate, too.

Site Planning

After the selection of land as per *Vāstu*, the sight was ploughed on a auspicious day as fixed by astronomical observations by a pair of specific oxen which had white spots on their heads and knees. The next step was with determination of cardinal directions using the Gnomon, which concluded with the fixation of *Vāstu-puruṣa-maṇḍala*. Different kinds of them were used depending upon the need of the applications. In fact circular *Vāstu-puruṣa-maṇḍala* symbolised the terrestrial world with constant movement. The square one showed rigidity and thus represented a perfect and absolute form. The posture of *Vāstu Puruṣa* has been different with different aspects of structural requirements. That is to say, *Vāstu Puruṣa* considered in residential buildings differs greatly in the application of temples constructions. Vāstu Śāstra describes 32 ways of constructing *Vāstu-puruṣa-maṇḍala.* The simplest among them is conceived with square or *pada* and the longest in this characteristics is of 1024 *padas.* The exact size and shape of *Vāstu-puruṣa-maṇḍala* is determined according to the requirements of the building constructions. There are thirty-two kinds of *Vāstu-puruṣa-maṇḍalas* and these are *Śākala, Pecaka, Pīṭha, Mahāpīṭha,* etc., ending with the 32nd one which is named as Indrakānta.

Mode of Application

In building towns and cities, the architect had to decide first, which *Vāstu-puruṣa-maṇḍala* holds appropriation depending upon the size of the town. Thus, fixation of the peripheral limits of a town used to be determined by configuring the alignment patterns of main streets which resembled the arms of the cosmic cross, attributed to avenues planted with shady trees. Thus, the longest arm used to be aligned East and West and named after *Mahākāla* or *Vāmana.* In fact there used to be ringroads planned surrounding the whole city or town and called as *Maṅgalavīthi.* Thus, the whole *Vāstu-puruṣa-maṇḍala* used to be fragmented into 81, 64, 49 pads or landed parcels and pushed into different zones. The innermost square or *pada* was called Brahmā and the next called after *Daivika* or the belt of gods, next to this is called *Manuṣya* or the belt of humans and the fourth ring was called *Paiśāca* or the belt of demons.

Different zones or squares used to be occupied by different classes of human being. But the central square which was called *Brahmasthāna* was always occupied either by a temple or a palace. While planning of roads in the course of conceiving the design for a town or a city, the cosmic cross was used for pinpointing the roads running East to West and North to South representing principal streets. Roads running in the Eastern axis ensured towards purification of the street by Sun rays from morning till evening and the North-South road profiles provided a perfect circulation of the air and benefit of cool breeze.

The roads were slightly aligned at 60 degrees to the North or South to ensure safety from the Sun glare falling on the eyes of horses dragging the chariots or the men holding the reigns of the horses.

Mode of Measurements

A definite mode of measurement was in vogue. It started with *Paramāṇu*, which in fact was visible only to the great Sages. Eight such Paramāṇus used to be called *Rathareṇu*, or grain of dust which arose from the wheels of a chariot, and out of eight such *Rathareṇus* came one *Vālāgras* compared to a lotus and eight such lice made up a grain of *Yava*. Three to four and a half Yavas made one *Aṅgula*, representing the inferior finger. Twelve *Aṅgulas* made one *Vitasta* or a span and two such *Vitastas* made one *Hasta* or cubit, which is almost equal to 25 Aṅgulas. 27 Aṅgulas made one *Dhanurgraha* or the handle of a bow. The next unit was called *Hasta*, which was fourfolded; the first was named after *Cishcu* which is employed in the manufacture of conches, vehicles; the second version called *Prājāpatya* was used to apply in building constructions like temples; the third version is *Dhanurmuṣṭi* used in the construction of residences; and the fourth was *Dhanurgraha* used in the construction of villages, towns and cities.

Placement Scenarios of Different Enclosures

While site planning a city or a town, *Vāstu* pertaining to placement of different building enclosures used to be observed very strictly. For example, the palace was to be placed exactly in the centre of the town by occupying one-ninth of the area of the whole of the fort. The palace faced exactly East with lands reserved for teachers and priests in the North-East direction. The royal kitchen including elephant stables and store houses used to be placed in the South-East. On the external sides, merchants trading in liquid, grains, and artists used to stay. The main treasury, accounts offices, etc., used to be placed in the South-East. The store houses containing forest produce and the arsenal used to be placed in the South-West. In the South, commercial buildings and merchants houses used to be placed, including those of army generals. Stables for asses, horses, etc., used to be placed in the South-West. In the North-West, the chariots and conveying vehicles used to be placed. In the West textile based materials, bamboo mats, armours and weapons used to be kept. In the North-West shops and hospitals and stables of cows were placed. To the exact North of the palace, the temple used to be decided upon. Residence for brahmins used to be found within the precincts of this area. In addition, landscaping and garden planning was also placed. Especially huge trees always dominated the centre of the town or a city. This tree was the Bodhi tree under which village communities used to meet. In fact, the city architect was assisted by a landscape architect or Aramakral Imavanakarinah in planning a city.

Concept of a Village

Vāstu describes various layouts and concepts. It suggests ramparts encircled with moats or surrounded by ditches compounded with a security wall. The village boundaries should always be marked by a river, mountain or bulbous planes, caves, artificial bundings (*setubandha*) or by trees such as *Śālmali* (silk cotton trees) and *Kṣīravṛksa* (milky tree). The *Vāstu* describes 12 types of village shapes. They are: (1) *Maṇḍūka*; (2) *Prastara*; (3) *Bahulika*; (4) *Paraka*; (5) *Caturmukha*; (6) *Pūrvamukha*; (7) *Maṅgala;* (8) *Viśvakarma*; (9) *Devarāta*; (10) *Viśveśa*; (11) *Kailāsa*; and (12) Nityamaṅgala.

Even optimum population density was fixed within these villages. For example, *Nityamaṅgala* type of village had a population of 6000 people.

Town Planning Concepts

The Indo-Aryan town planning principles are almost a blueprint copy of the concepts used in the village planning, especially the central cross roads which were running along with the *Maṅgalavīthi* or *Pradakṣiṇāpatha.* This ground was fragmented in the same style as that in the village planning techniques and the identifications of *Varṇas* depended upon the position of square or *pada* in the chess board patterns of roads, house plots, temple placements. Sometimes the amalgamated spatial patterns were followed which depended upon the urban planning contexts and, therefore, were free from a monotonous look. The city used to be developed after a lot of thinking in the initial planning itself, by the city architect, confined to the principles laid down in *Vāstu* sciences.

Thus, village plans and the town plans almost enjoyed many similarities and helped towards fusing of them when in due course, the village began to grow big. The existing example for this kind of *Vāstu* application is seen in Bijāpur.

Pāṭaliputra also had the same kind of developmental concept where grouping of several villages in due course of time became a city and functioned as capital of the dynasty of Candragupta Maurya. In the event of any unrest anticipated due to political instability, the capital cities used to be shifted to an important village in a group of villages and further encompassing them into a single city. Thus, *Vāstu* concept was in vogue even in villages and thus helped to shift capitals in a much lesser time.

The shape of towns and cities and their geographical locations were classified and determined as per *Vāstu* principles. Accordingly, there were twenty types of towns and cities, starting from *Padma* category to *Girinagar* type. The word '*Pura*' and '*Nagara*' actually belong to Vedic *Vāstu* periods. The most important shape used in the initial concept of towns and cities, as per the *Samarāṅgana-sūtradhāra,* is towards square shape, as it denotes limits to expanding life and also a perfection sans life an ultimately, sans death. Hence square shaped cities were endorsed fully by Rājā Bhoja as laid down in his abovementioned treatise on Indian architecture. The city of *Takṣaśila* was built as per the *Vāstu* principles (see the Plan of Taxila, p. 91).

As an example of expansion due to overflow of population, Dwārakā is notable. Dwārakā city was built by Viśvakarmā under the guidance of Lord Kṛṣṇa. Due to expansion which became necessary due to overflow of population, it enveloped nearby towns and satellite towns which were built in the square shape allowing faster and easier amalgamation process.

Conclusions

The detailed concepts of building and designing of ancient villages, towns and cities as per the *Vāstu* principles, as laid down in the *Samarāṅgaṇasūtradhāra*, act as a mirror even in today's context of town and city planning which are now facing the wrath of myopic planning. Today planners have pushed these *Vāstu* concepts to back benches where ancient concepts of a town or a village had the central embodiment that was pinned into the shaping process of a city by its citizens themselves. The foundation for shaping the cities was entirely dependent upon the social, political, religious and spiritual transformations, especially of *Vāstu* principles in view of the fact that the ancient concepts in this direction were founded by the ancient *Ācāryas* of great renoun. There was not a single instance where they succumbed to the pressures of political influences to spoil the town planning concepts in those days. The shapes and *Vāstu* concepts which existed in those days really held relevance to the symbolic expression towards the smooth national culture and also acted as the finest methods where inculcation of Vedic *Vāstu* principles fused into all kinds of buildings resulting in generation of ornamental buildings coupled with inspiring arches and beautiful domes which mirrored the soul inspiring achievements of the great Indian architects.

These value and *Vāstu* based concepts without an iota of doubt act as traditional linkages to the development of

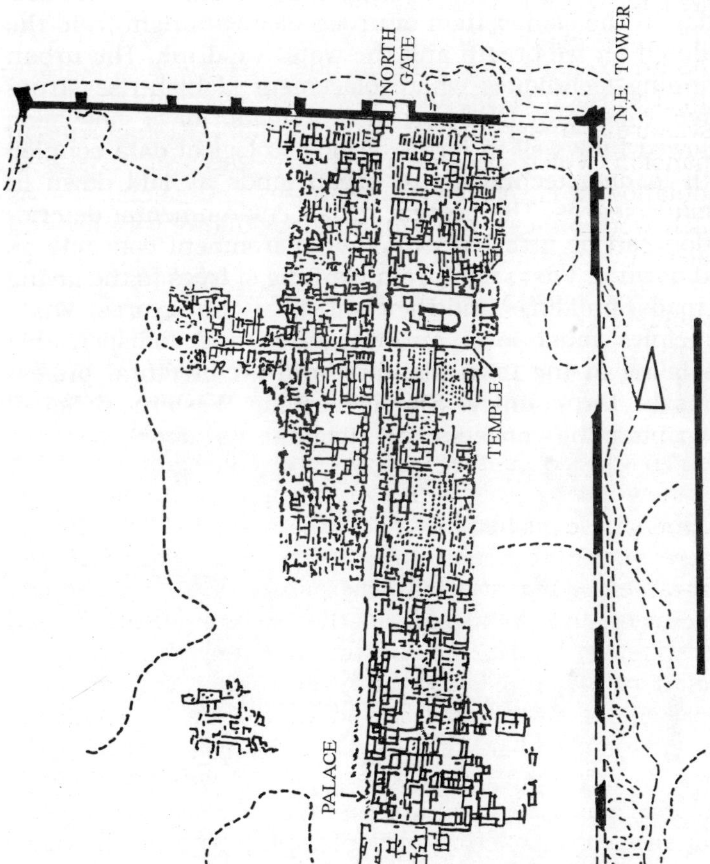

PLAN OF TAXILA CITY BUILT ON VASTU PRINCIPLES

modern cities especially the city of Bangalore where the urban planning and environment have become unlivable today in the composition of urban elements right from the polluted air we breath and the water we drink. The urban planning techniques where placement of high-rise structures especially CBD becomes crucial, have not been followed fully well in terms of meteorological data coupled with loading technology of urban lands as laid down in *Vāstu* sciences. The present urban environmental deterioration can be arrested with the environment concepts as laid down in *Vāstu* right from planting of trees to the laying of roads, buildings and their subsidiary annexures. *Vāstu* principles must form anti-integrated and indispensable discipline in the town planning and architectural professions in the country. Simply copying Western styles of town planning concepts will not take us anywhere.

Hospitals and Consulting Chambers

Dr. Bhargava C. Babu

Selection of the plot is to be done as per the procedure laid down, because plot shape, size and all other topographical features hold significant bearing in *Vāstu*.

After procuring the plot, the discrepancies or defects (*doṣas*) if any should be rectified, and then one should go in for a compound wall or fencing to ward off ill-effects of the neighbouring plots (*parisara vāstu*).

In entire plot, the hospital building should come up in the South-West without any "blocks" in the North-East, North, East, North-West or South-West. Wards should be in the South and/or West. The major operation theatre (M.O.T.) should be in the South-West. Pharmacy, registration, reception, billing, etc. are to be in the North-West.

The general ward should be in the South.

Placement of consulting chamber should be in the North or East of the building. In the consultation chamber, seat should be in the South-West corner of the chamber. Patients should sit on the left side of the doctor while conversing. Examination table should be in the South, West or South-West of the chamber. Hand-scrub for Doctor, if required, should be placed in the South-West, if consultant or specialist sits in the South-West, which automatically fits into appropriate position. The wash-basin is to be placed in the North-West corner of the consulting chamber.

All doors of the chamber should be in the exalted position.

For hospital building, one should avoid Eastern, South-East and South-West entrances, otherwise the hospital will gain notoriety and evil aura for illegal treatments like abortion, treating of criminals and finally end up in closure due to financial losses or bad reputation.

The dunghill or garbage dumping point or incinerator should be in the South-East of the plot.

The sterilisation unit should be planned in such a way that it occupies the South-East (*āgneya*) position of the building.

Miniature or emergency sterilisation for O.T. purpose may be kept in the South-East of operation theatre.

If the South-East portion of the building is utilised as the general ward, usually prognosis of patients will be hampered, and most of the times accident victims or prisoners and murder cases will get admitted.

Āgneya room or South-East portion of the hospital should be used as sterilisation unit preferably. If it is used as a labour room, female-births will be more than male births. Such is the case also when the main entrance is on the East (*pūrva*) or South-East (*āgneya*).

If the hospital has North-East entrance (aisanya-pravesa), then it will come into lime light because of its exalted entrance within no time.

The Pantry for the hospital can be provided in the South-East of the building. If this is not available, alternatively, pantry may be accommodated in the South-West or North-West of the building. In such a case, hospital administrator may feel uneasy to maintain the pantry.

The Mortuary (to keep cadavers) should be located in the South-West corner of the plot. The room should be constructed by following the principles of out-houses (*upagṛham*).

Washing of hospital linen (patients' drapes, aprons and bedsheets) may be done on the Eastern side of the plot. If they are subjected to sterilisation, the process should be carried on the South-East of the plot or building. If this is required to be done outside the building, the room should be constructed according to the principles of out-houses (*upagṛham*).

Vāstu: Yesterday and Day Before

*Prof. S.A. Deshpande**

The sudden emergence and the recourse to the tenets of the ancient *Vāstu Śāstra* is both surprising and understandable ! It is surprising because while the world moves rapidly towards the 21st century, propelled by the "faster-than-mind" super computers, the art of building in our country is pulling us back into the ancient wisdom of the *Vāstu* texts. It is, at the same time, quite understandable why we are allowing this to happen. With the break-neck speed of development in the West, even the Western society feels left behind. While, in India especially, the society is still in the pre-modern state of the art, the gap between the developed and the developing is an ever widening chasm which we are helplessly watching. Unable to accelerate and catch-up, we are left to ourselves. In all walks of our sociopolitical environment we seem to be wallowing in the mud of our past glory. As a nation we seem to be closer to the past than the future.

There is, however, nothing wrong in learning from the past. But the point is whether we are intellectually competent enough to do this. If tradition is to be believed, we simply lack the ability. The ancient wisdom of our great civilization had always remained within the coterie of the few *Rishis* and the wise men who isolated themselves from the people at large. The treatises containing the 'thought' were in accessible and beyond the understanding of the lay people. The concepts were ritualized. The rituals were simple and understandable. These were explained in the religious texts and enforced by the priests through the social institution. To facilitate enforcement, mortal fear and

* 88, West Park Road, Dhantoli, Nagpur-440012.

penalty on default were used as the means. With the passage of time, the ritual became more interesting complicated and overbearing. It was also more physical, tangible and gave an experience of 'having done something'. Thus, the metaphysical base on which the ancient wisdom stood was soon to be lost to the bizarre activity of the ritual. In the medieval period ritualism was further strengthened as the consequence of default or non-compliance was highlighted as an example of the fate of the 'non-believer'! It would be erroneous to believe that all this happened in our country only. In the pre-modern Europe witchcraft and sorcery were quite rampant. It was only the post-industrial revolution society in the West that moved it from faith to reason!

In ancient India, the learned and the enlightened *Rishis* divided knowledge into Metaphysical and Physical sciences. *Jñāna* was the outcome of the mind, while *Vijñāna* was the benevolent interface for the development of mankind. The abstract metaphysical thought was rendered into tangible scientific and engineering modes. Mutation of concepts was achieved by transition through Śāstra>> *vidyā>>Kalā*; i.e., *Theory* (thought), *methodology* (way of achievement) and *implementation* (art/skill of realizing it). It is well-known that ancient knowledge was preserved through *Śruti Smṛti Purāṇa*, i.e., "what was heard, memorised and committed to texts". It will be quite unnecessary to venture to guess at the time that has elapsed between the first and the third stages, and the changes that may have been caused by errors in understanding and due to individual interpretations. The *Vāstu* texts available today are no 'divine scriptures', nor could these be original 'words of the mouth'! However, these are enough to inform us how much the Rishis with their 'mind power' were able to relate the effect of the astral bodies in the universe and more specifically, solar radiation on the human bodies.

Śilpa Śāstra

The term '*Śilpa*' is commonly misunderstood only to mean 'sculpture'. This *Śāstra,* however, dealt with all the facets of the man-made world, *Vāstu* and *Nagara-racanā* being a part of it. It also dealt with engineering, biology, hydraulics, mining, marine, aeronautics, communication, defense, etc. The approximate time-frame in which these texts were created is synchronous with the age of the Vedas, which itself is a matter of research. Without getting into the controversy about the domicile of the Aryans, it is the product of the Vedic culture. The material text is found scattered in several treatises. There are commentaries and interpretations by many Rishis and *Munis*. These are found in the Vedas, Purāṇas and Saṁhitās which were the operative 'code books'. Although the territorial jurisdiction of the code cannot be precisely delineated, it is observed that the *Bhṛgu Saṁhitā* held its sway in the North, the *Mānasāra* in the middle and the *Mayamata* in the South of the Indian subcontinent. There are minor variations in the prescriptions as related to *Vāstu*.

Vāstu Śāstra

The awareness and the belief that energy (*ūrjā*) released in the cosmos was responsible for making of the universe (*viśva*) and for getting it going, is the very basis of our metaphysics. The knowledge is documented and graphically presented. The basis of the *Vāśtu Śāstra* seems to rest on the following :

1. *Cosmic Influence*: The heavenly bodies in the celestial space influence the activity on the surface of the earth;
2. *Solar Energy*: The energy levels and radiation from sun rays are not the same all over the surface of the earth;
3. *Geo-magnetic Fields*: The magnetic fields between the North and the South poles of the earth affect the bio-organisms. The magnetic field also creates sensitive spots on the earth's surface which were used to advantage, especially in communication whether marine or extra-terrestrial navigation;
4. *Geology of the Crust*: Materials for construction and other associated systems depend upon extractable minerals common to a region and hence the ability

to select appropriate materials;

5. *Hydrology and Eco-systems*: Habitable regions depend on perennial sources of water and the types of supportive vegetation; and
6. *Socio-Cultural Beliefs*: Emergence of the human society from primitive to organized levels of a structured society, and gradual shifting from a metaphysical view of life to a materialistic one, resulting in need for body comfort.

Vāstu-Puruṣa-Maṇḍala

It will, thus, be seen that the ancient texts were based on a scientific understanding of the phenomenon and looked upon the man-made structure as a reaction to its environment. The Hindu concept of architecture had always been that of a 'model of the cosmos'. This was further explained by the *maṇḍala* graphics, the various *Vāstu-puruṣa-maṇḍala* diagrams. The *Mānasāra* has described about thirty-two types of *maṇḍala* diagrams. These are similar to the horoscopes, which locate the positions of various planets at a given time. The effect of the celestial forces on the house and its occupants is capable of being studied. Much like the horoscope, the *Vāstu-puruṣa-maṇḍala* depicts the positions of the origin of the effects on a human body. These diagrams are, indeed, very complicated for the modern mind to understand and even more difficult for proper interpretation.

Vāstu Śāstra is indeed a time-tested science. Among many other things, it contains directives on:

1. Site selection;
2. Where and when to commence excavation;
3. Location and extent of the open spaces;
4. Location of a well;
5. Laying of the foundation stone;
6. Orientation of the entrance door;
7. Number and placement of windows;
8. Direction and location of stairs;
9. Position of the Pūjā room;
10. Placement of the Kitchen;

11. Suitable location of sleeping or bed rooms;
12. Position of the grain store and a safe;
13. Latrines and wash rooms; and
14. Types of vegetation desired around the house, etc.

Vāstu as the Third Skin

The effect of solar radiation on the body and the mind must have, indeed, been well understood by ancient thinkers. The rays of the sun that propelled photons at a fantastic speed create on the earth, geo-magnetic and electro-magnetic energy fields, which cause an effect on the nervous system of the human body. The solar spots and flares produce temperature variations at the source. The radiation levels are unbearable for any life form to survive. Fortunately, this radiation passes through several 'filters' that absorb most of the ill effects. The human body is built to withstand a temperature range of -40° to +40°C. But the ideal range lies between 25° to 35°C which was obtained in the Tropics. That is why the Tropical belt of 23°C along the Tropic of Cancer has been the 'Cradle of Civilization'. Also, it is known that the normal temperatures for the mind and the body are between 22° and 32°C. That would probably explain why the ancient sages migrated to the Himalayan heights for meditation after gaining complete control over the body functions. The role of the *Vāstu Śāstra* can, therefore, be seen to be restricted to the design of the *Third Skin* over the mind; the first being the *Body*, the second being the *Clothing*, and the third one being the *Shell* or the structure of the house!

The Vital Question

Although the antiquity of *Vāstu Śāstra* is beyond any debate, its antiquity itself is being quoted by the learned and by the pseudo-pundits as proof for its relevance today. The frontiers of knowledge may indeed be limited, but that of ignorance, infinite.

The question that needs to be boldly considered is the usefulness or otherwise of this great ancient wealth of scientific knowledge. Science as such is rational. It has to provide satisfactory answers to many questions. It can be understood that the basis of the *Vāstu Śāstra* must be the effect of the physical, climatological and social influence on the shelter and its occupants. The science, therefore, provided guidance to the extent it could foresee reaction. It is obvious that with intervention of modern technology, man has gained dominance and control over that aspect of Nature. It will be safe to assume that the sages themselves would have revised and amended the texts to suit contemporary situation. We should look for the secret behind the rituals that are now left behind for us, rather than follow them by way of a social weakness.

As architects we are stunned at the rapidity and cunningness with which the tribe of the so-called *Vāstu*-pundits has been operating in our domain. If we are really disturbed, the fault mainly lies with us. Our educational systems, thanks to Macaulay, are more British, even today, than those in Britain itself. The only past that we know of us is what they have told us! The relevancy of *Vāstu Śāstra* today is more academic than real. The menace of the pseudo-pundits can be countered only by us becoming more knowledgeable of the ancient science. Whether we use it for spiritual or professional reason is another matter. But we must not forget that the strength of this pseudo-pundit is in the gullibility and blind faith of his victim, our client.

Finally we know that *Śāstra* (science) is a vehicle between the mystique and its understanding. Science has to offer an explanation of the phenomenon. It must lead to better understanding by both the intellectual and the common people in society.

Could it be that for this purpose, the thinkers introduced the 'rituals' (*karmakāṇḍa*) ? And, is it therefore that the society today, which consists of a majority of the lay people, easily devolves its faith in only the ritual and spares itself the excruciating pain of understanding ? These and many more questions need to be boldly asked, if not answered!

---

* The author is Former Head of the Department of Architecture, V.R. College of Engineering, Nagpur; Immediate Past President, Indian Institute of Architects. Author acknowledges the benefit of previous discussion with S/Shri Himanshu Chhaya, Prabhakar Bedge and Vijay Deoskar.

General Vāstu Guidelines

C.H. Gopinath Rao, B.Sc., B.E., M.Sc. (Engg.)*

A number of principles and suggestions have been laid down by ancient astrologers. The reasons for many of them have not been understood. However, the principles have been found to be based on good reasons and sound in practice.

General

The building should be constructed parallel to the magnetic forces. Northern wall shall be exactly to North and the Southern wall exactly to South. However, when the street in a layout is not held parallel to the magnetic forces, the street can be taken as the base and the building can be marked with respect to the street. The variation between the magnetic direction and the direction of the site can be upto 12 degrees.

Preparation of Site

The site should be cleared of vegetation. Trees like jackfruit, peepal, neem tamarind, etc., if on the site, should be removed with roots at least six months before construction is started. If any tree is to be removed after occupation, a minimum of three months should be allowed to pass.

Commencement of Building

The building should be commenced on an auspicious day and time. The following inauspicious days should be avoided:

(a) When a member of the family is in mourning due to the death of his kith or kin;

*19, Oliver Road, Mylapore, Chennai-600 004.

(b) When a child is born in the family and the house is considered to be polluted;
(c) When a female member of the house is pregnant;
(d) When a female member has her mensus.

If two units are proposed to be constructed in a plot, the first one should be on South or West only.

Layout of Building

1. It is preferable if the building faces East or North-East.
2. The building should never face South-East.
3. The South-West corner should be an exact 90 degree angle.
4. The house should not face a mountain nor the shape of the house resemble a mountain.
5. The building should not be square, but could be rectangular.
6. The corners of any house should not be in line with the door or window of any other house.
7. The construction of the building should be such that the Sun's rays shall fall on the building for three hours after sun-rise and three hours before sun-set.
8. The setbacks on North and East should be more than on South and West by 1.25 to 1.5 times.
9. All corneres of rooms should be perpendicular to one another from base of the roof.
10. North-West and South-East should not project beyond the periphery of the building.
11. The colour washing can be as shown below: For houses facing East, white; South-East, gray; South, red; South-West, green; West, blue; North-West, white; North, green; and North-East, yellow.

Disposition of Rooms in the Building

1. The bedroom should be on the South-West.
2. The position of the bedroom where a couple is united has a bearing on the prospects of a child. If the

room is in the western part of the house, the child will be intelligent, prosperous and will become famous.

3. Bedrooms for couples should be only on the West or North.
4. The total number of rooms in a house shall be odd in number. For purpose of computing, any room provide with a door (including toilets) should be considered a room.

Kitchen

1. Kitchen should preferably be on the South-East corner of the building.
2. The person who cooks should face exactly East.
3. The sink in the kitchen should be in the North-East corner of the kitchen.
4. Storage for storing provisions provided in the racks should be on the walls which are on Southern or Western side and not on the Northern and Eastern side.
5. Wash-basin in the kitchen should be in the North-East.
6. For South facing houses, the kitchen can be on North-West. However, the oven may be in the South-East corner of the kitchen room.

***Pūja* Room**

Pūja room should preferably be in the North-East direction.

Servants' Quarters

Servants' quarters should be in the North-West.

Walking Space in Rooms

In all the rooms, more walking space should be provided on the North and East direction than on South and West.

Verandahs

1. Verandahs or sit-outs in the South or West should

be higher than the floor level of the main building, while in the North and East, verandahs should be lower than the floor level of the main building.

2. If verandahs or porticos are provided, the width on North should be more than the width on the South or West. Verandahs on the North and East should be continuous and there should not be any break between them.

Doors and Windows

1. Doors of rooms should be in North-East or North or East.
2. The main entrance to the house can be one or maximum two on front side. More than two should be avoided.
3. In case of main door, the shutter should open inside. If the main door has single door, the hinges should be on the left side, when viewed from inside the premises.
4. The shutters of the big door should be made using three planks, but should not be of the same variety.
5. The total number of doors and windows, taken separately, should be even in number and should not have zeros in the ending. Doors should normally be on North direction.
6. Exit of the house should be on the North or East or West in order of preference, and not on the South.
7. The main entrance door should not face the intersection of roads and no trees should obstruct the entrance. However, according to some experts, if the distance between the entrance door and the above obstructions is more than the height of the building, the obstructions will not be considered inauspicious.
8. The entrance steps should be an even number. The number of pillars should be an even number. Similarly, if beams are introduced in any room, or hall, this also should be an even number.

9. There should be no window on South-West side upto 12% of the length of the building.

Woodwork

1. Timber used in buildings should not be from the trees of Peepal, Silk-cotton, Ber, etc. Further, trees damaged by natural disasters and grown on burial grounds should not be used.
2. For wood works in a building, only new timber should be used and for renovation of an old building, old wood can be used.

Well

1. The well should be provided on the North-East direction of the plot.
2. If any fountain is to be provided, it should be only on the North or East side of the house and the distance of which from the main door should be the minimum height of the door.
3. The projected wall of the well from the base should be of round shape.
4. Even an edge of the wall of the well should not be on the line connecting North-East corner of the building and North-East corner of the plot, and the well should be only on the North-East corner of the plot.
5. According to some experts, the well should be exposed to sun rays for a period of about six hours after sunrise.
6. The above rules hold good for other sources of water like sump, corporation tap, etc.
7. Water tank should not be provided in the North-East or North-West direction.

Compound Around Building

1. The compound-gate should be on North-East or North-West or South-East only.
2. Trees grown on West and South direction can be taller than the height of the building.

3. On the East and North directions, trees should not be taller than the height of the building.
4. No flower pots should be kept on the compound wall or on the walls of the buildings of North and Eastern sides.
5. No arches for plants should be made on the compound wall or on the walls of the buildings of North and Eastern sides.
6. Shed or outhouse or water closet or bath should not be provided on North or Eastern side of the building.
7. Staircase should not be on the North-East.
8. The steps of the staircase should be provided in such a manner that climbing should be towards North or towards East.
9. Compound wall on the South or West can form part of a room or the building, while there should be a gap between the main building and compound wall on North or East.
10. The height of the compound wall on the West should be higher than that on the East. The height of the compound wall on the South or West should be higher than that on the North.
11. If any vertical addition is to be made, it should be on the South or West of the existing building.

Toilet

1. The commode should face either South or North and not East nor West.
2. Attached bathroom should be on the North or East of the bedroom.
3. In any room, North-East corner should not be used for keeping spoiled clothes or shoes, chappals, broom sticks, chairs, etc.
4. Bath water, waste water or water used for washing vessels should be disposed only on the East or the West or North or North-East only.
5. Septic tank should be either in the middle of the East or North and should not be on the compound

wall.

6. Overhead tank should preferably be on the South-West and the gap should be provided between the roof and the bottom of the tank. Overhead tank should not be on the North-East direction.

House Warming *(Gṛha-praveśa)*

1. House warming function shall be done only after laying the roof slab, fixing the shutters for doors and windows and satisfying the *Vāstu* sacrifice ceremony.
2. Name Plates: After deciding on the suitable name for the house and preparing the name plate/board, it may be prayed in *Vāstu Śānti* and embedded on the wall on the house-warming day itself.
3. There should be at least one lamp lighted during the period covering from the sunset to sunrise on the succeeding day.

Post-Construction

1. The house should not be kept vacant for more than three months.
2. If any portion of the building is to be let out, it is preferable that the South portion is occupied by the owner. The North or the North-East can be let out. South portion should not be kept vacant.
3. If any additional residential units are to be constructed other than the main building, these should be on the North or the East, leaving some vacant space on these directions.
4. The ground floor of the house should not be kept unoccupied, while the first floor can be kept unoccupied.
5. Partitioning of the house building is not advisable.

Section II

VĀSTU AND JYOTIṢA (ASTROLOGY)

Astrological Configurations for Vāstu

S.K. Kelkar*

Any land selected for National, Industrial units (small or big) or private purposes must be free from afflictions. Besides, proper *muhūrta* must be observed so that the *Vāstu* constructed on such land would last long. The *muhūrta* must be selected on astrological rather than religious considerations.

It is my general experience that people living in a palace or multistoried building are not happy because of reasons unknown to them, although sufficient care has been taken by builders, by architects, and interior decorators in constructing the dwelling place. After going through a number of horoscopes during the last two decades or so, thorough investigation carried out by me has led me to write the following lines.

Fourth House

In the *Jātakapārijāta*, an exhaustive list of various characteristics that can be judged from each house of the horoscope is described. So far as the fourth house is concerned, it has been stated that it implies everything concerning a building that could be constructed for safety and welfare of an individual. It is called as *Bhavana Saṁsthā*. If auspicious planets, such as Venus, Mercury and Moon are placed, one can enjoy vehicular and residential comforts. In short, such building or residential premises are free from various afflictions. There are some who purchase vehicles for their quick movement or for their

* Flat No. A 24, 3rd Floor, Saras Nagar, Near Sarasbaug, Shukrawar Peth, Pune-411 002.

own luxury, but the vehicles will either be defective causing heavy expenditure or the person concerned will meet with accident, and the vehicle and the individual are both likely to be damaged. The same principle can be applied for the residential quarters or industrial places.

Illustrations

Very recently I met an individual from an affluent family of Bombay staying near Marine Drive. His twenty-four years old daughter was ailing for more than three years. He had tried all systems of medicines but his efforts were in vain. After examining the charts of all the four members of the family, it was found that the fourth houses were afflicted severely. I questioned him about the location of the house. I told him that this building must have been constructed on certain temple which were buried underneath. He has nearly five buildings in Bombay and every building was causing him some trouble or the other. I have gone to the places and checked the building in which he was staying for over fifty years. On the ground floor, an idol mostly from the Ajanta Caves was installed but the gods and the goddesses that have been buried underground were troubling the family very much. The daughter's bedroom was exactly on the buried place. I made further investigations as to whether all the inhabitants of the flats of the seven storied building had problems. All of them reported 'yes'. My theory proved correct and some suggestions have been made to remove the inauspicious aspects.

Nobody has given any consideration to such factors for the failure or success of buildings constructed in such areas.

Planets in the Fourth House

1. In the *Jātakapārijāta*, it is said that when *Gulikā* is placed in the fourth house, the person born will be devoid of houses, happiness, lands and vehicles and thereby he becomes a wanderer.
2. If an eclipsed planet is in the fourth house, one should presume that one has to reciprocate the

obligations of the last birth, especially to the parents. It is called *Pitṛ-doṣa.* It shows the specific departed soul is haunting the place.

3. The three asterisms ruled by the Sun, viz., *Kṛttikā, Uttarā* and *Uttarāṣāḍhā* are not advisable on the house. These are to some extent cruel constellations. If one gets property by inheritance, the individual may not be able to enjoy peace and tranquility in such *Vāstu.* It should be ascertained from experts what type of rituals are required to be performed for removal of this *doṣa.*
4. Saturn-Mars conjunction: I need not put much emphasis on this combination of the planets which are of contrary nature. But when such a combination takes place in the fourth house, one can presume that he has taken birth in a house wherein there are a lot of obligations to be met. Recently I came across a case in which a Brahmin was engaged to look after some property during the Portugese regime. In course of time, the Portugese left India and the whole land comprising a number of acres came into the hands of this poor Brahmin. At present, the third or fourth generation is enjoying the property but it could neither dispose off the property nor take the advantage of the lands, which are lying as they are. One after another small pieces of the land have been disposed off at insignificant price by the present generation to make ends meet. When the question of disposing of the main land arose, they had to wait for fifteen years but no transaction was successfully made and the family has no source of income except this land. I have seen the premises myself alongwith an expert and located the area in which the secret situation was available there. Initially, I had advised all the members of the generation to pray to lord *Śiva* every day, and that after a year or so they should come to me. As the prayer was increasing day by day, they got the clue. In the past there was a number of gold coins occasionally found in that area. Besides, there are coconut trees

on the same land. There is a big well wherein all the year round ample water is available, but inside the well there is a tunnel. One of the *māntrikas* disclosed that the whole property was conditioned by the grandfather because the subsequent generations should not waste it for selfish reasons. After a number of rituals, the land has been freed from the clutches of the spirits and the family was able to dispose off the land for a huge amount.

5. Saturn-*Rāhu* conjunction: This is a very bad combination. Evil spirits may have their abode there. It is very difficult to remove such type of affliction.
6. In case residential premises are close to temples or *samādhis*, regular worship will have to be offered so that happiness will prevail. Otherwise, curses result.
7. Retrograde planets in the fourth house are not favourable. Even the auspicious planet when they are retrograde, do not favour *Vāstu* for one reason or the other.

The sum and substance of this paper is that the land on which *Vāstu* is to be constructed should be free from afflictions. Besides, the horoscope of the purchaser of the land and the buildings should be checked. The same principle can further be observed very critically when huge lands are purchased. A proper *Muhūrta* should be made use of; otherwise the very purpose of big projects is likely to be lost. While selecting a *muhūrta*, the astrological principles rather than religious ones should be observed very carefully. I shall quote an example of Koyna Dam Project. The inauguration of the dam was on *Dasarā* day, but the astrological principles were completely ignored. We are witnessing a number of earthquake tremors there. No one can predict the safety of the dam.

Vāstu in Astrology

*Dr. T.S. Vasan**

Vāstu Śāstra is one of the branches of Hindu Astrology. The Rishis of yore should have thought deeply on the *kārakatva* of the planets or their significations in formulating the principles of *Vāstu*. The principles given by our *Ācāryas* are of eternal nature in the changing world. The characteristics of the *kārakatva* of planets cannot be changed. Keeping in view the natural laws, the Rishis have given the basis to build houses, temples, cities, etc. By following these principles of *Vāstu*, i.e., the *kārakatva* of planets in building dwelling places, we can get peace and tranquillity and general happiness in our lives.

The whole world is a manifestation of the *Pañca-mahābūtas* or *Pañca-tattvas*, viz., *Pṛthvī*, *Āpa*, *Tejas*, *Vāyu* and *Ākāśa*. The *Ākāśatattva* works in higher dimensions of life, whereas the four basic *Tattvas*, viz., *Pṛthvī*, *Āpa*, *Teja*, *Vāyu*, are of great utility in man's day-to-day life. He himself is a product of the *Pañcamahābhūtas*. The house in which he dwells has three components of the Tattvas and if proper rules are not followed, there will be every likelihood of suffering with anxieties in life. In our day-to-day life, we have to cook our food, eat, sleep and do many other activities of our day-to-day life in our house. These can be grouped under *Sāttvika*, *Rājasika* and *Tāmasika* natures. Each direction and a portion of the house are earmarked for our different department of life, keeping in view the planetary *Kārakatvas*. If this rule is transgressed, there will be confusion and those dwelling in that place will encounter many problems of health and monetary affairs. Even for the mutual understanding between members of a family, there will be differences and stress.

Let us try to understand the different directions and

---

* 50/7, Aparna Complex, S.C. Road, Bangalore-560 009.

their rulers.

Rulers: The East direction is ruled by the Sun, and the West is ruled by Saturn. In the same way, the North is ruled by Mercury, and the South is ruled by Mars. The North-East is ruled by Jupiter, and the South-East is ruled by Venus. The North-West is ruled by the Moon, and the South-West is ruled by Rāhu.

East: The Sun, who rules this direction, is the promoter of health and that is why the sun-rays should enter a house early in the morning. Therefore, we have to keep doors and windows properly to get the sunlight in a house. Windows are, therefore, ruled by the Sun and the Moon who are called the luminaries, which, in other words, are planets responsible for light in human life, and more specifically, physical and mental health. The life-giving principles of the Sun should be followed by keeping doors and windows open so that the sunrays enter a house as the morning Sun has a property of purifying water. The entry of sunlight in the morning is life-protecting, and as the Sun goes up, his destructive force comes into play. By evening when it comes down, it again has a soothing influence. If by chance the kitchen is located in the East of the house, Venus being the enemy of the Sun, the housewife may suffer from bilious complains and nervous debility, and also there may be uterine disorders.

West: Saturn is the presiding deity of the West direction. This direction is very suitable for locating the dining room which will bring auspicious influence to the family. The person who has the main door in this direction will have come up from great difficulties and he ekes out his livelihood by physical labour as Saturn stands for labour and hard work. To keep food-grains in this direction is good.

North: Since the North is ruled by Mercury which is a planet of the mind, education etc., we can keep the study-room in this direction, in addition to the treasury of wealth. The presiding deity Mercury who is symbolic of God Viṣṇu is the Lord of Wealth. If the main door is kept in this direction the head of the family will be intelligent and will earn his living through business enterprises or intellectual activities as Mercury stands for *buddhi*; the *kārakatvas* for consultation and communication are good here. Generally, this is a good direction to keep the money-chest.

South: The South direction has Mars as its lord. This is the best direction for the bedroom. The husband-governing planet Mars and the wife-governing planet Venus are both friendly to each other. This, therefore, is a good direction for them to sleep and is very conducive to deep attachment and understanding between them. When the kitchen and the bedroom are in one direction, the couple will experience a lot of mental unrest. It is also not good to take food in this direction as they may suffer ill-health or other ailments. This direction is called the direction of the god of Death.

North-West: Vāyu is the presiding deity of this direction. *Vāyu* is the god of Wind, and the ruler is the Moon. If the main door is towards this direction, the lord of the house will have many travels. This is a very good place for storage of food-grains. The *Pūjā*-room here will also bring auspicious indications.

South-West: This direction is ruled by Rāhu. This is the place where the toilet has to be built. If by chance the walls of this direction are dilapidated, there will be visitations of spirits.

North-East: This direction is ruled by Jupiter and the presiding deity is *Īśvara*. This is the place where divine contemplation is done. Idols of worship should be kept in this direction. The owner of the house will have high honour, respect and prestige in society. It is said that the *Pūjā*-room and the bathroom in this direction will ensure auspicious results and will promote longevity, good health, good fortune and peace of mind.

South-East: The presiding deity of the South-East is Agni, the god of fire, and Venus is the governing planet of this direction. If the kitchen is kept in this direction, there will be peace and tranquility in the family. If by chance there is an overhead tank or large accumulation of food articles in this direction corners, the house-wife and her daughters will suffer from ill-health.

Therefore, to understand the good and bad aspects of different portions of the house, one has to understand the permutations and combinations of major planets and sub-planets joining them. In order to understand this, we have to identify each planet with different portions of the house. The Sun and the Moon representing the windows are found on the right and left side of the front portion of the house. The inside hall of the house is identified with Mars, Venus with the bedroom, Saturn with the store-room, and *Ketu* with ventilation of the front door. Generally speaking, *Ketu* represents the conservancy, stagnant water or a ditch. The moon generally stands for cowshed and also storage of grains. Though Saturn is also a planet connected with storage, he represents *Bhūtagaṇas*, which means, living beings who consume food. Therefore, the West direction is meant for dinning room. In addition to mercury's jurisdiction of the hall in the house, he represents the treasury room where treasures of the house in the form of jewels, money, cash and documents are kept. It may be also called as strong-room where the iron-chest is kept. Rāhu, the ruler of *Nirṛtya* is a planet ruling waste material. Therefore, the lords of eight directions are *Indra* (East), *Agni* (South-East), *Yama* (South), *Varuṇa* (South-West), *Śani* (West), *Kubera* (North), *Īśvara* (North-East), and *Vāyu* (North-West).

Just like the Four Classes (*cāturvarṇya*) of human beings, the soils are also categorised under four types. Red, white, yellow, and black or rocky soil. Therefore, each type of soil is suitable for a particular set of people who are engaged in a particular avocation, such as intellectual pursuits, public social affairs, business enterprises, and manual agricultural pursuits. If white soil is selected by people who pursue intellectual pursuits, they will prosper well. Red soil is useful for people who are engaged in public social affairs. Yellow soil is suitable for the business community, and black soil is useful for those who are engaged in physical labour. Then, among the mixed soils, white and red are good for prosperity. Then we have to infer the different materials used in the construction of the house. Lime is indicated by Mars. Hard stones are also indicated by Mars. Marble stones are indicated by the Moon, and black stones are indicated by Saturn. The wall in the house which is covered by darkness indicates miseries to the womenfolk of the house indicated by Saturn.

Let us study some of the *Kārakatvas* of the planet which can fit into the *Vāstu* principles: The Sun stands for fire, father, east direction, mental purity, copper and mouth. The Moon stands for mind, water, heart, silver, mother, pond, nourishment, pleasures of life, eating, good blood and vital energy. Mars stands for south, fire, affection, jewel, gold, beautiful clothes, management of wild elements, independence, etc. Mercury stands for treasury, education, writing, conversation, philosophy, doctor, astrology, flourishing of family and sacred prayer. Jupiter stands for cow, philosophy, gods, finance, religious duty, *Mantra*, holy water, movements in heaven, sweet juice, gentleness, Vedic text, and being engaged in one's duty. Venus stands for women, marriage, south-east corner, beauty, love-making, enjoyment, singing, happiness from wife and luck. Saturn stands for labour class, workers, servile duty, old age, strong at the conclusion of the day, black grains, iron, a room where weapons are kept and quality of *Tamas*. Rāhu stands for north-west direction, gambling, waste material and dirty things. Ketu stands for Lord *Gaṇeśa*, great penance, science of witchcraft, knowledge of *Brahma*, philosophy and luck.

Now we can understand how our Rishis built houses in conformity with planetary directions and their *Kārakatvas* for the peace and prosperity of man. They have also taken into consideration the benefic and malefic qualities of the planets. For example, Jupiter, Mercury and Sun are benefic with *Sāttvika* nature, and the Moon and Venus are benefic with *Rājasika* nature, and Mars, Saturn and Rahu are malefic with *Tāmasika* nature. In our daily life, we may segregate our actions into *Sāttvika*, *Rājasika* and *Tāmasika* activities.

Now, when we come to the actual picture of house, we see the rules of *Vāstu* for different activities as follows: Praying in the North-East direction, sleeping in the South direction, studying, commercial undertakings and keeping the treasury in the North, and storing of grains and having servants' quarters in the West of the house. When we take to the sleeping room, elders will sleep towards South-West. West ruled by Saturn is symbolic of old age and in other directions, young members of the house may be sleeping. Since the hall of the house is a communicating room where friends and relatives come and sit and discuss, it is ruled by Mercury, the planet of communication. The *Vāstu* principles strictly follow the enmities and friendships of planets. Certain *Kārakatvas* of one planets may not be suitable for another planets who is inimical to him. For example, fire will not go hand-in-hand with air. Fire stands for Mars, and Saturn stands for air. In the same way, South and North, East and West, North-East and South-West, and North-West and South-East are directions that do not harmonise mutually. Therefore, the *Kārakatvas* coming under one planet should not be exchanged or placed in the direction of the inimical opposite planet which creates disharmony and distress in the family. Since benefics and *Sāttvika Grahas* are bent on doing good to the native, they should be given more prominence than malefics and their directions. With regard to the loads, the malefic planetary directions should carry more load than the other benefic planetary side. In the same way, water should always run towards the benefic and *Sāttvika* direction, and not vice versa. With this simple planetary understanding of the *Kārakatvas*, it is very clear that *Vāstu* principles are akin to Astrology, and therefore *Vāstu* is within the purview of Astrology. If there is any problems or difficulties, proper remedies can be had, keeping in view the planets and their *Kārakatvas*, their enmities and friendships.

Vāstu and Jyotiṣa

A. Narasimha Alse

Vāstu and *Jyotiṣa* cannot do without each other, since they are like air and water; they are guiding factors. In the socio-economic context of the ancient and middle ages, there was close co-operation among the five groups of craftsmen dealing with (a) Iron, (b) Wood, (c) Copper, (d) Stone-Śilā and (e) Gold-*Suvarṇa*. The Purāṇic accounts refer to the creator 'Viśvakarman' himself as the primordial craftsman. Human beings depend upon traditional craftsmen like goldsmiths, blacksmiths, carpenters, stone-sculptors and masons. In the *Bṛhat-saṁhitā* of Varāhamihira, *Śilpa-śāstra* and Architecture (*vāstu*) are dealt with. Later, the tendency to write books on specific topics even in architecture like building of houses began. As a result we have works like the *Manuṣyālaya-candrikā* and the *Gṛha-vāstu-sāra* for ordinary houses, the *Prāsāda-kalpa*, etc., for palaces, the *Maṅdira-vāstu* for temples, the *Vāpi-kūpa-lakṣaṇa* for excavating Tanks and wells, and the *Vāstu-ratnāvali* for designing buildings.

The well-known texts of *Vāstu Śāstra* are the *Mānasāra*, the *Aparājita-pṛcchā*, the *Samarāṅgaṇa-sūtradhāra*, and the *Viśvakarma-vāstuśāstra*. With reference to the common residential buildings, there are four important designs: (1) *Ekaśāla*, i.e., those constructed on one direction; (2) *Dviśāla* (two sides); (3) *Triśāla* (three sides) and (4) *Catuḥśāla* (four sides). Of these the important one is the *Ekaśāla* one. The *Alinda* of house is its verandah. A house is again divided into three parts: (1) *Brahma-bhāga* is the Front Part; (2) *Gandharva-bhāga* is the Centre part; and (3) *Manuṣya-bhāga* is the Hind Part.

The *Brahma-bhāga* (front part) is good for study, planning, meeting friends and entertainment. The *Gandharva-bhāga* (centre part) is good for cooking, dining, bathing and for the work of the servants. And, the *manuṣya-bhāga* (hind part) for sleeping and keeping money, ornaments, etc.

Now, let us deal with planets and their effects on houses, in view of the science of Astrology.

Sun: Sun is the soul (*ātmakāraka*) besides being *Pitṛkāraka*, and governing planet of the fifth sign Leo of the zodiac (*bhacakra*). In *Gṛhavāstu*, the window on the East should be such as to allow maximum sun-light, otherwise it will disturb the prosperity of a family.

Moon: The left side of a house is indicative of mother or daughter. If the left window happens to be a puja room, women will enjoy divine perception, wisdom (Moon + Jupiter); in case a room is full of darkness with materials dumped, the house wife suffers ill-health.

Mars and Venus: The kitchen should be in South-East (*āgneyī*). Mars is the planet ruling the South. But it is Venus who governs a kitchen. If a kitchen is situated opposite to a bedroom, although there may a happiness, there will be ill-health. In some houses, where both the kitchen and bathroom are combined, great hardship is felt and earnings go the waste.

Mercury: Mercury governs the North, verandah, hall vistors' room and sit-out. If there is a puja room in the hall itself, the owner of the family enjoys great benefits from lands. If the hall is attached to bedroom, the house-wife will be earning well. If the hall suffers for want of ventilation or darkness, there will be immoral affairs and earnings through shady means.

Jupiter: Jupiter rules the direction of North-East which is suited for proper puja room. Suppose the door is directly facing a puja room, even though there be hardship in life, later on one would enjoy prosperity.

Saturn: It governs the West and is the best friend of Rahu. Rāhu and Ketu represent main door and rear door, respectively. Food material stored in the West (store room, etc.) is auspicious and leads to prosperity.

Rāhu: It governs the South-West. Unused materials, location of water closets and toilets here is good. As Rāhu governs the main door, the entrance door must be larger than the other doors.

Ketu: The direction of Ketu is also the North-East. Ketu governs small rear door, the bath rooms, ditches and staircase. If the staircase leading to the first floor is near the main door entrance, it indicates self-deception and is not auspicious.

Relevance of Muhūrta to Vāstu Śāstra

S. Krishna Kumar, B.E. (Mech.), FICAS*

Muhūrta normally means auspicious time at which various events of life are fixed. *Muhūrta* is as important as the methodology of building construction. As per Vāstu, an auspicious time for fixing the main-door frame, for digging the earth and the *Gṛha-praveśam* after the completion of the building plays an important role in one's life.

Good Days for Gṛhārambha (*Śaṅku-sthāpana* and *Guḍḍālī Pūjā*)

मृदुध्रुवस्वातिपुष्यधनिष्ठादिवतये रवौ ।
मूले पुनर्वसौ सौम्यवारे प्रारम्भं शुभम् ॥
mṛdu-dhruva-svāti-puṣya-dhaniṣṭhādi-vataye ravau /
mūle punarvasau saumyavāre prārambhaṁ śubham //

"*Mṛdu-saṁjñaka (Mṛgaśīrṣa, Revatī, Citrā), Dhruva-saṁjñaka* (*Uttarā, Uttarāṣāḍhā, Uttarābhādrapada, Rohiṇī*), *Svāti, Puṣya Dhaniṣṭhā, Śatabhīṣā, Hasta, Mūla* and *Punarvasu* are good to start the building construction activity".

आदित्यभौमवर्जं तु वाराः सर्वे शुभावहाः ।
द्वितीया च तृतीया च षष्ठी च पच्चमी तथा ॥
ādityabhaumavarjaṁ tu vāraḥ sarve śubhāvahāḥ /
dvitīyā ca tṛtīyā ca ṣaṣṭhi ca pañcamī tathā //

"All the days except Sunday and Tuesdays are auspicious. The second, third, fifth and sixth *tithis* are bad."

---

* 5, IV Block, III cross, Kumar Park West, Bangalore-560 020.

सप्तमी दशमी चैव द्वादश्येकादशी तथा ।
त्रयोदशी पञ्चादशी तिथयः स्युः शुभावहाः ॥
saptamī daśamī caiva dvādaśy-ekādaśī tathā /
trayodaśī pañcadaśī tithayaḥ syuḥ śubhāvahāḥ //

"The seventh, tenth, eleventh, twelfth, thirteenth and fifteenth (Full Moon) lunar days are said to be auspicious."

दारिद्र्यं प्रतिपत् कुर्यात् चतुर्थी धनहारिणी ।
अष्टम्युच्चारनं चैव नवमी शस्त्रघातिनी ॥
dāridryaṁ pratipat kuryāt caturthī dhanahāriṇī /
aṣṭamyuccāṭaṁ caiva navamī śastraghātinī //

"If a house is commenced on the first *tithi*, there is poverty, if on the fourth lunar day, loss of wealth, if on the eighth day eviction, and if on the ninth day, danger from weapons."

दर्शे राज्यभयं भूते सुतदारविनाशनम् ।
धनिष्ठापञ्चके नैव कुर्यात् स्तम्भसमुच्छ्रयम् ॥
darśe rājyabhayaṁ bhūte sutadāravināśanam /
dhaniṣṭhā-pañcake naiva kuryāt stambha-samuc-chrayam //

"If begun on *Amāvasyā* fear from the government, if on the fourteenth day, destruction of children and ladies. The house should not be commenced in *Dhaniṣṭhā-pañcaka.*"

सूत्रद्वार शिलान्यास प्राकारादि समारभत् ।
यामित्रं द्विविधं वर्ज्यं वेधोपग्रहकर्तरी ॥
sūtradvāra śilānyasā prākārādi samārabhat /
yamitraṁ dvividhaṁ varjyaṁ vedhopagrahakartarī //

"The *Lagna* at the commencement of the building should not be flanked on either side by malefics and Upagrahas."

कुलिकं कण्टकं कालं यमघण्टं तथैव च ।
जन्मतृतीय पञ्च सप्त तारा वर्ज्यानि भानि च ॥
कुयोगवन सञ्ज्रश्च तथा त्रिस्पृक्खलं दिनम् ।
पापलग्नानि पापांशाः पापवर्गास्तथैव च ॥

kulikaṁ kaṇṭakaṁ kālaṁ yamaghaṇṭaṁ tathaiva ca /
janmatṛtīya pañca sapta tārā varjyāni bhāni ca //
kuyogavana sañjraś ca tathā trispṛkkhalaṁ dinam /
pāpalagnāni papāṁśāḥ pāpavargās tathaiva ca //

"Bad days, bad *Lagna*, bad *Lagna-navamāṁśa* and malefic *Vargas*, *Gulikā*, *Yamaghaṇṭa-kāla*, the first, third, fifth, seventh stars from the native's birth star are not recommended."

कुयोगास्तिथि वारोत्था स्तिथिभोत्था भवारजाः ।
विवाहादिषु ये वर्ज्यास्ते वर्ज्या वास्तुकर्मणि ॥
kuyogās tithivārotthās tithibhotthā bhavārajāḥ /
vivāhādiṣu ye varjyās te varjya vāstukarmaṇi //

"The bad days caused by *tithis* and weekdays and *Nakṣatras*, and those prohibited for marriage-*muhūrtas* are prohibited for *Gṛhārambha* also."

Vāstu Puruṣa Diagram

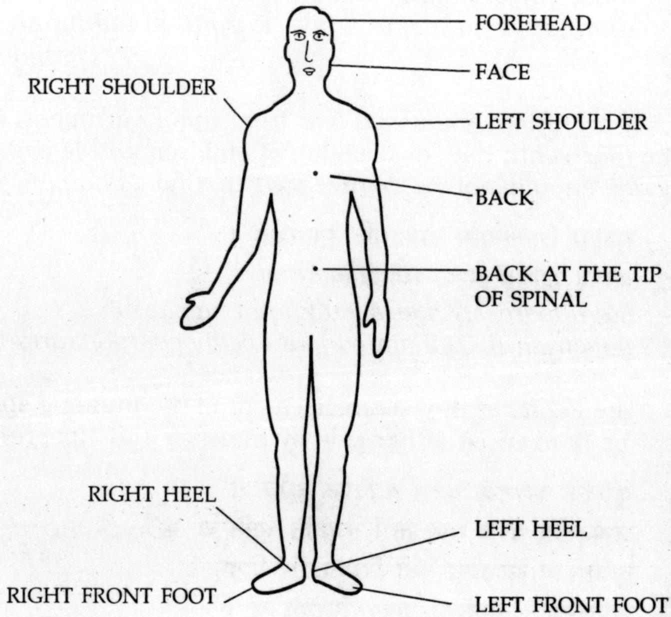

Vāstu Cakram

वास्तुचक्रं प्रवक्ष्यामि यच्च व्यासेन भाषितम् ।
यस्मिन्नृक्षे स्थितो भानुस्तदादौ त्रीणि मस्तके ॥
चतुष्कमग्रपादे स्यात् परश्चत्वारि पश्चिमे ।
पृष्ठे चे त्रीणि ऋक्षाणि दक्षकुक्षौ चतुष्ककम् ॥
पुच्छे चत्वारि ऋक्षाणि कुक्षौ चत्वारि वामतः ।
मुखे भत्रयमेव स्युरष्टाविंशति तारकाः ॥
शिरस्ताराग्निदाहाय गृहोद्वासोऽग्रपादयोः ।
स्थैर्यं स्यात् पश्चिमे पादे पृष्ठे चैवं धनागमः ॥
कुक्षौ स्याद् दक्षिणे लाभः पुच्छे च स्वामिनाशनम् ।
वामकुक्षौ च दारिद्र्यं मुखे पीडा निरन्तरम् ॥
पुनर्वसौ नृपादीनां कर्तव्यं सूतिकागृहम् ।

vāstucakraṁ pravakṣyāmi yac ca vyāsena bhāṣitam /
yasmin ṛkṣe sthito bhānus tadādau trīṇi mastake //
catuṣkam agrapāde syāt paraś catvāri paścime /
pṛṣṭhe ca trīṇi ṛkṣāṇi dakṣakukṣau catuṣkakam //
pucche catvāri ṛkṣāṇi kukṣau catvāri vāmataḥ /
mukhe bhatrayam eva syur aṣṭaviṁśati tārakāḥ //
śirastārāgnidāhāya gṛhodvāso 'grapādayoḥ /
sthairyaṁ syāt paścime pāde pṛṣṭhe caivaṁ dhanāgamaḥ //
kukṣau syād dakṣiṇe lābhaḥ pucche ca svāminā śanam /
vāmakukṣau ca dāridryaṁ mukhe pīḍā nirantaram //
punarvasau nṛpādīnāṁ kartavyaṁ sūtikāgṛham /

The *Vāstu Cakram* is as follows:

The stars from that occupied by the Sun indicate the different reckoned parts of the body as follows:

1-3 Stars	—	Forehead
4-7 Stars	—	Front toe
8-11 Stars	—	Heel
12-14 Stars	—	Back
15-18 Stars	—	Region under right shoulder
19-22 Stars	—	Back (tip of the spinal region)
23-25 Stars	—	Region under left shoulder
26-28 Stars	—	Face

If the star falls on the forehead, fire accident takes place; if on the front foot, prosperity of the house; if on the heels, permanancy; if on the back, financial benefits; if under the right shoulder, all types of profits; if on the tip of the spinal region, the owner will suffer very badly including destruction; if under the left shoulder, poverty; and if on the face, permanent problems. (A special note on *Punar-vasu* says that) the labour ward commenced on *Punarvasu* star is auspicious.

Now, for example, consider a man born in *Rohiṇī* asks a question about commencement of a *muhūrta* for digging of earth for his building (*bhūmi-pūjā*) when the Sun is in *Mṛgaśīrṣa.* According to astrology, *Mṛgaśīrṣa* being *Sampaṭa-tārā* is good for *bhūmi-pūjā.* But according to *Vāstu,* the first three stars commencing from *Mṛgaśīrṣa* will fall on the forehead as per the *Vāstu-cakra.* Accordingly, such a star causes fire accidents. Therefore, even though *Mṛgaśīrṣa* is a *Sampat-tārā,* it should be delected and a suitable star like *Uttarā-phālgunī* falling on the ninth star would be suitable. As per Vāstu-cakra, this star falls on heels which is auspicious indicating permanancy. Thus, *Uttarā-phālgunī* is suitable both astrologically and according to the Vāstu-cakra, and, therefore, is auspicious for the *Gṛhārambha-muhūrta.* In a similar manner, *muhūrtas* can be fixed for any given day by noting the star transitted by the Sun on a particular day.

Special Information on *Muhūrta*

श्रवणाभिजितोर्मध्ये प्रवेशं तत्र कारयेत् ।
चरलग्ने चरांशं च सर्वथा परिवर्जयेत् ॥ १ ॥
sravaṇābhijitor madhye praveśaṁ tatra kārayet /
caralagne carāṁśaṁ ca sarvathā parivarjayet //1//

Construction of the entrance of Labour Room (*sūtikāgṛha*) should never be undertaken during *Cara Lagna* and *Cara Navamāṁśa.*

जन्मभाच्चोपचये लग्ने वर्गे तथैव च ।
प्रारम्भणं प्रकुर्वीत नैधनं परिवर्जयेत् ॥ २ ॥

पापैस्त्रिष्ठायगतैः सौम्यैः केन्द्रत्रिकोणगैः ।
निर्माणं कारयेद्विमानमष्टमस्थैः खलैर्मृतिः ॥ ३ ॥

janmabhāc copacaye lagne varge tathaiva ca /
prārambhaṇam prakurvīta naidhanaṁ parivarjayet //2//

papais triṣṭhayagataiḥ saumyaiḥ kendratrikoṇagaiḥ /
nirmāṇam kārayed vimānam aṣṭamasthaiḥ khalair mṛtiḥ //3//

The *Upāśraya* house (third, sixth, tenth or eleventh) from *Janma Rāśi*, as well as the eight sign from it should not be the rising sign for starting construction.

Such constructions begun when malefic planets occupy the third, sixth, or eleventh house from *Lagna*, and benefics occupy *Kendras* and *Koṇas* from it, death is sure to take place in them, if malefics occupy the eighth house from the *Lagna*.

Yogas

गुरुर्लग्ने रविः षष्ठे द्यूते सौम्ये सुखे सिते ।
तृतीयस्थेऽर्कपुत्रे च तद्गृहं शतमायुषम् ॥ १ ॥

Gurur lagne raviḥ ṣaṣṭhe dyute saumye sukhe site /
Tṛtīyasthe 'rkaputre ca tadgṛhaṁ śatamāyuṣam //1//

1. If Jupiter is in *Lagna*, the Sun in the sixth, Mercury in the seventh, Venus in the fourth, and Saturn in the third, the house constructed will last for hundred years.

भृगुर्लग्नेऽम्बरे सौम्ये लाभस्थाने च भास्करे ।
गुरुः केन्द्रगतो यत्र शतवर्षाणि तिष्ठति ॥ २ ॥

bhṛgur lagne 'mbare saumye labhasthāne ca bhaskare /
guruḥ kendragato yatra satavarṣāṇi tiṣṭhati //2//

2. If in Ascendant Venus is posited, Mercury in tenth, Sun in eleventh and Jupiter in *Kendras* (i.e. first, fourth, seventh, tenth), the house will last for hundred years.

हिबुकेज्ञेऽम्बरे चन्द्रे लाभे च कुजभास्करौ।
प्रारम्भः कुरुते यस्य अशीत्याहुः क्रमा भवेत् ॥ ३ ॥

hibukejñe 'mbare candre labhe ca kujabhāskarau /
prarambhaḥ kurute yasya aśītyāhuḥ kramā bhavet//3/

3. If Jupiter is in the fourth from the Ascendant and Moon in the tenth, Mars and Sun in the eleventh, the house constructed in such a *Lagna* will last for eighty years.

लग्ने मृगे पुत्रगेऽन्ये षष्ठे भौमे तृतीयगे।
रवौ यस्य गृहारम्भः स च तिष्ठेच्छतद्वयम् ॥ ४॥

lagne mṛge putrage 'nye ṣaṣṭhe bhaume tṛtīyage /
ravau yasya gṛhārambhaḥ sa ca
tiṣṭhecchatadvayam //4//

4. If Venus is in the Ascendant, Jupiter in the fifth, Mars in the sixth, Sun in the third, the house constructed will last for two hundred years.

लग्नेस्थौ गुरुशुक्रौ च रिपुराशिगते कुजे।
सूर्ये लाभगते यस्य द्विशताब्दानि तिष्ठति ॥ ५॥

lagnasthau guruśukrau ca ripurāśigate kuje /
sūrye lābhagate yasya dviśatābdāni tiṣṭhati //5//

5. If Jupiter and Venus are in *Lagna* and Mars in the sixth and Sun in the eleventh, the house constructed in such a *Lagna* will last for two hundred years.

स्वोच्चे लाभगते मन्दे सहस्राणां समस्थितिः।
स्वोच्चस्थो वा भृमुर्लग्ने स्वोच्चे सुसंस्थिते ।।६॥

svocce lābhagate mande sahasrāṇāṁ samasthitiḥ /
svoccastho vā bhṛgur lagne svocce susaṁsthite //6//

6. If Venus is in exaltation in the *Lagna* (i.e. *Mīna* or Pisces *Lagna*) or Jupiter is exalted in the fourth and exalted Saturn is in the eleventh, the house will last for many thousand years.

कर्कलग्नगते चन्द्रे केन्द्रस्थाने च वाक्पतिः।
मित्रस्वोच्चस्थितैः खेटैर्लक्ष्मीस्त्वसय चिरं भवेत्॥ ७॥

karkalagnagate candre kendrasthane ca vakpatiḥ /
mitrasvoccāsthitaiḥ kheṭair lakṣmīs tvasya ciraṁ
bhavet //7//

7. If the Moon is placed in *Karka*, i.e. Cancer *Lagna*, Jupiter in a *Kendra* and benefics in friendly or exalted houses, the house commenced during such a *Lagna* will last long and will be a wealthy house.

इज्योत्तरात्रयाहीन्दुविष्णुघातृजालोडुषु ।
वारुणा सहितेष्वेषु कृतं गेहं श्रिया युतम्॥ ८॥
ijyottarātrayāhīnduviṣṇughātṛjāloḍuṣu /
varuṇā sahiteśv eṣu kṛtam geham śriyā yutaṁ //8//

8. The house commenced in the star *Puṣya, Uttarā Phālgunī, Uttarāṣaḍhā, Uttarābhādrapada Áśleṣā, Mṛgaśīrṣa, Śravaṇa, Rohiṇi* or *Pūrvābhādrapada* will be a house of wealth.

दिग्दैवत्वाष्ट्र वारीश रुद्रादितिवसूडुषु।
शुक्रेण सहितेष्वेषु कृते धान्यप्रदं गृहम् ॥ ९॥
digdaivatvāṣṭra vārīśa rudrāditivasūḍuṣu /
śukreṇa sahiteśv eṣu kṛte dhānya pradaṁ gṛhaṁ //9//

9. The house commenced in *Viśākhā, Citrā, Śatabhīṣā, Ārdrā,* and *Punarvasu,* when the Venus is in *Dhaniṣṭhā*, that house will always have the granaries full.

हस्तार्थभत्वाष्ट्र दस्र चानुराधीडुभेषु च ।
बुधेन सहितेष्वेषु धनयुक्तसुखप्रदम् ॥ १०॥
hastārthabhatvāṣtra dasra cānurādhīdubheṣu ca /
buddhena sahiteṣv eṣu dhanayuktasukhapradam//10/

10. A house commenced in *Hasta, Uttarā-phālgunī, Citrā*, with Mercury in *Aśvinī* and *Anurādhā*, will bestow financial happiness to children.

Evil Yogas

शत्रुक्षेत्रगतैर्वा नीच स्थैर्वा पराजितैः।
प्रारम्भे यस्य भवने लक्ष्मीस्तस्य विनश्यति ॥ १॥
śatrukṣetragatair vā nīcasthair vā parājitaiḥ /
prārambhe yaśya bhavane lakṣmīs tasya vinaśyati//1//

1. If the Ascendant is in inimical or debilitated or defeated sign, a house constructed then will be trouble-some with destruction of wealth certain.

एकोऽपि परभागस्थो दशमे सप्तमेऽपि वा।
वर्णाधिपे बलैर्हीने तद्गृहं परहस्तगम् ॥ २ ॥
eko'pi parabhāgastho daśame saptame 'pi vā /
varṇadhipe balair hīne tadgṛhaṁ parahastagam //2//

2. If the lord of any house is posited in the seventh or tenth inimical house and if the *Varṇādhipa* is devoid of strength, then such a house commenced in such a *Lagna* will go to others.

पापान्तराले लग्ने न च सौम्ययुतीक्षिते।
अष्टमस्थेऽर्कपत्रे चाशीत्यब्दादि हन्यते ॥ ३ ॥
pāpāntarāle lagne na ca saumyayutīkṣite /
aṣṭamasthe' rkapatre cāśītyabdādi hanyate //3//

3. If the *Lagna* is between two malefics and if benefics do not aspect it, and if Saturn is in the eighth, the house gets destroyed in the eightieth year.

मन्दे लग्नगते चैव कुजे सप्तमसंस्थिते।
शुभैरवीक्षिते वापि शतवर्षाणि हन्यते॥ ४॥
mande lagnagate caiva kuje saptama-saṁsthite /
śubhair avīkṣite vāpi śatavarṣāṇi hanyate //4//

4. If Saturn is in the Ascendant, Mars in the seventh and if benefic planets do not aspect the *Lagna* then also the house will last in hundred years.

लग्नभे शशिनि क्षीणे मृत्युस्थाने च भूसुते।
प्रारम्भः क्रियते यस्य शीघ्रं तद् विनश्यति ॥ ५ ॥
lagnabhe śaśini kṣīṇe mṛtyusthāne ca bhūsute /
prārambhaḥ kriyate yasya śīghraṁ tad vinaśyati//5//

5. If in the Ascendant *Lagna*, Moon is posited and in the eighth house is Mars, the house constructed in such a *Lagna* collapses early.

दशापतौ बलैर्हीने वर्णनाथे तथैव च।
पीडितर्क्षगते सूर्ये न विदध्यात् कदाचन॥ ६॥
daśapatau balair hīne varṇanāthe tathaiva ca /
pīḍitarkṣagate sūrye na vidadhyāt kadācana //6//

6. If the tenth lord is devoid of strength as also as the *Varṇanātha*, and if Sun is in *Duṣṭasthāna* (bad house), one should never start the construction of a house.

पितृमूलेज्यभाग्यार्कं पौष्णभेषु च यत्कृतम्।
कुजेन सहितेष्वेषु गृहं सन्दह्यतेऽग्निना ॥ ७॥
pitṛmūlejyabhāgyārkaṁ pauṣṇabheṣu ca yat kṛtam /
kujena sahiteṣv eṣu gṛhaṁ sandahyate'gninā //7//

7. The house commenced during the transit of Mars in *Maghā, Mūla, Puṣya, Pūrvāphālgunī, Hasta*, and *Revatī* is ravaged by fire.

मूलं च रेवती चैव कृत्तिकाषाढमेव च ।
पूर्वाफाल्गुनी हस्तं च मघा चैव तु सप्तकम् ॥
एषु भौमेन युक्तेषु वारे तस्यैव वेश्म यत् ।
अग्निना दह्यते कृत्स्नं पुत्रनाशः प्रजायते ॥८॥
mulaṁ ca revatī caiva kṛttikāṣāḍhameva ca /
pūrvāphālgunī hastaṁ ca maghā caiva tu saptakam//
eṣu bhaumena yukteṣu vāre tasyaiva veśma yat /
agninā dahyate kṛtsnaṁ putranāśaḥ prajāyate //8//

8. If the house is commenced on Tuesday and if in transit Mars is in *Mūla, Revatī, Kṛttikā, Pūrvāṣādhā, Pūrvāphālgunī, Hasta* or *Maghā*, then that house is sure to be ravaged by fire, and there will be loss of children in that house.

अग्निनक्षत्रगे सूर्ये चन्द्रे च तत्र संस्थिते।
निर्मितं मन्दिरं नूनमग्निना दह्यतेऽचिरात् ॥ ९॥
agninakṣatrage sūrye candre ca tatra saṁsthite /
nirmitaṁ mandiraṁ nūnam agninā dahyate'cirāt//9//

9. If the Sun and the Moon are in *Kṛttikā*, the house built

during such time will burn due to fire.

ज्येष्ठानुराधके चैव भरणीस्वाति पूर्वभे।
धनिष्ठास्वपि ऋक्षेषु शनिस्तिष्ठेद् दिनेऽस्य च॥
कृपणो न मतः प्रोक्तो धनधान्याधिके गृहे।
पुत्रे जातेऽथवा तस्मिन् गृह्यते यक्षराक्षसैः॥ १०॥
jyeṣṭhānurādhake caiva bharaṇīsvāti pūrvabhe /
dhaniṣṭhāsv api ṛkṣeṣu śanis tiṣṭhed dine 'sya ca //
kṛpaṇo na mataḥ prokto dhanadhānyādhike gṛhe /
putre jāte'thavā tasmin gṛhyate yakṣarakṣasaiḥ//10//

10. If during the transit of Saturn in *Jyeṣṭhā*, *Anurādhā*, *Bharaṇī*, Svāti, *Pūrvāsādhā* and *Dhaniṣṭha*, and the week day happens to be Saturday, there will be wealth in the house, but if children are born, they will not live due to reasons that cannot be detected.

मध्याह्ने तु कृतं वास्तु कर्तृवित्तविनाशनम्।
महानिशास्वपि तथा सन्ध्ययोर्नैव कारयेत्॥ ११॥
madhyāhne tu kṛtaṁ vāstu kartṛvittāvināśanam /
mahāniśāvapi tathā sandhyayor naive kāryet //11//

11. The commencement of the house in the midday, afternoon or midnight leads to destruction of money of the owner.

नाशं दिशन्ति मकरालिकुलीरलग्ने मेषे घटे धनुषि कर्मसु दीर्घमुक्तम्।
कन्याधने मिथुनगे ध्रुवमर्थलाभं ज्योतिर्विदः कलशसिंहवृषेषु सिद्धिम् ॥ १२॥
nāśaṁ diśanti makarālikūlīralagne meṣe ghaṭe dhanuṣi karmasu dīrgham uktam /
kanyādhane mithunage dhruvam arthalābhaṁ jyotirvidaḥ kalaśasiṁhavṛṣeṣu siddhim //12//

12. The *Gṛhārambha* in Capricorn, Scorpio or Cancer *Lagna* leads to destruction; delays in Aries, in Libra, Virgo, Pisces and Gemini profit of money; in Aquarius, Leo and Taurus auspicious results and fulfilment of objectives.

Planetary Combination in *Lagnas*

लग्नेऽर्के वज्रपातः कोशहानिश्च शीतगौ।
मृत्युर्विश्वम्भरापुत्रे दारिद्र्यं रविनन्दने॥
जीवे धर्मार्थकामाः स्युः पुत्रोत्पत्तिश्च भार्गवे।
चन्द्रजे कुशलावाप्तिर्यावदायुः प्रवर्तते॥ १॥
lagne 'rke vajrapātaḥ kośahāniś ca śītagau /
mṛtyur viśvambharāputre daridryaṁ ravinandane //
jīve dharmārthakāmāḥ syuḥ putrotpattiś ca bhārgave /
candraje kuśalāvāptir yāvadāyuḥ pravartate //1//

1. At the commencement of the house, if:
Sun is in the Ascendant, *Vajrapāta* (calamity) takes place;
Moon is in the Ascendant, destruction of the wealth or of money;
Mars is in the Ascendant, death takes place;
Saturn is in the Ascendant, poverty (*dāridrya*);
Jupiter is in the Ascendant, *Dharma*, *Artha* and *Kāma* are obtained;
Venus is in the Ascendant, birth of son; and
Mercury is in the Ascendant, healthy life till the end.

द्वितीयस्थे रवौ हानिश्चन्द्रे शत्रुक्षयो भवेत्।
भूमिजे बन्धनं प्रोक्तं नाना विघ्नानि भानुजे॥
बुधे द्रविणसम्पत्तिर्गुरौ धर्माभिवर्धनम्।
यथाकामविनोदेन भृगौ कामं व्रजेत् फलम् ॥ 2॥
dvitīyasthe ravau hāniś candre śatrukṣayo bhavet /
bhūmije bandhanaṁ proktaṁ nānā vighnāni bhānuje//
budhe draviṇasampattir gurau dharmābhivardhanam /
yathākāmavinodena bhṛgau kāmaṁ vrajet phalam//2//

2. If the Sun is in the second, loss will take place;
if moon is in the second, destruction of enemies;
if Mars is in the second, imprisonment;
if Saturn is in the second, many obstructions;
if Mercury is in the second, increase of wealth and money;

if Jupiter is in the second, *Dharmavṛddhi* takes place; and
if Venus is in the second, high sexual satisfaction.

तृतीयस्थेषु पापेषु सौम्येष्वेव विशेषतः।
सिद्धिः स्यादचिरादेव यथाभिलषितं प्रति ॥ ३॥
tṛtīyastheṣu papeṣu saumyeṣveva viśeṣataḥ /
siddhiḥ syād acirād eva yathābhilaṣitaṁ prati //3//

3. If malefics are in the third, delays in all spheres will take place; and
if benefics are there, the aim will be fulfilled quickly.

चतुर्थस्थानिने जीवे पूजा सम्पाद्यते नृपात्।
चन्द्रजेयार्थलाभः स्याद् भूमिलाभश्च भार्गवे ॥
वियोगः सुहृदां भानौ मन्त्रभेदो महीसुते।
बुद्धिनाशो निशानाथे सर्वनाशोऽर्कनन्दने ॥ ४॥
caturthasthānine jīve pūjā sampādyate nṛpāt /
candrajeyārthalābhaḥ syād bhūmilābhaś ca bhārgave //
viyogaḥ suhṛdām bhānau mantrabhedo mahīsute /
buddhināśo niśānāthe sarvanāśo'rkanandane //4//

4. If Jupiter is in the fourth, respected by king;
if Venus is in the fourth, acquisition of lands;
if Sun is in the fourth, destruction of friends;
if Mercury is in the fourth, profit of money;
if Mars is in the fourth, treating of men differently;
if Moon is in the fourth, destruction of intelligence; and
if Saturn is in the fourth, destruction of all matters.

पञ्चमे तु सुराचार्ये मित्रवसुधनागमः।
शुक्रे पुत्रसुखावाप्तिः रत्नलाभस्तथेन्दुजे॥
सुतदुःखं सहस्रांशो शशाङ्के कलहः स्मृतः।
भौमे कार्यविरोधः स्यात् सौरे बन्धुविमर्दनम्॥ ५॥
pañcame tu surācārye mitravasudhanāgamaḥ /
śukre putrasukhāvāptiḥ ratnalābhas tathenduje //
sutaduḥkhaṁ sahasrāṁśau śaśāṅke kalahaḥ smṛtaḥ /
bhaume kāryavirodhaḥ syāt saure
bandhuvimardanam //5//

5. If Jupiter is in the fifth, good friends and acquisition of money;
if Venus is in the fifth, bestowal of son;
if Mercury is in the fifth, bestows precious stones;
if Sun is in the fifth, difficulties for progeny;
if Moon is in the fifth, quarrels;
If Mars is in the fifth, opposition in works; and
if Saturn is in the fifth, destruction of relatives.

षष्ठस्थानगते सूर्ये रोगनाशं विनिर्दिशेत्।
चन्द्रे पुष्टिः कुजे प्राप्तिः सौरे शत्रुबलक्षयः॥
गुरौ मित्रोदयः प्रोक्तो भृगौ विद्यागमो भवेत्।
सम्यग्ज्ञानार्थकौशल्यं नक्षत्रपतिनन्दने॥ ६॥
ṣaṣṭhasthānagate sūrye roganāśaṁ vinirdiśet /
candre puṣṭiḥ kuje prāptiḥ saure śatrubalakṣayaḥ //
gurau mitrodayaḥ prokto bhṛgau vidyāgamo bhavet /
samyagjñānārthakauśalyaṁ nakṣatrapatinandane//6//

6. If the Sun is in the sixth, destruction of diseases;
if Moon is in the sixth, development in all;
if Mars is in the sixth, profits;
if Saturn is in the sixth, destruction of enemies;
if Jupiter is in the sixth, speciality in mantras (in chanting);
if Venus is in the sixth, bestowal of education; and
if Mercury is in the sixth, good knowledge and profit of money.

सप्तमस्थानगे जीवे बुधे दैत्यपुरोहिते।
गजवाजिधरित्रीणां क्रमाल्लाभो विनिर्दिशेत्॥
भास्करे कीर्तिभङ्गः स्यात् कुजे विपदमादिशेत्।
हिमांशो क्लेश आयासः पतङ्गे व्यङ्गताययम्॥ ७॥
saptamasthānage jīve budhe daityapurohite /
gajavājidharitrīṇāṁ kramāl lābho vinirdiśet //
bhāskare kīrtibhaṅgaḥ syāt kuje vipadam ādiśet /
himāṁśau kleśa āyāsaḥ pataṅge vyaṅgatāyayam//7//

7. If Jupiter, Mercury and Venus are in the seventh, profits from elephants, horses and lands;

if Sun is in the seventh, fear from enemies and destruction of fame;
if Mars is in the seventh, danger foreseen;
if Moon is in the seventh, tragedy and painful menses;
if Saturn is in the seventh, physical deformity or handicaps.

नैधने च सहस्रांशौ विद्वेषो जनितापदः।
शनिः शीतमयूखे च भौमे सौरे च रुग्भयम्॥
बुधे मानधनप्राप्तिर्जीवे च विजयो भवेत्।
शुक्रे स्वजनवेधः स्यान्मन्त्रस्यापि देहिनः॥ ८॥

naidhane ca saharāṁśau vidveṣo janitāpadaḥ /
śaniḥ śītamayūkhe ca bhaume saure ca rugbhayam //
budhe mānadhanaprāptir jīve ca vijayo bhavet /
śukre svajanavedhaḥ syān mantrasyāpi dehinaḥ//8//

8. If the Sun is in the eighth, fear from enemies;
if Moon is in the eighth, loss;
if Mars is in the eighth, diseases;
if Saturn is in the eighth, fear;
if Mercury is in the eighth, gain of money and fame;
if Jupiter is in the eighth, success; and
if Venus is in the eighth, discrimination from relatives in treatment.

वागीशे नवमस्थाने विद्याभोगाभिनन्दनम्।
बुधे विविधभोगाश्च शुक्रे च विजयो भवेत्॥
चन्द्रे धातुक्षयः प्रोक्तो धर्महानिश्च भास्करे।
कुजे चार्थक्षयं विद्याद् रविजे धर्मदूषणम् ॥ ९॥

vāgīśe navamasthāne vidyābhogābhinandanam /
budhe vividhabhogāś ca śukre ca vijayo bhavet //
candre dhātukṣayaḥ prokto dharmahāniś ca bhāskare /
kuje cārthakṣayaṁ vidyād ravije dharmadūṣaṇam//9//

9. If Jupiter is in the ninth, *vidyā*, happiness, etc.;
if Mercury is in the ninth, bestowal of pleasure in many ways;
if Venus is in the ninth, success;
if Moon is in the ninth, Tuberculosis;

if Sun is in the ninth, loss of *Dharma*;
if Mars is in the ninth, destruction of wealth; and
if Saturn is in the ninth, *Dharma-doṣa*.

दशमस्थानगे शुक्रे शयनासनसिद्धयः।
सुराचार्ये महत्सौख्यं विजयः स्त्रीधनं बुधे॥
मार्तण्डे च सुहृद्बुद्धिश्चन्द्रे शोकविवर्धनम्।
भौमे रत्नागमः प्रोक्तः कोणे कीर्तिविलोपनम् ॥१०॥
daśamasthānage śukre śayanāsanasiddhayaḥ /
surācārye mahatsaukhyaṁ vijayaḥ strīdhanaṁ budhe//
mārtāṇḍe ca suhṛdbuddhiś candre śokavivardhanam /
bhaume ratnāgamaḥ proktaḥ koṇe kīrtivilopanam //10//

10. If Venus is in the tenth, sex-pleasure;
if Jupiter is in the tenth, extreme happiness;
if Mercury is in the tenth, success, attainment of financial profits from women;
if Sun is in the tenth, development in friendship;
if Moon is in the tenth, increase in tragedies;
if Mars is in the tenth, availability of precious stones; and
if Saturn is in the tenth, destruction of fame.

लाभस्थानेषु सर्वेषु लाभस्थानं विनिर्दिशेत्।
व्ययस्थानेषु सर्वेषु विनिर्दिश्यो व्ययः सदा ॥११॥
lābhasthāneṣu sarveṣu lābhasthānaṁ vinirdiśet //
vyayasthāneṣu sarveṣu vinirdiśyo vyayaḥ sadā//11//

11. All the planets in the eleventh give profits and in the twelfth give losses.

स्वोच्चे पूर्णफलः प्रोक्तः पादोनां स्वर्क्षगो ग्रहः।
स्वत्रिकोणेऽर्धफलदः पादमित्रगृहाश्रितः॥
समर्क्षे रिपुराशौ च समकष्टफलौ ग्रहौ।
नीचस्थो निष्फलः प्रोक्तो वर्गे तु सत्फलः शुभः ॥१२॥
svocce purṇaphalaḥ proktaḥ pādonāṁ svarkṣago grahaḥ /
svatrikoṇe'rdhaphaladaḥ pādamitragṛhāśritaḥ //

samakṣe ripurāśau ca samakaṣṭaphalau grahau /
nicastho niṣphalaḥ prokto varge tu satphalaḥ
śubhaḥ//12//

12. It is said that planets in exaltation give full results; half results in own *Rāśi* and *Mūla Trikoṇa*; quarter in friendly house; neutral results in neutral *Rāśis*, and bad results in inimical house. In debilitation, no results at all. Planets in *Śubha Vargas* bestow good results.

द्वंद्वाङ्गराशिगते सूर्ये माघे भाद्रपदे तथा।
वृक्षाणां च्छेदनं काष्ठसञ्चयार्थं न कारयेत् ॥ १३ ॥
dvandvāṅgarāśigate sūrye māghe bhādrapade tathā /
vṛkṣāṇāṁ cchedanaṁ kāṣṭhasañcayārthaṁ na
kārayet //13//

13. Do not cut trees when the Sun is in *Dvisvabhāva* or Common *Rāśis*, and in the months of *Māgha* and *Bhādrapada* (i.e., during September and October).

One can conclude that however well the building might be constructed as per the principles of *Vāstu*, if the important *Muhūrta* combinations are not achieved to the owner is likely to suffer the effects of bad *Muhūrta* as enunciated and outlined above.*

* Editorial Note: The author of this article has not revealed the sources of the verses quoted by him. This has precluded the editor from correcting the readings of some of the verses, which are obviously deficient due to a few missing words or syllabhs, e.g. vs. 6 under yogas—N.M.K.

The Efficacy of Vāstu Śāstra

*Kowtha Lalith Manohar**

The word '*Vāstu*' is derived from the Sanskrit Dhātu *Vasa* which means 'to live'. So, *Vāstu Śāstra* is the science which deals with the layout of the site and the building to be constructed. It also gives elaborate details about the construction of townships, palaces, complexes, etc. The main objective of this *Śāstra* is to make humanity live in as perfect a harmony as possible with Mother Nature. This *Śāstra* was given to us by the *Maharṣis*.

The area is divided into eight parts: East, South, West, North, North-East, South-East, South-West and North-West. Each of these directions has a deity called *Dikpāla*. The *Dikpālas* are as follows:

East	- Indra	South-East	- Agni
South	- Yama	South-West	- Nirṛti
West	- Varuṇa	North-West	- Vāyu
North	- Kubera	North-East	- Īśāna

The Vedic texts have given different hymns to the eight *Dikpālas*. Indra is the king of the *Devatās*. The Sun rises on the Eastern Horizon. Hence East is given the most prominent place followed by North, the direction of Kubera, the lord of wealth. East is the point of health, virtuous living, and fame. North is the point of wealth, name, prosperity. North has astronomical significance also as it points towards the Pole-star or the *Dhruva Nakṣatra*. Whenever we discuss about the *Vāstu* of a plot or building, we first fix the North and East points and then proceed with the mapping out of the building.

*"Ananda Nilayam", Kowtha Bhavan, 6-1-294/10, Padmaraonagar, Secunderabad-500 025.

While fixing the norms for a dwelling house, *Vāstu Śāstra* has fixed the Southern side for the bedroom. It also states that more space is to be left on the Northern side of the plot. Let us examine the logic behind this. Cool breeze comes from the Southern direction which is described as *Malaya-māruta*. To enjoy this breeze we require space on the Southern side. 'A' and 'B' construct one building each, side by side. The Northern side of 'A' will be the Southern side of 'B'. So, automatically when 'A' leaves more space; on the Northern side, 'B' will have more open space on his Southern side which will facilitate free flow of air. The bedroom which is supposed to be the Southern side will have a lot of fresh air. This means that when one retires to bed after a tiring day's work, he will enjoy the beautiful cool Southern breeze which will induce good sleep. On the Eastern side also one is supposed to leave more open space. This enables the early morning Sun rays to fall on the front-yard and the building. The Sun rays are an antidote for many evils.

The *Vāstu Śāstra* has been discussed in our scriptures, as well. We find references to *Vāstu* in the *Rāmāyaṇa* at many places. *Vāstu Śāstra* lays down separate norms for dwelling houses, palaces, complexes, public utility buildings, etc. For the capital of a kingdom to be constructed, the layout is given in detail. For the palace of an Emperor or king the layout is given. One can get a broad idea about the layout of a capital and more so of the palace of king from the Sundarakāṇḍa of the *Rāmāyaṇa*. What we now know as "lung space" has been described as "*Udyāna*" or "*Vana*" in the texts. They have also listed the types of trees to be grown in these Parks. Water fountains, wells with steps to go up to the water, ponds, lakes and the surrounding greenery are vividly described. Imagine the kingdom of Rāvaṇa, Laṅkā, the total area of that land, the size of the people at that time and the millions who lived in that kingdom as described by Vālmīki. Inspite of all these, the layout could be so well designed. We may refer to Cantos 6, 7, ślokas 1 to 8 of Canto 9 and ślokas 1 to 8 of Canto 15 of the Sundarakāṇḍa.

Nowadays, we argue that cities are overpopulated. It

does not mean that the regulatory authorities should allow haphazard constructions. Persons with clear perspective of *Vāstu Śāstra* should head the town planning departments, exercising full control over the construction activities adhering strictly to the laid down norms without fear or favour. Had this been done, the present state of affairs could have been avoided. "Better late than never". Let the people who matter take the initiative in this regard and bring out a code for construction of building in the whole of the country.

For construction of temples also, Vāstu Śāstra coupled with *Āgama Śāstra* is scrupulously followed. There are varieties of *Āgama Śāstras*. *Śaivāgama, Vaikhānasāgama, Pāñcarātrāgama* are a few to be mentioned. For preparing idols in the temples, *Śilpa Śāstra* is followed in consonance with *Āgama Śāstra*. All these are independent *Śāstras* and are very vast. These are mentioned here to enable the readers to understand our glorious and rich traditions and culture. A good knowledge of Sanskrit is a prerequisite to understand these traditional texts. But, over the years, the Sanskrit language was totally ignored by successive governments and the people also did not evince interest in learning it. The results are obvious.

Vāstu Puruṣa—Rituals

The presiding deity of *Vāstu* is called *Vāstu Puruṣa*. While laying the foundation stone for a new building or while entering a new building, *Vāstu Pūja* and *Vāstu Homa* are performed as prescribed by our scriptures to propitiate the *Vāstu Puruṣa* and to ward off the evil aspects. I invite the attention of the readers to Canto 56 of the *Ayodhyākāṇḍa* and Canto 15 of the *Araṇyakāṇḍa* of the *Rāmāyaṇa*. In the first reference *Śrī-Rāma* mentions to *Lakṣmaṇa* the efficacy of *Vāstu* and *Vāstu Pūjā* as follows: ''कर्तव्यं वास्तुशमनं सौमित्रे चिरजीविभि:।'' (*Kartavyaṁ vāstu-śmanaṁ saumitre cirajīvibhiḥ*) which means, 'this *Vāstu Pūja* has to be done by those who wish to live long.' In his commentary on this passage, Maheśa Tīrtha states: ''वास्तुशब्देन गृहाधिष्ठित शिखिपर्जन्य प्रभृति पञ्चचत्वारिंशद्देवता उच्यन्ते। तासां शमनं होमनैवेद्यबलिभिः पूजनं बोधायनेनोक्तम्।''

(*Vāstuśabdena gṛhādhiṣṭhita śikhiparjanya prabhṛtipañca-catvārimśad-devatā ucyante / Tāsāṁ śamanaṁ homanaivedyabalibhiḥ pūjanaṁ bodhāyanenoktam*) 'By the *Vāstu* is meant the forty-five deities starting with *Agni, Parjanya* etc., who occupy the house. Sage Bodhāyana has given in the *Gṛhyasūtras* the procedure to propitiate these deities with *Havana*, offerings, etc.' this has to be done by everyone while entering the new house to have a long and happy life.

If one takes the initiative and pains to delve deep into our age-old texts, he will find clear-cut instructions for keeping the idols of different gods in the Pūjā in different directions. Even in *Pañcāyatana Pūjā* the idols of the five gods Āditya, Ambikā, Viṣṇu, Gaṇapati and Śiva have to be kept in a particular order placing them in different directions. When we do the *Pūjā* of *Śrī Satyanārāyaṇa Svāmī*, we place the *Grahas, Dikpālas* and others in different places. All these indicate that each direction (*dik*) is controlled by one invisible power called *Dikpāla*.

This power is like electricity which is not visible to the naked eye. Electricity can only be seen through a light, fan or any other appliance. If one does not have the required apparatus, this electricity energy cannot be experienced. Similarly, to experience this divine invisible power one has to be thorough with this subject and must possess the power of concentration. Without these pre-requisites, one will definitely not be able to understand or experience the efficacy of this *Śāstra*. It is not proper to advise with half-baked knowledge, which, in the long run, will prove dangerous to all concerned. Of late, we find some people trying to interpret this science with their own logic. By mere chance some of their versions may come out correct. But unless it is supported by the authority of the *Śāstra*, it cannot be confirmed as right.

Let us take a case where a house was constructed by the ancestors. The grandfather and father have prospered well in that house. But in the third generation, the person living in the same house has lots of problems. What could be the reason? *Vāstu paṇḍitas* examine the building and state that all troubles are only due to *Vāstu*. If the *Vāstu* was good for his ancestors, how could it become suddenly bad now? This will be a valid question. One answer for this will be that the horoscopes of the grandfather and father must have been very powerful such that the impact of the *Vāstu* defects was not felt by them. Since the horoscope of the present person has some lacunae, the *Vāstu* defects have come to the fore. So, it is observed that while one looks at *Vāstu* he should also look into the natal chart of the resident and corroborate the readings. If the placement of planets in the natal chart is such that the native has to undergo troubles, however much we try to set right the *Vāstu* defects, the troubles persist. *Vāstu* defects play their part and contribute to the overall bad situation. Corrections made to rectify the defects will reduce the intensity of the problems.

Vāstu and astrology are the two divine sciences with the help of which one can plan to have a peaceful and happy life. These two sciences deal with invisible forces which make one's life happy or otherwise. Let the persons practising these two sciences exercise proper care while giving predictions or advising their clients about their future. They should also be conversant with the remedial measures as detailed in our traditional scriptures.

From the above we find that *Vāstu* is not of modern origin but it has been a part and parcel of our traditional glorious past. Before I conclude, I would like to touch upon the most important saying from our scriptures:

किं कुर्वन्ति ग्रहाः सर्वे शन्यर्काङ्गारकादयः ।
एकादशस्थे गोविन्दे वासुदेवेऽखिलात्मनि ॥
kiṁ kurvanti grahāḥ sarve śanyarkāṅgārakādayaḥ /
ekādaśasthe govinde vāsudeve 'khilātmani //

"When one's mind is filled with the thoughts of the lord of the universe, Govinda, and one's body is engaged in the service of Vāsudeva, what effect can the planets like Saturn, Sun, Mars have on such a noble person?" The same theme was propounded by Saint Thyagaraja in the last century when he sung: "I have no work with the planets as long as the merciful Śri Rāma is with me."

Vāstu: A Result-Oriented Science

*Arvind Pandurang Vaze**

Vāstu Śāstra has grown out of life. It has its techniques of identification with Nature. Life and destiny are a part of the universal fabric of Nature. In Marathi, this is described as "*Piṇḍī te brahmāṇḍī*".

Today, *Vāstu Śāstra* is yet to be discovered and systematised. And that is why some intellectuals may have a reckless urge to dismiss it as totally irrelevant, groundless and even superstitious. But as a matter of fact, this science has outlasted the history of modern science and it continues to yield amazing powerful results on many people in their lives and work.

In the present day of urbanisation and sophisticated modernisation, the principles of *Vāstu Śāstra* are still applicable. The effects, good or bad, which have been ascribed to particular directions are still found to work.

I have found that even in the concrete jungle of Mumbai, if the rules of *Vāstu* are implemented, people can get positive results. Thus it is rightly described in the Vedas as eternal (*śāśvata*) science. Not only in the flat-system, but even in two-room tenement chawl system, one can get positive results and get relief from problems.

In the buildings that have already been constructed, a common man is helpless in making structural changes. Even then, if he effects changes in the arrangement of rooms, he can reduce ill-effects at least to the extent of 30 to 40% and gain about 25 to 30% positive effects. *Vāstu* is a great boon to any grief-stricken and financially overburdened family.

* Advocate, High Court, Bombay, II Floor, Waknis Building, Mugbhat Street Corner, Girgaum, Mumbai-400 004.

Unfortunately, modern builders and architects do not care at all as to how happy a person is who purchases a flat and occupies it for years together. I do not blame them, because they have never been taught this age-old science. They feel that once they design and erect the building or structure, their responsibility is over. But no, this should never be the attitude of an architect. And that is why *Vāstu Śāstra* specifies as to how an architect should be. Even the Roman architect Vitruvius specifies as to how an architect should be.

It is unfortunate that our entire teaching system in architecture colleges is based upon British and French methods. A student of architecture knows the names of Bannister, Charles Correa, LaCaribonzer, etc., but he is totally ignorant of such great names as Maya, Viśvakarmā, Nandīśa, Kaśyapa, Parāśara, etc., and other ancient masters of India.

In the construction of house, flat, or a building, the well-being of the occupant from every angle is of prime importance in *Vāstu Śāstra*. Orientation of any premises considering the cardinal principles of every direction is an essential part while planning the constructions. An occupant should be able to lead a happy and peaceful life, once he occupies and starts residing in a flat or bungalow, and this is possible only if the principles enunciated in *Vāstu Śāstra* are implemented by architects and builders.

In the Vedic period, the Rishis and their *Āśramas* and *Parṇakuṭis* on the bank of rivers, and those were placed in such a way that at no time would there be any imbalance between Nature and the *Āśrama*. All the rules of *Vāstu Śāstra* were followed and that is why we have not heard of any *Āśrama* being swept of Jānhavi Rishi at Janwad which had a tree known as Ājānvṛkṣa. Even the Krishna river had to take a turn without touching the Asrama during the floods. Till 7th July, 1941, the *Ājānvṛkṣa* and the Parṇakuṭi of Jānhavi Rishi were in good shape. Unfortunately, thereafter all sorts of bad elements took shelter in the Āśrama and the *Ājānvṛkṣa* tree was uprooted in the year 1962-63. The Ājānvṛkṣa tree had all sorts of properties to give maximum benefits provided your behaviour is good; it will shower all beneficial blessings on you provided its sanctity is kept.

The importance of trees has been specifically mentioned in the *Vāstu Śāstra*. That is why it is said:

वर्जयेत् पूर्वतोऽश्वत्थं प्लक्षं दक्षिणस्तथा।
न्यग्रोधं पश्चिमे भागे उत्तरे चाप्युदुम्बरम्॥

varjayet pūrvato 'śvat thaṁ plakṣaṁ dakṣiṇastathā /
nyagrodhaṁ paścime bhāge uttare cāpyudumbaram //

Which trees should be planted in which direction? What are its positive and negative aspects? The *Pipal* tree is the most powerful tree amongst all. It gives strength and wealth in abundance if planted at its proper place and worshipped regularly; so also, it totally annihilates the family if one tries to cut it down. A person cutting down the Pipal tree is bound to suffer an attack of paralysis or may become a pauper or some such adverse incident will take place within a very short span. The age of the *Pipal* tree is very important as it gives results only after it is eight years old.

In a recent case from Pune, a *Pipal* tree was uprooted after performing perfect ritual meant for it. The couple was told to sprinkle ritual water only where a *Tulasī* plant stood, by evening. Unfortunately, the couple poured the water on a fully grown Sandal-wood tree. The next morning the Sandal-wood tree was totally dry. The couple could not get a child for seven years. Principles laid down in *Vāstu Śāstra* regarding tree plantation and cutting must be followed to avoid mishaps and tragedies.

Why is importance given to the selection of land in *Vāstu Śāstra*? Just as in the case of the human body, the mind or brain is supreme, so also in the case of the earth (*pṛthivī*), some parts of the land are supreme, strength-wise. That means one can show his supremacy over others by residing thereon or by performing Tapas there.

Apart from the selection of land, equal importance is given to water. It may be in the form of a well or borewell or storage tank. It is not possible for one to change the river, stream or rivulet. But digging of well or borewell or construction a storage tank is within one's power. However, the direction of such a water-place is very important. A well or borewell on the South-East, South or South-West direction gives ghastly results, while if it is on the North or North-East direction it will give riches.

A trader in Sangli District having an annual turnover of ten crores found that his business was dwindling to the extent of two crores for no apparent reason. When I visited his house, I found a well in the middle of the bungalow. Much against his wishes, he agreed to fill up the well with stones and mud. Within three months, he found his business flourishing again with the same machinery, same staff and same rates. When a borewell is dug in the South, the death of a lady inmate takes place.

I would like to elaborate the principle areas on which a common man should concentrate more. A minimum of four aspects must be considered while implementing the principles of *Vāstu* in one's house.

1. **Aiśānyāṁ Devatā-gṛham**: The placement of God is to be in the *Aiśānya Diśā* or the North-East corner. Many people feel that if God is placed in the North-East, it faces South-East or South-West and is, therefore, inauspicious. If it is placed on the Eastern side in the North direction, it faces West, again it may appear proper. And, therefore, to suit their convenience, they keep God in the West facing the East direction. My personal experience reveals that the placement in proper direction is most important, not the direction which it faces.

2. The second important factor is about cooking one's food. I need not dwell upon this aspect more as all of us certainly have unanimity on the sūtra: *Āgneye pāka-sadanam.* Only one thing has to be borne in mind while implementing this sūtra, and that is, while cooking, even in this corner, i.e. *āgneya*, one must face East and cook food. If one tries to cook food facing South, as *Āgneya* is also 15^0 towards South, one is bound to face one medical problem or the other.

3. The third important aspect is the position of the cash-box or treasury or the cupboard wherein cash, jewellery or

valuable documents are kept. The placement of this must be on the North, though it faces South. By and large, people do not like to keep such cupboard facing the South. According to them, opening of such cupboard towards South is not good. But this is a misconception.

4. The fourth important aspect is about keeping photographs of dead persons in the shrine. My experience has shown that in whichever house, the photos of dead relatives, i.e., father, grandfather, mother, wife, etc., are kept in or around the shrine, that family suffers in many ways. Either there is a constant ailment in the house or financially such a family goes down day by day; or even marriages in such families are performed very late. This reason is that no one can equate mortals with the Immortal.

The difference between astrology and *Vāstu* is that astrology gives general direction of one's life. It defines one's weakness, tendencies and strength, which one can try to overcome by improving oneself and minimise the weakness through efforts. It gives some solace to one in difficult circumstances.

By using the principles of *Vāstu* one can definitely, within a reasonable span, improve one's financial stability and also relationship with the outer world. Once you make the necessary and requisite changes in your house or workplace, other things automatically follow.

I desire to place before you that I consider the *Aiśānyā* as the best direction in any human life along with the water flow. Thought-provoking mind development is hastened if we face the *Aiśānyā* or North-East direction. Concentration of mind is made easy if we sit facing that direction. This forced me to probe into various biographies and life histories of great saints and Rishis. Take, for example, Saint Ramdas of Maharashtra. He always used to sit in a cave in front of which there was a stream. Similar was the case of Swāmi Raṅgāvadhūta or Swāmi Nṛsiṁhasarasvatī who lived on the banks of the river Narmadā in Gujarat. Pondering over this I have come to the conclusion that there is a definite nexus between the North-East direction and the existence of water and the destiny or well-being of man. And, therefore, I say that life without water and the *Aiśānyā* direction is zero. Life will become beautiful and *bountiful* if a man observes the tenets of the *Aiśānyā-diśā* and properties of water. If the sanctity of the North-East direction is not respected, I have observed devastating results whether it is a house or a factory or industry.

Whenever there is a toilet block constructed in this direction, total destruction of the factory or industry is seen. Such a family will be ruined, without knowing or understanding as to what wrong they have committed. I have visited many factories with such location of toilets and have found that they always suffer losses which ultimately lead to closure.

Vāstu Śāstra exists because, as they say, this is proved by Āgama as it presents the result in front of one's eyes: "*Idam āgama-siddhatvāt pratyakṣa-phala-darśanam*". Not only has this science been proved, but its effects or results are also perceived.

Vāstu or the Heavenly Planets in Human Houses

*R.G. Rao**

Each direction is governed by the planets. Thus, Sun governs the East, Venus governs the South, Saturn governs the West, Mercury governs the North, The Lord of Fire governs the South-East, the Moon governs the North-West, the Dragon-Head governs the South-West and the Dragon-Tail governs the North-East. The comparison between Astrology and *Vāstu* is given clearly in the *Uttarakālāmṛta.*

In terms of Astrology and *Vāstu* there is a rapport between Venus and the Lord of Fire, because Venus (the house-wife) being in kitchen must be using fire for preparation of food. There is rapport between Agni and Venus.

For a house facing the East, we have first the main entrance (*dvāra*), next the visitor's hall, then the bedroom in the South, Dragon-head in the South-West direction (including stores for old things, dustbins, toilet, etc.).

Saturn is for the West direction and so inside the house (before the dead end to the West) there must be a store room and on the West direction there must be a small door (as compared to the main door). This design helps to discharge and vent out the polluted air of the house through the rear door which serves as ventilation; just as man eats the food through the mouth and discharges the excerta through the rear (i.e. the anus).

The Moon is for the North-West direction covering washing area also and Mercury is for the North (also called *Kubera-dik*).

In this way, it can be observed that Astrology and *Vāstu*

* Manjunathana Extension, Kartiguppa Main Road (Near Vidyapeeta), Bangalore-560085.

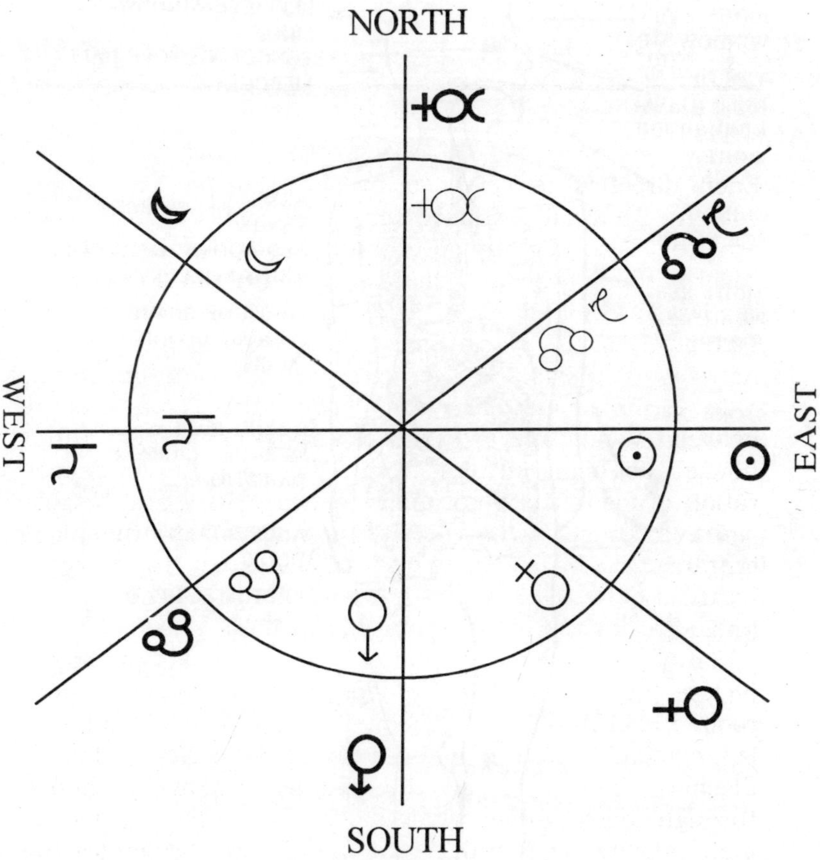

Fig. 1

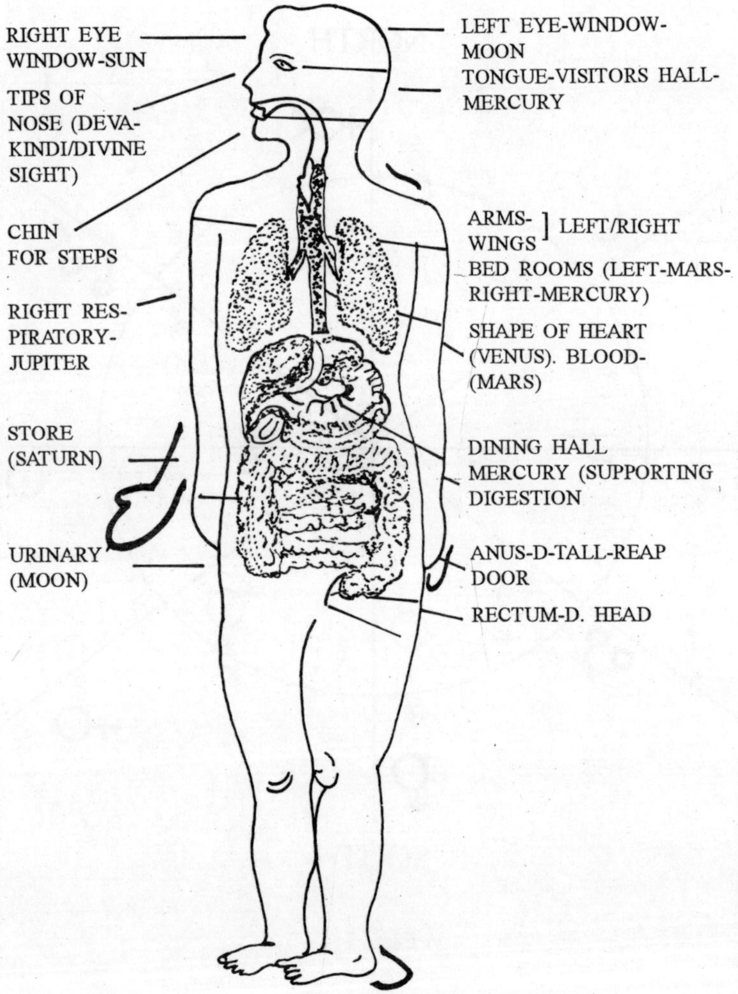

RIGHT EYE WINDOW-SUN
TIPS OF NOSE (DEVA-KINDI/DIVINE SIGHT)
CHIN FOR STEPS
RIGHT RES-PIRATORY-JUPITER
STORE (SATURN)
URINARY (MOON)
LEFT EYE-WINDOW-MOON
TONGUE-VISITORS HALL-MERCURY
ARMS- WINGS] LEFT/RIGHT
BED ROOMS (LEFT-MARS-RIGHT-MERCURY)
SHAPE OF HEART (VENUS). BLOOD-(MARS)
DINING HALL MERCURY (SUPPORTING DIGESTION
ANUS-D-TALL-REAP DOOR
RECTUM-D. HEAD

Fig. 2

NINE PLANETS IN THE HUMAN HOUSE

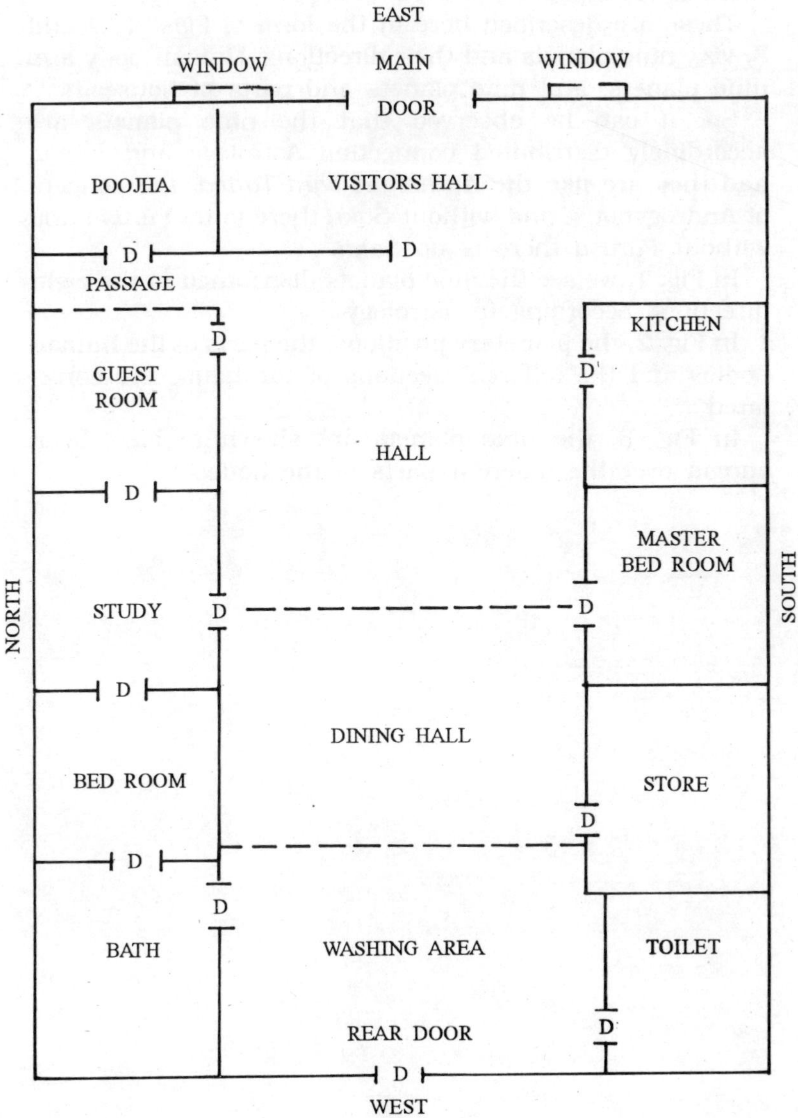

Fig. 3

must be going together like the flesh and blood of the body and without the blood there is no body and without flesh there is no blood.

These are described here in the form of Figs. 1, 2 and 3, viz., nine planets and their directions; Human body and nine planets; and nine planets and parts of houses.

So, it can be observed that the nine planets are accordingly distributed connecting Astrology and *Vāstu*, and they are like the *Ardhanārīśvara Tattva*, the concept of Androgynous, and without *Śakti* there is no *Puruṣa* and without *Puruṣa* there is no *Śakti*.

In Fig. 1, we see the nine planets distributed in the eight directions according to astrology.

In Fig. 2, the planetary positions, the parts of the human bodies and the different sections of the house are correlated

In Fig. 3, the nine planets are shown to have been spread over the different parts of the house.

Hindu Geomancy

*U.S. Pulippani**

Food, clothing and dwelling are the basic needs of man. From times immemorial man has been trying to achieve the best standards in these three things. In other words, achievement of these three things makes the man really blessed.

Our ancients were real scientists who have blended the science of Architecture and Astrology in a unique way, following which a dwelling place promises a bright and happy life for the owners.

Man's breath (*prāṇa*) is vibrative with cosmic *prāṇa* or *prāṇic* energy of the Universe, the place in which it functions. If both are tuned to function positively in a dwelling, then the owners or residents will have all success. Our ancients personified this in the form of a human figure called *Vāstu Puruṣa*.

References to the *Vāstu Śāstra* are found in the *Rāmāyaṇa* and *Mahābhārata*, etc. We can also trace elements of *Vāstu Śāstra* in the sites at Mohenjo Daro and Harappa, Dwārkā, Kāñcī, Ayodhyā and Kāśī.

There are thirty-two texts of *Vāstu Śāstra*, of which the *Viśvakarma-vāstu-śāstra* and the *Mayamata* are the important ones. *Vāstu Śāstra* is a separate branch of Astrology which deals exclusively with building of houses for individuals, palaces or dwellings for rulers, choultries or caravanserais, schools, hospitals, offices, temples, etc. I shall confine myself in this paper to *Vāstu Śāstra* with reference to individual houses only.

Basic Points

The main points to be considered are the omens observed

* 32/C, Anand Flats, Ground Floor, Hindi Prachar Sabha Street, T. Nagar, Madras-600 017, Tel: 044-4347702.

before entering the site of a building, the nature of the earth, the time of laying the foundation, the direction the house should face, the location of individual living sections like bedroom, *pūjā* room, drawing room, kitchen and dining rooms, cattle shed, car shed, well, garden, sewerage ways and overhead tanks. Apart from these, the position of the main doors for houses facing different directions, the proportion of height and width of the main and other doors, and the wood to be used for such doors are also to be considered. Particular timings called the waking state of *Vāstu Puruṣa* in which the building is to be started is very much important. How the total area (i.e. the length × the width) of the house will be in auspicious proportion to particular values called *Āyādi-Garbha*, arriving at the auspicious *Tithi*, *Nakṣatra*, *Yoga*, etc., as also the cumulative bad or good effects for each area in square feet of the house, the best month and timing for entering into the new house, etc., are some of the salient points to be considered.

(A) Omens

When the plot for a building itself has been finalised, the owner officially enters the plot along with the building craftsmen to consider starting the construction. The omens occurring at that time should be beneficial and good. Seeing beautiful women with their husbands, pots filled milk, etc., washerman, cooked rice, young married women, temple courtesans, bundles of sugarcane, and twin Brahmins are some of the good omens.

(B) Doors and Rooms

1. For reckoning area, the area of the house should include the base of all the four walls.
2. The ratio of height to the width of entrance including the main entrance should be 9:5, which will endow upon the owner all wealth and comforts.
3. Teak wood and a special wood called *veangai* are good for houses.
4. The number of doors in a house should be odd.

5. All planks should belong to one variety of wood. Planks of varied woods should not be used.
6. The main entrance should be a little higher than the other doors.
7. The different rooms should be planned in different directions of the house as shown below:
   - (i) Northern Direction—treasury (place of keeping money), bedroom.
   - (ii) North-Eastern Direction—*pūjā* room, granary, and bedroom.
   - (iii) East—*pūjā* room, bedroom, bathroom; the sewerage should go out in this direction through backyard.
   - (iv) South-Eastern Direction—kitchen, dining room and guest room.
   - (v) South—*pūjā* room, dining room; oven should be located in south-eastern corner of the kitchen.
   - (vi) South-Western Direction—all instruments, study room, etc.
   - (vii) West—bedroom.
   - (viii) North-West—*pūjā* room, labour room (i.e. the place for women to give birth), place of stocking grains, storeroom, etc.
8. The well should be in the South-Western direction for houses facing the North or East. It should be located in the North-Eastern direction for houses facing South or West.
9. If more than one dwelling are planned in the same house, the calculations are to be made separately for both the houses.
10. If there is more than one floor, it is better to have staircase steps facing North or East.
11. The drainage water going out of a house should go out in any one of North, East or North-Eastern directions.
12. If open space is to be left inside a house, the length should be more in the East and West and less in the North and South.
13. The main door or gate of the house should have

a thoroughfare up to the backyard and some open space should be left at the back which should be clearly visible from outside the main entrance; i.e., all the doorways reckoned from the main door should be in one line.

(C) Site

1. The Earth of the ground should be of sweet taste, good smell, white, light brown and of other pleasing colours.
2. The level of the ground should be lower in the Eastern and Northern directions than in the Western and Southern directions. The effects of levels of the ground either in elevation or in depression

Table 1: Effects of Directions

Direction	*Elevation*	*Depression*
1. East	Loss of progeny.	Wealth, long life, fame.
2. South-East	If higher than South-West it is bad. If higher than North-East and North-West it brings wealth.	If lower than South-West it is good. If lower than North-West and North-East there will be fire accidents, criminal mind and rivalry.
3. South	Prosperity and health.	Sickness and poverty.
4. South-West	All round progress and fame.	Long sickness, premature death and vices.
5. West	Fame and name and children.	Ill health and loss of children.
6. North-West	If higher than North-East it is all round success and wealth. If higher than South-East it is good for all matters.	If lower than North-East it is illness and rivalry. If lower than South-West and South-East it is good.
7. North	Drives away wealth.	Brings in wealth.
8. North-East	Brings poverty	Brings wealth from many sources.

in all the eight directions are as shown in Table 1.

3. The directions that are auspicious for the four classes of society are:
   (i) Houses facing North for teaching and priestly class;
   (ii) East facing houses for rulers;
   (iii) South facing houses for traders and business men; and
   (iv) West facing houses for manual workers and labourers.

Table 2: Effects of Dimensions

Length or Breadth in feet	*Results*
6	Good
7	All activities will fall.
8	All endeavours will succeed, removes enemies even the withered plants grow well.
9	Disease, lack of longevity, wife will pass away earlier.
10	Growth of cattle and agriculture as well as good.
11	Abundance of food, milk, and agriculture.
12	Destruction of wealth, sorrow.
13	Endeavours fail, relatives turn into enemies, all obstacles.
14	Destruction of happiness, loss of life.
15	Death due to chronic illness. Sins, wealth will not accumulate—poverty.
16	Growth of wealth, birth of children, enemies will disappear.
17	Winning over enemies, God's blessing, Governmental ocupations of high status.
18'	Death of wife, quarrel, fear, death of children, especially sons.
19	Same as above.
20	Birth of children, growth of business, happiness, and growth of wealth.

Note: Effects are given even upto 44 feet in old Tamil manuscripts.

4. The length and width of the rooms also hold good or bad indications, as shown in Table 2.

(D) Wood

1. There are three varieties of trees: Male, Female and Eunuch. Trees that are of uniform diameter from top to bottom are male. They are suitable for main door frames, windows and pillars. The trees larger at the bottom and smaller in diameter at the top are female ones. These are useful for cross-beams, etc. The trees with greater diameter at the top and bottom but less in the middle are eunuch. These are to be used only for miscellaneous purposes.
2. Wood from Mango trees are good for Devas, i.e., for temples.
3. Neem wood (*margosa*) is good for thinkers.
4. Teak wood is good for ruling people.
5. Other wood, except those with thorns and bitter taste trees, are suitable for other people. Wood from the following trees should be avoided: Fig, Banyan, Aśvattha, Silk cotton, etc., especially the following that are named in Tamil, viz., Ichi, Parasu, Kucham, Elandhai, Peeli, Magizam (*vagula*), Vilva, etc. These will bring extinction of progeny and lead to poverty. Cotton, Agathi, Palmairah, Naval, Neeli, Arkam, Tamarind, and other trees should not be grown in houses. These will destroy wealth.

(E) When to Build Houses

1. Houses facing East should be built in the lunar months when the Sun is in the Nirayana signs of Cancer and Leo.
2. South facing houses should be built during the months when the Sun is in Libra and Scorpio.
3. West facing houses should be built during the months when the Sun is in Capricorn and Aquarius.
4. North facing houses should be built when the Sun is in Aries and Taurus.

(F) Directions and *Rāśis*

1. East facing—Scorpio, Pisces, and Cancer.
2. South facing—Taurus, Capricorn and Virgo.
3. West facing—Libra, Gemini, and Aquarius.
4. North Facing—Sagittarius, Aries, and Leo.

(G) The Main Doorway

The width of the complete house including the walls on both sides should be divided into nine portions. The main entrance should be so positioned that it should contain portions of both the 4th and 5th portions of the width divided by 9. The parts should be reckoned from the following directions:

1. For houses facing East, reckoning should be done from the North.
2. For houses facing South, reckoning should be done from the East.
3. For houses facing West, reckoning should be done from the North.
4. For houses facing North, reckoning should be done from the East.

The nine parts reckoned from the first part belong to the planets as follows: Sun, Moon, Mars, Mercury, Jupiter, Venus, Saturn, *Rāhu* and *Ketu*, respectively. The portion of Jupiter is good for temples, that of Venus good for houses, but money will be wasted on sensual pursuits and will bring scandals to the lady of the house. That of Mercury is good for cattle-sheds and business centres in particular. Usually, the main door is kept combining Jupiter and Mercury portions to attract and bring prosperity.

(H) Time to Start

Rules of ordinary electional astrology do not apply in house building. The North and the South poles of the Earth are centres of magnetism. Taking this into account in addition to other forces and pulls (gravitational and interplanetary, etc.). Ancient sages found out that certain periods of time carried positive vibrative forces, during which if the building work was started, it would make the owner successfully complete the house. They personified this force in the form of an effective individual called *Vāstu Puruṣa*. The period when these positive forces were active, the *Vāstu Puruṣa* was said to be awake. At other times they said that he was sleeping. The building of the house was to be started when *Vāstu Puruṣa* was waking up from sleep.

Before entering into the details of the above, we will look into the meaning of the word '*Vāstu*' and what it signifies. Yāska in his *Nirukta* gives the following explanation: '*Vāstur Vasater nivāsakarmaṇaḥ*', which means 'the place where one lives'. The saviour who protects the dwelling is termed as '*Vāstoṣpati*'.

Vāstu or the place (earth) is vibrating and alive. Similarly, the inner core of all living creatures is also vibrating. The Universe is also vibrating. These three vibrative forces are set in a positive rhythm and when building work is started at such a time it brings success for the residents as well as the house. This protective deity is termed as *Vāstu Puruṣa*. He is said to be placed in the plot selected as follows: The plot is divided into 64 squares forming the grid of *Maṇḍūkapadam*. The *Vāstu Puruṣa* has to be placed within four squares of each direction. In actual practice his head occupies the four squares of each corner direction as explained below.

He is said to change his direction in the following manner. In the first quarter of the day he lies down horizontally placing his head towards North, feet towards South and faces East. In the second quarter of the day, he places his head towards East, feet towards West and faces South. In the third quarter of the day, he places his head towards South, feet towards North and faces West. In the fourth quarter of the day, he places his head towards West, feet towards East and faces North. Before starting building work, the location of his navel is selected for *Śaṅku-sthāpana* (Sacred Shell). Laying the foundation at the location of his feet is prohibited. This means that the vision of *Vāstu* should not fall on that location. However, the said *Vāstu Puruṣa* is said to sleep and wake up from sleep in certain lunar months of the year, during certain dates of lunar months for a period of one *muhūrta* (one and half hours) and again goes to sleep. He is always keeping his head in the North-East direction and sleeps, which is his permanent position apart from his daily changing

Vāstu Puruṣa (The Spirit of the Building)

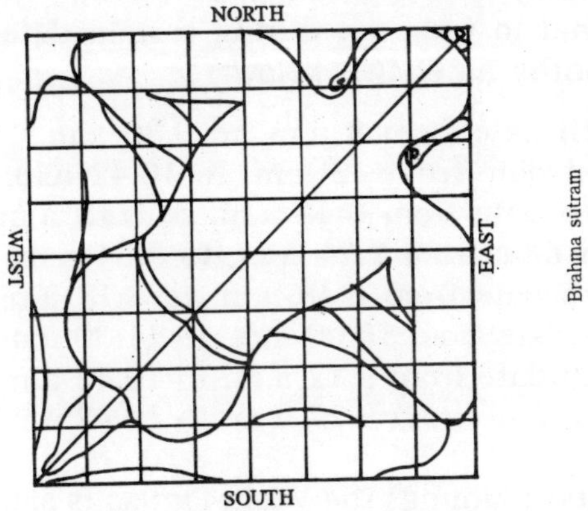

The *Vāstu Puruṣa* has to be placed within four parts of each direction.

The energy contained in the earth known as *Vāstu Puruṣa* is perceived as a male figure tightly coiled into the grid of the *Maṇḍūkapadam* or 64-part modula.

All buildings can be set out based on this measure. This is beneficial.

positions. The diagram below will explain this:

Each building has a living force which is called *Vāstu Puruṣa*. It can be described as the "spirit of the building". It is said: "The *Vāstu Puruṣa* has six bones, a single heart, four vulnerable points, and four vessels, and he is said to lie upon the ground his head towards the East."

It is said that the divinity named *Arya* is his head, that *Savindrā* is his right arm and *Savindrā* his (right) hand, that *Apa* and *Apavatsā* are his left arm and (left) hand, that *Vivasvant* is his right side and *Mahindra* his left, that in the middle his trunk is *Brahmā*, that his testicles are *Mitra*, that his right foot (and leg) are *Indra* and *Indrajā* and his left foot (and leg) are *Rudra* and *Rudrajā*. He rests with his face to the ground; his six bones, oriented to the East and North, are in the middle (centre) of the site. In the centre of the site are found the vulnerable points and the heart which is *Brahmā* and it is from there that the veins start. Thus the spirit is described.

It is known that it is He who, in every human dwelling,

is responsible for good and for bad fortune. That is why the wise must avoid tormenting his limbs with the 'limbs' of the house, for, if not, sorrows innumerable will fall upon the limbs of the owner of the house. Thus, the sage must always spare the body of the spirit (in the course of construction). As he wakes up from the sleep, he is said to perform five main activities. Cleaning of teeth, bathing, prayer, eating and finally taking *tāmbūla*, i.e., eating the betel leaves. He is said to wake up during certain dates of selected lunar months as shown below:

1. Aries 10th date from 8 a.m. to 9.30 a.m.
2. Taurus 21st date from 12 a.m. to 10.42 a.m.
3. Cancer 11th date from 6.48 a.m. to 8.18 a.m.
4. Leo 6th date from 2.24 a.m. to 3.54 a.m.
5. Libra 11th date from 6.48 a.m. to 8.18 a.m.
6. Scorpio 8th date from 10.00 a.m. to 11.30 a.m.
7. Capricorn 12th date from 9.12 a.m. to 10.42 a.m.
8. Aquarius 20th date from 9.12 a.m. to 10.42 a.m.

Starting from the above timings the *Vāstu Puruṣa* is said to do the five activities already explained taking 18 minutes for each. It is auspicious to start building or the foundation itself during the period of 36 minutes comprising of the last two activities of eating and taking *tāmbūla*. The foundation should always be started from the North-East corner of the plot where the *Vāstu Puruṣa* keeps his head.

The foundation should be laid in following months:

1. For the houses facing the East, work should be started when the Sun is in Cancer and Leo.
2. For houses facing North, the work should be began when the Sun is in Aries and Taurus.
3. For houses facing West, the work should be started when the Sun is in Capricorn and Aquarius.
4. For houses facing South, the work should be started when the Sun is in Libra and Scorpio.

Astrological Considerations

1. According to conventional astrological canons, it is

auspicious to start building of houses only during the two lunar months when the Sun is in Capricorn and Aquarius.

2. Houses should not be built when the Sun is passing through the second half of *Bharaṇī*, the four *padas* of *Kṛttikā* and the first *pāda* of *Rohiṇī*.
3. Houses should not be built when Mars is in *Kṛttikā*, *Puṣya*, *Maghā*, *Pūrvā*, *Hasta*, *Mūla* and *Revatī*.
4. House building should be undertaken when Mercury is passing through *Aśvinī*, *Mṛgaśīrṣa*, *Hasta*, *Uttarā*, *Citrā* and *Rohiṇī*, or when Mercury is exalted or is in *Lagna*.
5. House building should be undertaken when Jupiter is in *Śravaṇa*, *Uttarā*, *Uttarāṣāḍhā*, *Uttarābhādrapada*, *Purvābhādrapada*, *Mṛgaśīrṣa*, *Āśleṣā*, *Rohiṇī*, and *Puṣya*, or when Jupiter is exalted or when he is in *Lagna*.
6. House building should be undertaken when Venus is passing through *Ārdrā*, *Punarvasū*, *Dhaniṣṭhā*, *Viśākhā*, *Śatabhīṣā*, and *Citrā*.
7. House building should not be undertaken when Saturn is passing through *Śatabhīṣā*, *Pūrvābhādrapada*, *Svāti*, *Uttarābhādrapada*, *Bharaṇī*, *Dhaniṣṭhā*, *Anurādhā* and *Jyeṣṭhā*. Every alternative star from that occupied by *Rāhu* will be considered inauspicious. This covers 14 stars (the ninth star *Maitra* is not considered so good by some). Hence building work should not be started in these 14 stars.
8. The following *Lagnas* are auspicious: Aries, Taurus, Gemini, Leo, Libra, Scorpio, Capricorn and Aquarius. Of these the *Sthiralagnas* (fixed) are more auspicious.
9. The third, fifth, eighth and thirteenth lunar days of the bright half and Full Moon days are good.
10. Mondays, Wednesdays, Thursdays, and Fridays are auspicious among the week days.
11. *Rohiṇī*, *Mṛgaśīrṣa*, *Pūrvā*, *Puṣya*, *Uttarā*, *Śravaṇa*, *Dhaniṣṭhā*, *Śatabhiṣā*, and *Utttarābhādrapada* are auspicious for starting of houses.

12. Sundays coinciding with *Bharaṇī*, Mondays with *Citrā*, Tuesdays with *Uttarāṣāḍhā*, Wednesdays with *Dhaniṣṭhā*, Thursdays with *Jyeṣṭhā*, Fridays with *Pūrvāṣāḍha* and Saturdays with *Revatī* are to be avoided.

(J) Āyādi Matching

There is yet another way of finding out the suitability of the house for the owner. It is based on its area, i.e., the length × width which includes external limits. It is called *Āyādi-Garbha* matching of the following aspects:

1. *Āya* (income)	2. *Vyaya* (expenditure)	3. *Āyuṣa* (longevity)
4. Birth (*yoni*)	5. Star	6. *Tithi*
7. Day	8. *Lagna*	9. Creed (caste)
10. *Aṁśa*	11. Aspect	12. *Garbha*

In this the total area is divided by certain factors for each of the above aspects and the remainder shows whether it is good or bad. For instance, the plinth area of the house is divided by 8 and if the remainders be 1, 3 and 5, these are called *Garuḍa Garbha*, *Siṁha Garbha* and *Ṛṣabha Garbha*, which are auspicious. Hence the area should be adjusted to get an auspicious remainder. Like this, rules are given for other aspects also. Among these the longevity aspect should be fully considered carefully. (The total area should be divided by 100 and if the remainder is more than 45, it is good and if more than 60, this will be very good.)

There is yet another but simple way of arriving at this *Āyādi-Garbha*. This is classified into eight types based on the calculations. The length × breadth of the house, i.e., the area, is multiplied by 9 and divided by 8. The remainders 1 to 8 are good or bad as indicated below:

1. *Dhavajāyam* (Money Dimension) : Good and brings all wealth.
2. *Dhūmāyam* (Smoke) : Brings ill-health for the head of the family and also for his wife.

3. *Simhāyam* (Lion)	: Brings victory over enemies and assures health, wealth and prosperity.
4. *Śvāsyāyam* (*Prāṇa*)	: Brings ill-health and bad omens.
5. *Vṛṣabhāyam* (The Bull)	: Good and brings all finance and fortune.
6. *Kharāyam* (Donkey)	: The head of the family will turn vagabond, premature death of the members of family.
7. *Gajāyam* (Elephant)	: The life of the head of the family and members brightens and their health and wealth grow immense.
8. *Kākāyam* (Crow)	: This brings sorrow to the head of the family with no peace at home.

The basic dimensions of rooms, their location, their levels, the doors and space through the doors as given in *Vāstu* can be easily accommodated in modern planning. In the case of flats also, location and direction of rooms and also those for bed, kitchen, finance, store-room, etc., can be followed as per *Vāstu Śāstra* with advantage.

Due to very many constraints in which the modern man is not able to provide all the provisions reflected in the ancient texts. For these, adjustments and remedial measures can always be provided. Remedial measures are to be followed according to local conditions. For example, if the main entrance falls at Saturn's portions, by placing a mirror at a suitable place on the side wall therein, the reflections of the Jupiter's portion fall in, and thereby the evil of Saturn is greatly reduced. Similarly, the Chinese and Japanese traditional architects suggest hanging bells (sound of music) at the doors to drive away the evil forces. The provision of modern calling-bell with a musical sound somewhat resembles this.

I have based this synthesis on an ancient Tamil manuscript *Manai Nool* published by an International Institute of Tamil Studies, which again was brought out from palm-leaf manuscripts available with the Institute. In addition, the salient features of the *Vāstu Śāstra* mentioned in Sanskrit text were also considered.

REFERENCES

1. *Hindu:* Article, 31.10.1993 (Sunday).
2. *Mayamata* (by Bruno DAGENS).
3. *Manai Nool,* International Institute of Tamil Studies, Madras.
4. *Nirukta* by Yāska, and other Sanskrit works.

Rectification Through Vāstu Principles

*K. S. Anand Kumar**

Vāstu Śāstra or Astrology, and *Mantra Śāstra* are meant for the improvement of man's social, intellectual, economic and health conditions. By following these *Śāstras*, we can develop ourselves.

For thousands of years India was under the rule of foreigners, like Moghals, Britishers, Frenchmen, Dutchmen, etc., who tried to destroy its ancient culture and *Śāstras*. Having lost our roots, we are now at the crossroads, not able to follow the ancient *Śāstras*. *Vāstu Śāstra* is to be followed for building new constructions. Buildings are not being built as per *Vāstu Śāstra*, but they can be remodelled on its principles.

One need not be under the impression that many things can be achieved by building a house as per the *Vāstu Śāstra*. For example, Avenue Road in Bangalore is a busy commercial centre. Most of the merchants have their residences on the top of their shops. All houses are crowded and there is no lung space between shops or the houses. They are also not in conformity with *Vāstu* principles. Even the downward gradient or slope of the road is from North to South. With all this there is roaring business going on there as compared to other areas. This reveals that merits of former birth (*pūrva-janma-puṇya*) and luck play their role in the life of man. Adopting astrological Mantric remedies will be helpful in such cases.

In constructing a house or a building, four factors must be taken into account: (1) Location of a well; (2) laying the

* No. 144, 'Nandagokula', 20th Main, I Block, Rajajinagar, Bangalore 560010.

foundation; (3) locating the front door; and (4) *Gṛha-praveśam.* Even if one has strictly gone by the Vāstu considerations in these four phases, construction of the house must be started at an auspicious time, i.e., *Muhūrta.*

The other important points to be taken into consideration are: (1) Making changes as per Vāstu; (2) Tāntric and Māntric guidance; and (3) fixing of mirror or polished granite.

Important aspects to be taken care of at the site of the buildings are: (1) Well or water tank; (2) Corners and compound wall; (3) Location of entrance door and inside doors; and (4) High and low levels of the house.

Muhūrta

All the work must be taken up at an auspicious time. This will help in completing the work without any delay or obstructions. For instance, in the *Rāmāyaṇa,* when Śrī Rāma wanted to instal a Śiva-Liṅga, Hanūmān was asked to fetch one. As Hanūmān did not come in time, Śrī Rāma prepared a *Liṅga* out of the sand and finished the installation ceremony. When Hanūmān came with the *Liṅga,* Śrī Rāma informed him that the installation ceremony was over at the appointed time (*muhūrta*). This highlights the importance of *Muhūrta.*

Location of the Well

The well must be located at the North and East side of the site. There is nothing wrong if another well such as a bore-well is also dug. Wells located in the South-East, South, South-West can be closed without any fear of sin. The remedy for this is to dig a deep well on the Eastern or the Northern side.

Compound Wall

The compound wall should be built on all the four sides of the building. The walls may be of stone slabs or mud; they should be of the same size and height. No side should be vacant. At least a mud mound should be built. The compound walls should be higher, specially in the North or the East. In other directions, they must be even. There should be no growth in the North-East and South-East. If by any chance, it has a growth, it must be rectified. In any direction, if there is growth, we must be prepared to leave space in that direction. It can even be sold.

If there is a pit, it can be rectified by purchasing the land by its side. This extra land can be transferred to any member of the family. The same principle should be followed in the case of the house corners. If there is a compound wall between a factory and the residence, there must a window on the North-East, North and East. If this is not possible, at least an opening should be left in the North-Eastern or Eastern portion of the ceiling. If there are trees on the North and East side of the site, they can be removed after planting new trees on the South and West of the site.

Front Door

The main door of the house should not be in the direction of (1) South-East, (2) North-West, or North side, and (3) South-West or South side. If it is already there, it should be closed, and there is no further option to it. There must be only one front door. There is nothing wrong in closing a door when there are two. There should not be three doors in a row behind the main door inside the house. If there are three such doors, one more door should be fixed, which may be made of aluminium or plywood. The same rule applies to windows also. The main door of the house facing the North, West, and East is important, and auspicious. But recent experience has proved that the main door should be facing the North side between North-East, in the East between the South-East, and in the South or between North-West. In West, North-West is very suitable.

Mirror

The mirror has a special significance in our culture. It has been used from ancient times in temples and at the time of marriages and *Gṛhapraveśam.* Care must be taken to fix the mirror so that the higher points or sections of the building should be reflected in the mirrors. It should not reflect South, South-East or North-West. Fixing mirrors and placing colourful flower pots adds to the beauty of the commercial centres and also strengthens the *Vāstu.* The mirror helps ward off the evil eye (*dṛṣṭi*). It is of no use to fix mirrors everywhere. For example, the Glass House at Lalbagh in Bangalore, has been the meeting place for many political parties and their conferences. The glass house is the plus (+) shape. The result is that the parties which held conferences here are now in shambles or on the verge of disappearing.

If there is a pillar, pole or tree or towers in front of the building and which is conspicuous, it is good to fix a mirror in the house to reflect it. The mirror must be so fixed that as far as possible it would not reflect South-East, North-West and South-West.

Tantra Sādhanā

Fixing the *Śrī-cakra, Hanūmān-cakra* and *Matsya-yantra* help to mitigate the ill effects of *Vāstu-doṣas,* etc. Holy places like the *Śṛṅgerī, Udipī, Śrīśaila* and *Tirupati* have these *cakras* laid in their premises and even today they attract large number of pilgrims.

Mantra Sādhanā

Combination of *Havana, Japa* and prayer helps to rectify the defects of *Vāstu.* The *Vāstu-havana* should be performed before starting a new building to ward off the evil powers. *Sudarśana* and *Gaṇapati Havanas* should be performed for best results.

Vāstu and Remedial Measures

*K.R. Dasa Setty, B.Com.**

Vāstu Śāstra is relevant to prosperity and happiness in residential premises, commercial buildings and industrial undertakings. The directions East, South-East, South, South-West, West, North-West, North, and North-East are governed by the Sun, Venus, Mars, Rāhu, Saturn, Moon, Mercury and Jupiter, respectively. In the light of these two aspects, we shall deal with the main and important points to be observed according to *Vāstu Śāstras* for the construction of residential buildings. The following points themselves make for defect-free dwellings, which act automatically as remedial measures.

1. The *Pūjā* room should be in the North-East. Avoid it in the South-East and South-West. God should be faced in either North or East.
2. The Bath Room should preferably be in the East. The next best is the North.
3. The Kitchen should be located in the South-East corner. The person who cooks should face the East or the South.
4. The Bed Room could be in the South. The master bed-room is to be in the South-West corner. Avoid sleeping with the head in the North.
5. The Dining Room should also be attached to the kitchen. It could be in the West.
6. The Store Room is to be located in the North-West. Avoid it in the South-East.
7. Treasury or the almirah containing cash and jewellery is to be in the Northern wall so as to face

* MIG-39, 6th Cross, K. H. B. Colony, Yelahanka, Gandhinagar, Bangalore 560064.

South so that it can be operated by facing the North ruled by *Kubera*, the Lord of Wealth.

8. The Toilets are to be provided preferably between the South and South-West. Avoid the North-East.
9. The Varandah, Hall and Sit-out could be located in the North or the East.
10. Flooring, or the floor level of the house should be such that water flows towards the North or the East.
11. The *Āyas* of the house are to be fixed considering the houses surrounding it. To quote an example, a building with *Gaja Āya* should not face a building of *Siṁha Āya* as otherwise the former will collapse. In my opinion, this was what exactly happened in the Gangaram Building at S.C. Road, Bangalore.
12. The sump and tank are to be provided in the North-East, North or East.
13. Extend the North-East (deva-mula) by a section of the building diverging.
14. Converge South-East corner and ensure that South-East does not get diverged at any cost.
15. The total number of doors should be of even number.
16. The total number of the windows should not be either three or six or eleven.
17. There should not be any big tree in the front of the main door (simhadvara).
18. The main door is to be fixed at a point one-third the length of the wall.
19. The Śanku-sthapana is to be at an auspicious time. Adherence to *Vāstu-muhūrtams* is a must, since the convention of *Gudāli Pūjā* is not contemplated in the text books.
20. The Staircase may be provided in the Southern or Western side. Avoid it in the North-East.
21. As far as possible, the floor of the constructed building should be a minimum three feet above the ground or road level.
22. A sufficient number of windows is to be provided in the East and the West so as to get sunlight as

the Sun is *Kāraka* for health in Astrology.

23. Do not start construction at corner points. The mid-points between the South and South-East, West and North-West, North and North-East and East and North-East are always safe.
24. A *Tulasī* plant, which is a healthy shrub, grown anywhere in the house is a great remedial measure.
25. Avoid growing thorny plants in the house.
26. Fragrant flower plants growing in the house bring prosperity.
27. Avoid dirty water coming into your house from any direction; and if it comes, it should be cleared by the fresh water of the house in front of which it is flowing.
28. Rain water pipes may be attached to external Northern or Eastern wall so that the water collected at the top of the building can flow towards the East or the North.
29. Grow plants in the East or the North and trees in the West or the South.
30. Avoid providing the guest house in the North-East and South-West. Provide it in the South-East only.
31. The intersection of the boundaries of the houses is called Kuttu, and it should be avoided by worshipping the *Matsya-yantra* in the house.
32. The distance between the South-East and the North-West should not be more than the South-West and the North-East in the plinth area of the building.
33. An overhead tank may be provided in the South or the South-West or the West. Avoid it in the North, North-East and the East.
34. Perform the *Aṣṭa-dig-bandhana* for total prosperity at the house-warming time.

Section III

VĀSTU AND TEMPLE ARCHITECTURE

References to Vāstu in the Scriptures

M.V. Janardana M.A.*

Throughout the centuries, a predominant medium of creative expression in India has been sculpture. Natural calamities, internecine wars, foreign invasions and conquests, including long occupation by alien rulers have disrupted and even destroyed many ancient cultures of the world. The inhabitants of this land have faced such events without loss of identity. This basic continuity of life of maturity of the population following ancient patterns of culture, is clearly demonstrated in the uninterrupted evolution of the art of sculpture in India.

Just as in modern architecture all buildings are being constructed with geometrical and mathematical ground plans, Vāstu is based on mathematical, geomagnetic, philosophical and metaphysical concepts. These concepts are no abstractions, but living forces which become operative in determining the direction of our lives. Branching out of sculpture, the Science of *Vāstu* or *Śilpa* finds numerous references, implicit and explicit in the Vedas, Brāhmaṇas, Upaniṣads and Purāṇas. *Vāstu* is derived from the verb '*vas*' meaning 'to dwell', or place of residence (vide *Nirukta* 10.17). *Vāstoṣpati*, the lord of a house, is a deity in the *Ṛgveda*. It also applies to conveyances, furniture and all constructed structures. The principal Vāstu, however, is the ground on which others rest.

The sacred writings are arranged in four groups: (1) the Vedas; (2) the Upavedas or Supplementary Vedas; (3) the Vedāṅgas or Limbs of the Vedas; and (4) the Upāṅgas or Supplementary Aṅgas. The four Upavedas are: (1) *Āyurveda*,

* 443, 44th cross, I main, 8th Block, Jayanagar, Bangalore-560 070.

or the science of life and medicine, derived from the *Ṛgveda;* (2) *Gandharvaveda*, or the science of music, derived from the *Sāmaveda*; (3) *Dhanurveda*, or military science, derived from the *Yajurveda*; and (4) *Śilpa* or *Sthāpatyaveda*, or the mechanical arts and architecture, derived from the *Atharvaveda*.

The text-book of *Vāstu Śāstra* are records of oral traditions which go back into an undefined past. The *Bṛhat-saṁhitā*, for instance, compiled by Varāhamihira in the middle of the sixth century A.D., is based on the authority of Master Architects Maya, Viśvakarmā, Gārgya and Manu. It is the earliest datable source on Vāstu Śastra.

The *Viśvakarmānvaya-pradīpikā* explains that creation is another name for Śilpa, and the origin of Śilpa or 'form' is *Brahmā*, *Tvaṣṭra* and *Prajāpati* put together, called *Viśvakarmā*. Viśvakarmā is Prajāpati as the universal constructive principle. He is called Viśvakarmā because he created the activity of everything (*Bṛhaddevatā*, 2, 50). The five heads of Viśvakarmā are Sadyojāta, Vāmadeva, Aghora, Tatpuruṣa an Iśāna, representing East (*Ṛgveda*), South (*Yajurveda*), West (*Sāmaveda*), North (*Atharvaveda*) and North-East (*Praṇavaveda*), respectively. The fifth direction North-East arose from the middle of these four heads. While destroying he is called Rudra, while protecting Viṣṇu and while creating Brahmā (*Mulastambha Mahāpurāṇa*).

Vāstu Śāstra belongs to, and is, applied Astrology. Varāhamihira, in his *Bṛhat-saṁhitā* introduces Chapter 52 saying: "Vāstu-jñāna will be explained by me for the pleasure of astronomers and astrologers, as it has been transmitted from Brahmā to our days through an unbroken series of sages." Building is begun under favourable stars. The regents of the planets and the stars have their allocation in the diagram of the temple and their images are carved.

Vāstu Śāstra, in its fullest exposition, belongs to aesthetics. Three prominent schools of philosophy had deep theoretical impact on the evolution of philosophical postulates in Indian aesthetics, viz. *Rasabrahma-veda*, *Nādabrahma-veda* and *Vāstubrahma-veda*.

The Dikpālas or the guardian deities of different quarters

are in important concept in Vāstu Śastra. They are eight in number: Indra, Agni, Yama, Nirṛti, Varuṇa, Vāyu, Kubera and Iśāna, representing East, South-East, South, South-West, West, North-West, North and North-East, respectively. It is interesting to note that with the exception of Kubera and Īśāna, the *Dikpālas* are principal gods of the Vedic pantheon.

We find considerable variation in their names and numbers. In the *Vālmīki Rāmāyaṇa* Indra, Yama, Varuṇa, and Kubera are the guardians of East, South, West and North, respectively. In the *Mahābhārata* there is Indra, Yama, Varuṇa and Agni at one place, and Indra, Yama, Varuṇa and Kubera at another. Hopkins says: "The grouping of Indra, Yama, Varuṇa and Agni seems older than when Kubera is substituted for Agni."

The *Atharvaveda*, however, refers to six regions or *lokas* and their six respective guardians - Agni (South), Indra (East), Varuṇa (West), Soma (North), Viṣṇu (Fixed quarter) and Bṛhaspati (Upward quarter). In the *Kṛṣṇa Yajurveda (Taittirīya Saṁhitā)* the same six regions and their respective regents are mentioned, but Visnu is replaced by Yama.

The *Manusmṛti* explains the eight *lokapālas* thus: Soma (Candra), Agni Arka (Sūrya), Anila (Vāyu), Indra, Viśpati (Kubera), Appati (Varuṇa) and Yama. In this list Sūrya and Soma have been enumerated in place of Nirṛti and Īśāna of the later Purāṇic texts. The *Gobhila Gṛhyasūtra*, while describing the rites connected with building of a house, states that offerings should be made to the regents of ten regions (*diśas*), namely, Indra (East), Vāyu (South-East), Yama (South), Pitṛ (South-West), Varuṇa (West), Mahārāja (North-West), Soma (North), Mahendra (North-East), Vāsuki (Nadir) and Brahmā (Zenith).

The Buddhist texts speak of only four lokapālas: Dhṛtarāṣṭra (East), Vidūdhaka (South), Virūpākṣa (West) and Vaiśravaṇa (North).

The colours that are associated with the directions are red for East, violet for South-East, orange for South, yellow for South-West, white for West, blue for North-West, rose for North, and white for North-East. The space directions impart their specific character and function to movements on all planes of existence. These life currents which are ever at work transform a house into a functional organism.

The *Ṛgveda* postulates only water as the primordial element or matter, from which the other five elements of later philosophy evolve. Varuṇa is the upholder of physical and moral order. By his power of *māyā* he sends forth dawn and makes the Sun (who is also described as his eye) traverse the sky. Varuṇa, with Mitra, is most frequently invoked as the bestower of rain. Dual divinities like Mitrā-Varuṇa and Dyāvā-Prthivī are a special characteristic of the *Ṛgveda*. The release of waters and the breaking forth of dawn or emergence of light are described as simultaneous events originating from the same source (*Ṛg*. 1.164.51). These waters are described as moved upwards by Indra when set free for movement after killing of the demon Vṛtra. Their onward movement is, as described in the Ṛgveda (8.69.11), where seven rivers are said to flow into the jaws of Varuna as into a surging abyss or ocean. The universe is said to have consisted of nothing but undifferentiated waters in the beginning (*Ṛg*. 10.82.6; 129.3). This cosmic circulation of celestial waters is also stated in the *Zend Avesta*, the Greek and Egyptian mythologies. Probably this explains the reason why water should flow from west to east in a house.

The *Vāstusūtra Upaniṣad* is more fundamental than the other known texts. It is a profound study of the principles of origin of the '*how*' and '*why*' of form figuration and of its ultimate necessity and purpose. Dealing exclusively with the composition and layout of sculpture, it contains an esoteric doctrine, in which the production of *śilpa* is considered as a sacrificial act. In sage Pippalāda's conception, the language of *form* is equivalent to the spoken or written word or '*Vāk*' giving expression to a vision of divine truth.

In the *Matsyapurāṇa* (Adhyāya 252), Lord Matsya explains the origin of *Vāstu Puruṣa* to King Vaivasvata Manu. Perspiration trickled from the fore-head while fighting fiercely with the demon Andhaka in course of which the latter was killed. Out of this sweat was born an attendant who began to drink the blood of Andhaka, but was not satisfied. With the object of devouring three regions (*lokas*) this attendant performed penance in honour of Śiva. Highly pleased, Śiva appeared and told him to ask a boon. The devotee asked the boon of eating all the three lokas. Consequently, he brought all the *lokas* under his clutches and fell on the earth with his face downward to devour it. The terrified Brahmā, Devas and Rākṣasas got around and captured him from all sides; the being, thus imprisoned remained there and since then owing to all the Devas remaining there and living around him, came to be recognised as *Vāstu Deva.* Finding himself overpowered by the Devas, he prayed for liberation. The Devas replied: 'You will enjoy the sacrificial offerings of the *Vaiśvadeva* sacrifice, the offerings that will be given in any dwelling house and those of one who will perform sacrifices without the prescribed method.'

Based on this position of Vāstu Deva, the *Vāstu-puruṣa-maṇḍala* is drawn. The shape of this Yantra is a square with 64 or 81 small squares in it. This name consists of three parts, Vāstu, Puruṣa and Maṇḍala. *Vāstu* is the extent of existence in its ordered site, *Puruṣa* the source of existence, and *Maṇḍala* a closed polygon. It can be converted into a triangle, hexagon, octagon or a circle retaining its symbolism. The Vāstu-puruṣa-maṇḍala is the plan of all architectural forms of the Hindus. The square is the essential and perfect form of Indian architecture symbolising perfection beyond life. It houses the movement of the Sun and the course of the Moon.

All the cyclical numbers in Hindu cosmology are essentially based on the astronomical period of the precession of equinoxes. It is said that, they are exact fractions of the number 25920. It is also the number of solar years in the Pythagorean great year. The principal base of cyclical periods in the cosmical order is an astronomical period of the precession of the equinoxes, the duration of which is 25920. The period of the precession of equinoxes multiplied by 100 is the number of years which must be added to 71 times the number of years contained in the four Yugas × 14 (*Viṣṇupurāṇa, Pūrvārdha, Adhyāya* 3), i.e. 4,320,000,000 years, which is equal to one day of Brahmā which is also equal to 71 times a Mahāyuga multiplied by 14. It could be for this reason that the *Vāstu-puruṣa-maṇḍala* is laid out in 64 or 81 squares; either number is submultiple of 25920 which is 64 × 81 × 5.5 is the number of a Samvatsara.

So, on this Vāstu dial of cosmic movement, care must be taken not to interfere with the movements and their ways, for the order of the Universe and the destinies of human lives depend on it. The science of architecture is a part of the science of the luminaries; the time for setting up of a building, its place and direction it has to face are ascertained on this magic diagrams of the *Vāstu-puruṣa-maṇḍala*.

Briefly, the principles of *Vāstu* mainly cover the elevation (depression) of a plot, floor level of a house, number of doors, position of doors and rooms and the weight put by way of furniture and other things. Elevation and more weight in the South or West gives positive results whereas depression in the North or East or North-East is capable of attracting wealth and fame. The water source in a structure is as important as other factors. A well, underground sump or borewell in positions other than North-East, North or East gives disturbing results.

The *Matsyapurāṇa* further says that a house having only two rooms on the West is very auspicious, and that with those on the South is inauspicious. A house having room only on the West and North has fear from the king, and fire is the destroyer of the family. The one that has rooms only on the East and North gives unnatural death to the owner. The one that has fire places built for cooking purposes on the East and West causes death of the owner and widowhood to the womanfolk. North-East is the place for *pūja*. East for bathroom, South-East for kitchen, North for treasure, South for bedroom, West for dining, South-West for godown and North-West for toilet.

Application of Vāstu

An open space in the centre of a house serves the purpose of creating an artificial convection current of air during day and night. The creation of open spaces between the buildings of the same area gives a perennial breeze which can be seen in numerous lanes of Thanjavur.

It is quite interesting to note that the principles of Vāstu can be applied to boundaries of nations. On the study of the physical map of U.S.A., it could be seen that the Rocky mountains (13,000 ft.) in the West or more in altitude than Appalachian mountains (3,000 ft.) in the East, apart from the extension in the North-East, as also the five lakes and St. Lawrence river running out of U.S. from the North-East, gives her the position of the most powerful nation in the world.

With Mt. Blanc (15,771 ft.), Jura mountains, Vosges, and Alps in the East, the position of France has not reached the top. The Napolean Empire had two extensions in the South-East which resulted in the break-up of his empire. The plateau of Brittany, sea-level altitude in the West, North-East cut, North-West and South-East slightly extended leaves France vulnerable for future invasions and wars.

Germany has 'North German plain' in the North and the whole of Southern region is covered with mountains, which helped her to gain power through united Germany.

The principles of *Vāstu Śāstra* are not based on individual theories, but were realized in a penetrating analysis of the deepest mysteries of existence. In the absence of our ability to comprehend the true nature of Vāstu, the alternative is to embark on research of our scriptures. The chief source of complexity and difficulty in understanding is the symbolism adopted in the underlying cosmic pattern which opens up profound visions of the spiritual aspects of the Universe.

It may be concluded that this ancient knowledge of art, the sacred *Vāstu Śāstra*, is not an end in itself, but leads to that supreme spiritual knowledge which results in liberation.

The Vāstu of Temples

*V. Bala Naidu**

The term '*Vastu*', derived from the Sanskrit root (*dhātu*) '*Vas*' means 'dwelling'. The Āgamas are the basis for Indian Vāstu and sculpture. *Kriyāpāda* of each Āgama deals with temple construction and sculpture installation procedure, house construction, *Vāstu-pūjā*, specialities of *Śilpa*, etc. The *Vāstu-lakṣaṇas* are specially discussed in the Āgamas such as the *Kāmikāgama*, *Aṁsumadbhaedā-gama*, *Karṇāgama*, *Suprabhedāgama*, and *Vikhanasāgama*. The *Kāmikāgama* is one of the *Śaivāgams* which divides *Vāstu* into two categories, viz., Site and water. The Site *Vāstu* is further classified into two types, viz., '*Harmyādi Vāstu*' and '*Paryaṅkādi Vāstu*'; the former dealing with permanent structures, while the later dealing with the temporary amenities like tents and other movable structures and furniture. Water *Vāstu* is classified into three types.

Though *Vāstu* is primarily intended for selection of dwelling house sites, it is also applicable for selecting sites for other purposes such as cultivation of lands, gardens, bridges and water tanks.

With reference to the *Kāmikāgama*, the Temple *Vāstu* is classified into sixteen kinds and the *Gṛha Vāstu* into forty-five kinds. Temple *Vāstu* is also classified into '*Nāgara*', '*Vesara*' and '*Draviḍa*'. The main object of Indian sculpture from the ancient age is to establish the relation between man and the material world. Body is temple and soul is God. To signify God's power of creating the body construction, and its survival for the devotee, through *Śilpa Vāstu*, the temples are constructed.

For performing the Yajñas, halls called as *Vaṁśas*, Terraces and Platforms were constructed with bamboos,

* Astrologer, Nannoor, Post Kurnool-2, Andhra Pradesh.

bricks and timber. They were called '*Vedikās*'. For different *Yajñas*, different types of *Vedikās* were available.

The inspection of the ground plan was important, as ground plans were square, circular or semi-circular. The square and circular ground plans were important for religious performances. The square was called '*Sthaṇḍila*' and the circular was called '*Maṇḍala*'. Most of our temples are constructed in the shape of square, rectangle and semi-circular.

The ground plan (*tala-vinyāsa*) of circles was used for offerings to forefathers. Hence the Chief Architect (*sthapati*) gave no importance to these in construction of temples. Besides, the *Kāmikāgama* emphasises that circular (*maṇḍalākṛti*) plan should be rejected. A few temples of Kerala have this plan.

On the authority of the classification in our authentic works, this *Vāstu* can be divided into three types based according to the differences in the construction of Temple (*vimāna*):

1. *Nāgara:* The construction from the bottom to the upper dome of the temple (*vimāna*) in the shape of circular (*maṇḍalākṛti*) was called as Nāgara.
2. *Vesara:* The construction from the bottom to the top in mixed form is called as Vesara kind.
3. *Draviḍa:* The construction from the bottom to the top in the shape of sexagon or octagon was called Draviḍa tradition.

Temples are of two kinds, viz., cave temples and constructed temples. Temples constructed by drilling the caves are called cave temples, and temples constructed on plain and open area are called constructed temples. Constructed temples fall under the three categories of *Nāgara, Vesara* or *Draviḍa.*

Temple construction includes various halls in one complex, such as *Garbhagṛha* and *Antarāla, Mukha-maṇḍapa, Vimāna, Prākāra, Mahādvāra, Dvāramaṇḍapa,* Kitchen, Resting Hall, Car hall, etc., and such temple complexes could be *Eka-Kūṭa, Yugala, Trikūṭa, Catuṣkūṭa,* and *pañca-kūṭa.* Additional buildings or annexures for fine arts, education, music, dance, medical centre, choultries, etc., were also constructed as multi-purpose temple complexes.

The Indian architect was expected by the *Śāstras* to have learnt the occult sciences through *Anuṣṭhāna.* The *Sthapati,* the *Sūtragrāhi,* the *Vārdhakī,* and the *Takṣaka* are four castes and categories under Indian architecture.

Different planes for construction of villages, towns, temples, buildings, etc., are given in the *Śāstras.* The selection of site, testing of soil, selection of direction (*dig-nirṇaya*), Ground Plan, Digging base, *Garbha Vinyāsa* are important. On some occasions *Śānti-homa* and *Bali-vidhāna* are to be performed to lay down the *Pañca-loha* or copper vessel in the ground in the central building or *Mahadvāra,* and it is called *Garbha Vinyāsa.* This is more or less known as *Śilā-nyāsa.* There is a religious ceremony called *Aṅkurārpaṇa* performed before the construction starts. The main object of this ceremony is to facilitate the fruition of the work without obstructions and obstacles. This rite consists of placing different varieties of seeds in sixteen copper vessels in front of Soma and offering them to the concerned deity after germination.

The construction above the base and below the building is called *Adhiṣṭhāna* which must be strong. This is not required for ordinary dwelling houses, but is used in thousand-pillered *Maṇḍapas, Rāja-prāsādas* and *Mahādvāras* of the temples. There are many internal parts and each has got a specific name. These are mentioned in the *Śāstras.* The *Adhiṣṭhanas* are different for different lands of construction.

Garbha-gṛha, Maṇḍapa, the path for circumambulation and surrounding walls are constructed on the *Adhiṣṭhāna.* According to the direction of the *Mūla Vigraha,* i.e. the image of the principal deity, the entrance will be determined either on the Eastern side or the Northern side.

In olden days pillars were erected around the temple. These pillars have different names according to their form and architecture. There are two forms of pillars, viz., ordinary (*sādhāraṇa*) and ornamented (*sālaṅkāra*). Ordinary pillars are divided into nine types and the ornamented ones into twelve types. Pillars too have internal parts and have separate names for each part. Beams are erected on the pillars and on the beams the roof is erected. After the *Garbha-gṛha, Praveṣa* and other *Dvāras* will be constructed. The *Dhvaja-stambha* will be erected before the *Dvara* in front of the *Viśāla Maṇḍapa.*

In *Vāstu,* an auspicious moment with the best *Muhūrta* is selected for each stage of work to be started. Such a *Muhūrta* itself gives a long life to the construction. Starting a work without auspicious *Muhūrta* is 'just like giving treatment to a dead body'. Electional astrology has got its own significance and plays a vital role in deciding the fate of the structure. *Vāstu* must, therefore, be followed in concurrence with electional astrology.

The Śabda-Doṣas in Ārṣeya Vāstu Grantha*

*Sri Ramakavacham Venkateswara Sarma***

Colours of the Soil

The *Samarāṅgaṇa-sūtradhāra*, the *Mānasāra*, the *Aparājitapṛcchā*, the *Muhūrta-mārtaṇḍa*, the *Nirṇaya-sindhu* and the *Dharma-sindhu* are some of the important works on *Vāstu*. They are in Sanskrit. Modern *Vāstu* pundits have not studied the subject in depth. The following example is cited to this end, to enlighten the readers in this article on the errors that have crept into some of the Sanskrit words. E.g., the *Samarāṅgaṇa-sūtradhāra* says :

सिता रक्ता च पीता च कृष्णा चैव क्रमान्मही।
विप्रादीनां हि वर्णानां सर्वेषामथवा हिता॥

(*Sama. Sū.* 8.48)

sitā raktā ca pitā ca kṛṣṇā caiva kramān mahī /
viprādīnāṁ hi varṇānāṁ sarveṣām athavā hita //

'Different colours of the earth are allocated to different classes, i.e., the white to *Brāhmaṇa*, the red to *Kṣatriya*, the yellow to *Vaiśya* and the black to *Śūdra*'.

Herein, the word '*Pīta*' means yellow colour. A number of books quote the word as '*Pīta*' without looking into its meaning. But this is an error. We are familiar with white, red and black coloured land. But nowhere in the world do we see yellow coloured land. This is because the word '*Pita*', somewhere in the past, was mis-spelt, and this continued.

The author of the *Muhurta-marthanda* has clearly said

---

* Translated into English from Telugu by M.N. Subba Rao.

** Door No. 3-353, Vidyalaksmipuram, 4th Cross, Bapatla-522101 (A.P.)

'Kapittha' which means brown colour:

श्वेता रक्त कपीत कृष्ण वसुधाः।

(Muh. Mar, 6.2, p. 83)

śvetā rakta kapīta kṛṣṇa vasudhāḥ /

we find brown colour soil on the banks of the river Yamuna near Delhi. If the sand of the river is dried in the sunlight, it gets a brown colour. White and red coloured sand is not to be found. So the word 'pita' is incorrect, and the reading should be '*kapittha*'. Such mistakes are carried in books due to poor knowledge of Sanskrit. Many so-called *Vāstu* pandits criticised these colours of the soil as absurd. I request all such scholars to correct such incorrect (*aśuddha*) words.

Types of Śaṅku-sthāpana

There are three types of Śaṅku-sthāpana, one each for Deva, Mānava and Rākṣasa. The North-East corner is allotted to Devas (temples); the South-West corner is best for Demons (*rākṣasānāṁ tu nairṛtyam*), although this race is not in existence. But we find some people conducting it in the South-West also in some parts of Andhra Pradesh.

The South-East (*āgneyam*) is allowed for men (human beings) as the best for *Śanku-sthapana* in all *Vāstu* works. Thus, the *Bṛhat-saṁhitā* says:

दक्षिण पूर्व कोणे कृत्वां पूजां शिलां न्यसेत् प्रथमम्।
शेषाः प्रदक्षिणेन स्तम्भाश्चैवं समुत्थाप्याः॥

(*Brh. Sam* 53.112)

dakṣina pūrva koṇe kṛtva pujāṁ śilām nyaset prathamaṁ /
śeṣaḥ pradakṣiṇena stambhāś caivaṁ samutthāpyaḥ //

It means the South-East is first selected for *Saṅku-sthāpana*, in the case of human beings. Kaśyapa has also approved it. Bhaṭṭotpala opines that the North-East is best for *Sthapatis*.

But all people now conduct it in the North-East. It has gained good following. But as per the above śloka, *Śaṅku-*

sthāpana is to be done in the South-East (*dakṣiṇa-pūrva-koṇe*). The classical texts like the *Dharmasindhu*, the *Nirṇayasindhu*, the *Kṛṣṇa-vāstu*, the *Samarāṅgaṇa-sūtradhāra* and the *Bṛhat-saṁhitā* have said that *Saṅkusthāpana* is to be done in the South-East. But in practice, this has been overlooked.

Flooring Levels in Houses

The height of the basement in all directions should be equal. The heights of the room in the buildings should also be equal. The ground in the compound should be higher in the South and the West than in the North and the East. But, this principle is not applicable to the main building on any side. Contrary to this, the *Vāstu* pandits are preaching that the flooring should slope towards North-East in each room of the building.

The study of *Vāstu* texts available in Sanskrit will enlighten the readers the value of the treasure handed down by our ancient Rishis for the better and overall welfare of the society.

Indian Architecture

*Dr. S.R.N. Murthy, Ph.D.**

Introduction

Before the discovery of the Indus Valley Civilisation, i.e., prior to 1930 A.D., there was a belief that the Indians were ignorant of the science of architecture (Seshadri, 1962). However, the town planning, residential house construction and great bath and other structures of the Indus Valley brought to light that the people of this civilisation knew as much of civil engineering as their counterparts in the West like Greeks and Romans. This idea was given a fillip when in 1934 a text in Sanskrit called the *Mānasara* was discovered by Ramaraj who published an article on that work. Later the architectural information of that book was brought out by P.K. Acharya in 1943. This set at rest the erroneous opinion that Indians were ignorant of this science.

Many Sanskrit texts have come to be known to deal with the science of architecture. In Sanskrit the science of architecture and that of sculpture are not separated; and they are dealt with under the common title *Vāstu-Śilpa*. Amongst the numerous texts, mention may be made of the *Sanatkumāra-Vāstu-sāstra*, the *Mayamata*, the *Manuṣyālaya-candrikā*, the *Aṁśubobhini*, the *Vāstu-vidyā*, the *Suprabhedāgama*, the *Bṛhat-saṁhitā*, the *Śilpa-ratnākara*, the *Abhilaṣita-cintāmaṇi*, the *Samarāṅgaṇa-sūtradhāra*, the *Kāśyapa-śilpa*, the *Tantra-samuccaya*, the *Aṁsumad-bhedāgama*, the *Vāstu-ratnāvalī*, the *Kāmikā-gama*, the *Pratimālakṣaṇa*, the *Pratimā-māna-lakṣaṇa*, the *Rūpa-maṇḍana*, the *Vāstu-maṇḍana*, etc.

According to the *Viśvakarma-Vāstuśāstra*, the celestial

* 307-C/10, 18th Main, Vijayanagara, Bangalore-560 040.

architect got the thorough knowledge of this science from Lord Śambhu. The *Aparājitapṛcchā* of Bhuvanadeva (13th century A.D.) speaks of this lore as the gift of the celestial tree (*kalpataru*). Another version of this work of Viśvakarman mentions the succession of teachers from Lord Śambhu as follows: Parāśara, Bṛhadratha and Viśvakarman (Bhat, 1986). According to Venkoba Rao (1959), the science of architecture was revealed by *Brahmā, Viṣṇu* and *Maheśvara* to Indra, Bṛhaspati and Nārada. Further, he mentioned that, according to the *Matsya-purāṇa*, there were eighteen sages who have taught this science and include the names of Bhṛgu, Vasiṣṭha, Viśvakarmā, Yama, Nārada, Anagnacit, Viśālākṣa, Purandara, Brahmā, Kumāra, Nandī, Īśa, Śaunaka, Garga, Vasudeva, Śarad-daśva, Śakra and Bṛhaspati. It is also observed by him (ibid) that from the four facets of Brahmā originated Viśvakarma, Maya, Tvaṣṭr and Manu, who gave birth to Sthapati, Sūtragrāhī, Vardhakī and Takṣaka, respectively. Amongst them the Sthapati is the most important person who should know the Vedas and other sciences; Sūtragrahī is sculptor, Vardhakī is the painter, and Takṣaka is the carpenter.

Vedic Origin of Indian Architecture

Lord of the ground is referred to as Kṣetrapati in the *Ṛgveda*. He is described in the first three *Ṛks* of the Hymn 57 of Maṇḍala 4. The meaning of the Ṛks as translated by Griffith (1986) is given below:

1. We, through the Master of the Field,
   Even as through a friend, obtain
   What nourisheth our kine and steeds.
   In such may he be good to us.
2. As the cow yieldeth milk, pour for us freely,
   Lord of the Field, the water that beareth sweetness,
   Distilling meath, well purified like butter,
   and let the lords of the holy Law be gracious.
3. Sweet be the plants for us, the heavens, the waters,
   and full of sweets for us be air's midregion.
   May the field's Lord for us be full of sweetness,
   and may we follow after him uninjured.

Civil Engineering and Architecture are called Vāstu in Sanskrit, since it is mentioned in the Vedas that the eight Vasus, viz., Agni, Pṛthivi, Anarikṣa, Āditya, Dyaus, Candramā and Nakṣatras are held by the ground. Hence the earth is also called *Vasundharā* (Murthy, 1994-a). The lord of such a ground is addressed as Vāstoṣpati. Vāṣtospati has been addressed by the sages by the three *Ṛks* forming the Hymn 54 of the 7th Maṇḍala of the *Ṛgveda*, as also by the first *Ṛk* of the next Hymn. The English rendering of the *Ṛks* is given below, as per Griffith (ibid):

1. Acknowledge us, O Guardian of the Homestead: bring no disease, and give us happy entrance.
   Whatever we ask of thee, be pleased to grant it, and prosper thou quadrupeds and bipeds.
2. Protector of Home, be our promoter; increase our wealth in kine and steeds, O Indu !
   May we be ever-youthful in thy friendship; be pleased in us as in his sons a father.
3. Through thy dear fellowship that bringeth welfare, may we be victors, Guardian of the Dwelling!
   Protect our happiness in rest and labour.
   Preserve us evermore, Ye Gods, with blessings.

The first *Ṛk* of the next Hymn is:

1. Vāstoṣpate, who killest all disease and wearest every form,
   Be an auspicious Friend to us.

These mantras are being recited even to this day in every civil work specially in the entry of a newly constructed dwelling called *Gṛha-praveśa*. Employment of these *Ṛks* is itself self-evident, requesting the Lord of the Ground and the Guardian of the Homestead for prosperity and happiness.

Origin and Description of Vāstu-puruṣa

According to Bhat (ibid): "There was, it is said, some Being which obstructed the earth and the sky with its body. The gods suddenly caught hold of it and laid it upside down. Whichever limbs were held by different gods and those very gods as their presiding deities. The creator ordained that being to be the House-god of the nature of gods."

Hence, the ground for civil construction is given to be divided into 81 parts by drawing 10 lines from east to west and 10 lines from north to south in which Vāstu-maṇḍala deities are installed. In addition to the above, the deities of the *Sarvatobhadra-maṇḍala* are also established and worshipped duly after performing what are called *Rakṣoghna-śānti* and *Vāstu-homa* before entering the dwelling place. (For the description of the *Vāstu-maṇḍala*-devatās, Bhat [ibid] may be referred to.)

The *Vāstu-puruṣa* is given to sleep during Bhādrapada, Āśvayuja and Kārtika months facing east; in Mārgaśīrṣa, Pauṣya and Māgha months facing southwards; in Phālguna, Caitra and Vaiśākha months facing west; and in Jyeṣṭha, Āṣādha and Śrāvaṇa months facing north; it is advisable to fix doors in those specific directions respecting the months.

It is also observed that a house owner wishing for happiness should guard very carefully Brahmā - the central squares in the *Vāstu-maṇḍala* - for his affliction would harm the owner.

This plan of the *Vāstu-maṇḍala* is applicable to all civil constructions, be it a dwelling house, palace, town, etc. The ground must be levelled for alround prosperity. Easterly raised forebodes loss of wealth and children, and enmity with friends; south raised gives fear to death; west raised indicates loss of wealth; and north raised produces mental affliction.

It is also observed that flow of water must be towards north or east for prosperity. Situation of water sources to the east is given to indicate loss of children; to south-east danger from fire; to south fear or enemies; to south-west poverty; to the north increase of wealth; and to the north-east prosperity of children.

Location of well from the North-Eastern direction to northern direction clockwise is indicative of prosperity, good health, loss of children, death of spouse, death of owner, wealth, trouble from enemies and very little happiness, respectively. A well in the centre of the house forebodes destruction of house and wealth.

Testing of Ground and Rocks

There are several methods reported in various texts on architecture for testing the ground for civil constructions and for employing rocks for the purposes of making idols as per the canons of Indian sculpture. One of the methods of testing the ground used to be to make a pit of suitable dimensions and fill it by the scouped out material. If the material stands excess over the pit, then it indicates prosperity; if it is filled just to the level of the ground it indicates no loss no profit; and if the pit is filled leaving some portion, it indicates losses. This is very clearly suggestive of the porosity of the ground and the density of the material. The denser the material, the ground indicated its strength to hold prosperity and civil construction. It is modern and scientific.

Another method is to put water into such a pit, when the water takes a circular course inside the pit. If it is clockwise it indicates prosperity; otherwise it is negative in effect. This may not stand scientific rationale. But the water circulation of the wind and a wind of clockwise circulation is desirable. Probably, this may suggest removal of smoke, etc., emanating from the building to outer atmosphere since the north-easterly or South-Westerly winds bringing the monsoon rains in the sub-continent have to do much cleansing of the atmosphere surrounding the constructions. This is to be noted by modern architects in designing houses and other buildings.

The testing of rocks is something ingenious. They used to determine the nature of rocks by their acoustics or property of sound vibrations, at the hammer weight. Those rocks which gave bronze sound at the hammer weight are called Male; those which gave brass sound are called Female; and those which did not produce either sound are called Hermophrodite. It was also suggested that male rocks must be employed for sculpting male deities; female rocks for sculpting the female deities; and the hermophrodite for constructing the base, etc.

Highly compact rocks like some dolerites, bronzites, pyroxenites and peridoties as well as lamprofires give male sound; some of these rocks as well as dyka rocks of other igneous rocks produce female sound; most of the rocks produce neither female nor male sound and are hermophrodite. But it is doubtful whether sculptors of yore have selected their material approved as per the canons of Śilpa, since they did not have any knowledge of petrology.

Speaking about acoustics, it is interesting to recall here the compound pillars in some of the temples in South India producing the musical octave at hammer weight. One can see such pillars in the Vijaya Viṭṭhala temples of Hampi, Meenakshi temple, Madurai, Sundareshwarer temple at Tiruchendur and other places. The compound pillars are made of granites and charnockites and of different girth to produce the correct octave.

Speaking about the construction of temples and forts, the architects of yore in the subcontinent were nothing but experts. The plan of the temples, the spring supported water tanks, etc., are simply marvellous. From this point of view, it is easy to construct surface temples. But it is sometimes superb carving temples in the caves as of Ajanta and Ellora. The cave temples have been carved in rocks called basalt which are highly jointed and brittle. It is next to impossible to carve the cave temples with such perfect symmetry. There is nothing comparable to them in the whole world.

The Astrological Basis of Vāstu

Just like any other science originating from the *Vedas*, the science of Vāstu also bases its observations on the science of time, i.e., astrology. Time is the devourer of the Universe and the earth being a representative of the Universe, is no exception. Hence, any civil construction has a life period and it was known to the architects of yore. The life of a civil construction depended upon the *Lagna* of the foundation and the instalment of deity in a temple. Since the material of the temples is obtained from the earth which is subjected to weathering and denundation incessantly, any construction out of the earthly material would be destroyed in the course of time.

For constructing a civil building, be it a dwelling house, a public office, a temple, a fort, a palace, etc., It is suggested to commence the construction work on Wednesday, Thursday or Friday; especially on the third, fifth, seventh, tenth or thirteenth day of the bright fortnight; on the days ruled by the stars Aśvinī, Rohiṇī, Mṛgaśīrṣa, Puṣya, Uttarāphālgunī, Hasta, Citrā, Uttarāṣādhā, Śravaṇa and Uttarābhādrapada; especially in the Vṛṣabha, Siṁha, Kumbha Ascendants. Time may be Meṣa, Karkaṭaka and Tulā also, when it will be midling.

For locating wells and water resources, Monday, Wednesday, Thursday and Friday are recommended identical with Rohiṇī, Puṣya, Maghā, Hasta, Anurādhā, Śravaṇa, Uttarābhādrapada and Revatī. The *Tithis* recommended are Dvitīyā, Tṛtīyā, Pañcamī, Saptami, Daśamī and Trayodaśī. Karkaṭaka, Makara and Mīna with the Moon, it will be a certain source of perennial water. Civil construction may be undertaken during the months of Caitra, Vaiśākha, Śrāvaṇa, Kārtika and Māgha. The solar months Meṣa, Vṛṣabha, Karka, Siṁha, Tulā, Vṛścika are also recommended, excepting *Sūnya Māsa*. The *Lagna* must have the fourth and the eighth houses clear.

The civil constructions, especially bridges, dams, barrages, tanks, palatial buildings, etc., should be undertaken commencing from a favourable *Lagna*. The time of foundation laying is the most important. Depending upon the Lagna being strong in all respects, the construction may last long. If it is weak, then it will get destroyed early. If all the planets are favourable then the construction will go smoothly and get finished in time. If any of the planets are adverse—if the Moon, then there will be hardly any progress; if Mars, then there will be lack of attention from engineering quarters; if Mercury, then the plan may be adverse; if Jupiter, then shortage of wise advice; if Venus, then lack of funds, etc.; and if Saturn, then there will be trouble from labour.

Traditionally much information is present in many

Sanskrit texts on *Vāstu* for construction of dwelling houses and the direction in which a particular kind of room must be located. These facts insist on the happiness and prosperity that accrued by following the traditional methodologies. The latest methods of modern architecture do not yet support such traditional observations. They are trying new methods of construction and study must be done with reference to the changed conditions. In the absence of such information, it is advisable to follow the tradition. That does not mean that no change should be effected at all. If modern architecture takes into consideration the traditional data also, then it would be good. The modern architect should have an eye on the traditional information, astrology and Mantra-śāstra. There is no doubt that modern architecture is much advanced in the field of construction. But it is not sure that such constructions ensure happiness. For example, Varāhamihira (Bhat, 1986) has made observations on the location of doors to dwelling houses. Accordingly, he describes that location of door on the east side following the first eight divisions of total nine divisions as per the Vāstu-maṇḍala indicate danger from wind, birth of daughter, immense wealth, royal favour, extreme wrath, falsehood, cruelty and theft, respectively. From this it can be seen that locating the eastern door in the third and the fourth divisions is advisable, but locating the doors to the corner and entry from a side, etc., planned by modern architects go against the tradition. If they take the above advice and plan a house on the lines suggested by tradition, it would be good to them as well as to society.

Similarly, location of *pūja* room in the north-east, bath room in the east, kitchen in the south-east, bedroom in the South, toilet in the South-West, storeroom in the West, cattle in the North-West and treasury in the North is recommended. One may see the identification of these rooms as per the notation of the *Dikpālas*. That would reinforce and increase prosperity being added up. For whatever reason, if this set-up is disturbed, the head of the family will suffer the effects. Utility of total plinth area to the maximum and giving an attractive or novel look to the house, etc., the most important items of modern architecture, should be superimposed on the traditional lines. This is true of a temple, a palace, a town or a nation.

Even geologically, it is well known that the subcontinent of India which forms a part of the erstwhile Gondwana island along with Africa, Australia, South America and Antartica, some two hundred million years ago, has drifted some 9000 kms., during the above period from its original place to the present place moving at the rate of about 6 cms. per year in the north-eastern direction. This is unique and portends a unique history of India. It may be gathered that even from the earliest times India is enjoying a unique position in world history. Its prosperity, its history, its spiritualism and its Vedic lore, etc., are unique of any land mass in the world. Even to this day it commands respect in the United Nations for many things. The world history surrounds its history and in search of India, the land masses of the third world were rediscovered by European countries. It is said 'rediscovered' since it was already discovered by Indians long back in the human history as per the geography given by the *Sūrya-siddhānta.* Its successive civilisations, its art and architecture, its spiritual and scientific bases, its system of education, etc., are incomparable. This is biggest of all democratic nations in the world even to this day. Such claims as have been made by India are hardly possible for any nation in the world. Should one not describe these prospects to its "North-Easterly" movements from its original place ? (Murthy, 1994b).

A Critic of Erroneous Practices of Vāstu

Although the traditional school of Architecture has laid sound rules to be followed, the people and rulers of various parts in the country throughout history, have taken pride in flouting them as a result of which the nation has paid dearly. It is not known when actually the *Śiva-liṅga* of Prabhāsakṣetra, i.e. *Somanātha*, was installed; but it was destroyed by invasions from abroad. The same fate overtook the *Viśvanātha-liṅga* of Banaras. The present one is noted to have been installed by Rānī Ahalyābāi. Similarly, numerous temples and kingdoms have been installed and destroyed during the course of its long history. It is observed that the temples and deities must be constructed and carved as per the directions of measurement mentioned in the texts. Those temples or buildings, deities, etc., which have been constructed or carved with little regard to the rules are noted to destroy the nation or family (Iyyengaryaha, 1978).

It must be mentioned that marble, steatite, khondalite, sandstone, besalt, etc., are not fit for construction of deities. They may be good for construction of temples. Since the rulers who constructed the temples of these rocks found nearby their capitals, they have used them for carving the deities also out of them, flouting the rules of Śilpa. As a result they have met with destruction. Hence it is always advisable to follow the traditional principles, of course with superimposed modern architecture, for the prosperity of the people and the land.

In this connection it is very essential to impart training in the study of rocks to modern *Sthapatis* and temple architects so that they may select the right rock for right purpose, as per *Śilpa Śāstra.*

Conclusions

The Indian science of architecture and sculpture is as old as the *Ṛgveda.* There are many treatises in Sanskrit in this field. Indian architecture is unique in many respects. It is the best of the arts with relatively permanent basis. It has a long record of observations extending over several thousands of years. It is suggested that the modern science of architecture should take advantage of this science exposed to the branch of geology which deals with rocks, called petrology, for a really scientific method of practising *Vāstu* the *Śilpa.*

REFERENCES

Bhat, R.K. (1986): *Varāhamihira's Bṛhatsaṁhitā*, Motilal Banarsidass, Delhi, pp. 450-499.

Griffith, R.T.H. (1986): *The Hymns of the Ṛg Veda*, Motilal Banarsidass, Delhi, p. 707.

Iyyengaryaha, A.S. & T. (1978): *Indian Temples* (in Kannada), Bangalore, p. 135.

Murthy, S.R.N. (1993): *Glimpses of Hindu Astrology and Some Aspects of Indology*, Sadguru, Delhi, p. 308.

—(1994 a): *The Vedic Theory of the Earth* (submitted to Maharshi Sandipani Rashtriya Veda Vidya Pratishthanam, Ujjain), p. 342.

—(1994 b): *Geological Foundations of Indology*, Kalpataru, Bangalore, p. 91.

Sheshadri, M.: "Bhāratīya Vāstu Śilpa" in Krishna (ed.), *Bharatiya Sanskrit Darshana*, Bangalore (in Kannada), pp. 490-508

Venkoba Rao, B. (1959): *Mysore Deshada Vāstu Shilpa* (in Kannada), Vichara Sahitya, Bangalore, p. 180+18.

Vāstu Principles in the Construction of Theatres

*Dr. B.V. Venkatakrishna**

Theatres, cinema halls and auditoriums are important public buildings in modern commercial society. They provide place for entertainment. The important facets of refined entertainment are literature, fine arts, music, dance and drama, and now, the cinema. This concept of enlightening entertainment and entertainment halls has been studied by ancient sages and prescription for *Vāstu-lakṣaṇa* have been specified.

The construction of buildings is generally covered under the traditional disciplines or *Vāstu Śāstra* and *Śilpa Śāstra*. The tradition records about eighteen schools of Vastu thought attributed to the following sages: Bhṛgu, Atri, Vasiṣṭha, Viśvakarmā, Nārada, Nagnajit, Maya, Viśālākṣa, Purandara, Brahmā, Kumāraswāmī, Nandīśa, Śaunaka, Bharga, Vāsudeva, Aniruddha, Śukra and Bṛhaspati.

The concepts of *Vāstu* are based on the Vedic truth that the whole creation analysed from the aspect of the Five Elements, called the *Pañca Mahābhūtas*, viz., Earth (*pṛthivi*), Water (*āpaḥ*), Fire (*tejas*), Air (*vāyu*), and Space or Ether (*ākāśa*), has an interactive influence on the human beings, whose physical constitution is made up of these same *Pañca Mahābūtas*. The external physical buildings and Nature in the form of land exerts an influence (a natural force) which can be reoriented for the benefit of the individual. It is similar to the harnessing of any other natural energies like the wind energy and solar energy and tidal forces for the benefit of the mankind. The authors of *Vāstu Śāstras* recommend the building plans to suit the

* Director, International Sanskrit Research Academy (Regd. Trust), 627, I-B, Main Road, 7th Block (West), Jayanagar, Bangalore-560 082.

individual using it, for the maximisation of benefit from these natural forces, eternally in operation.

Nāṭya Śāstra is a classical text authored by sage Bharata (2nd cent. B.C.) consolidating the principles of earlier works, right from the Vedic times. In the second and third chapters of the *Nāṭyaśāstra*, Bharata details the *Vāstu* of the entertainment hall (*nāṭyagṛha* or *prekṣāgṛha*), an equivalent for today's theatre, auditorium or cinema hall, offering public entertainment:

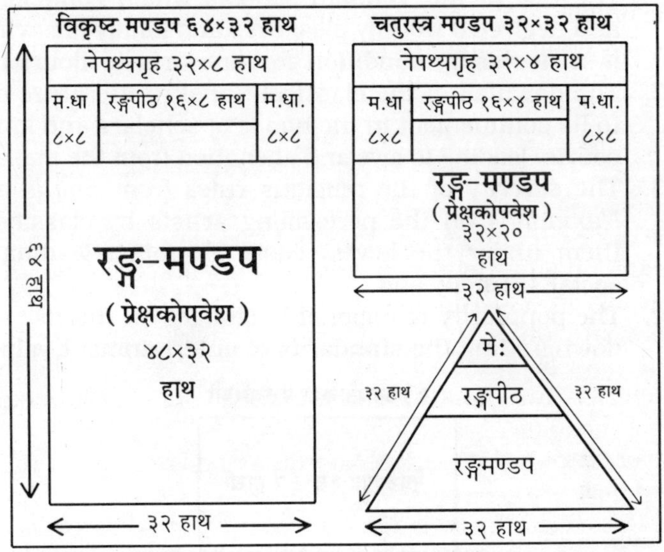

The salient features to be noted from the bulk of about two hundred Sanskrit ślokas in the text are the following:

Sage Bharata, following Viśvakarmā, feels a need to record the *Vāstu* details exclusively for an entertainment hall in contrast to the standard prevalent concept of uniform *Vāstu* rules for all types of constructions. This establishes the need to study the *Vāstu* requirement based on the purpose of the building, in a specialised way. For example, a temple is also a public building, but the purpose is to sustain and support *Dharma* and reduce *Kāma*. In contrast, an entertainment hall is a public building wherein the purpose is to cater to emotional appetite and provide an opportunity for healthy entertainment.

As early as the 13th century A.D., the *Vāstu* tradition for entertainment halls seem to have been lost. Probably the permanent structure type of entertainment halls were merged into the palace construction or temple construction. As a matter of historical fact and interest, this period of Circa 13th century A.D. is characterised by the following:

1. The rise of the *Vedānta* schools which condemned and neglected worldly pleasures and family life, which is a necessary condition for fine arts to flourish;
2. The dawnfall of the classical Sanskrit literature due to its confinement in the house of scholars and kings' courts, leading to awe and alienation from the masses;
3. The severity of the religious rules from *Smṛtis* and *Nibandhas* on the performing artists by classifying them under the lowest caste grouping, leading to social turmoil; and
4. The popularity of regional languages on the rise and downgrading the standards of entertainment values.

(२) आयताकार मत्तवारणी

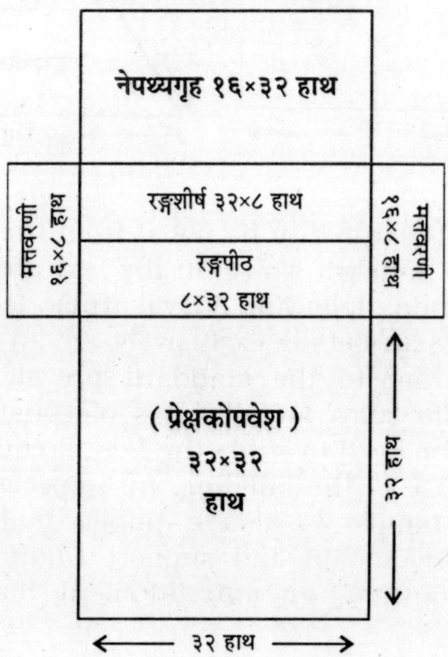

The entertainment hall is a place where people of different age groups, sex, temperament and disposition sit together and watch the performance. They open up totally to the presentation in the most receptive way. The time for which they sit together in the hall is a short duration (relatively). This short duration of staying together, yet not inter-acting, but open to the same influence, is a unique feature which normally does not happen in other places or other activities. The experience of the act of entertainment has a long influence on the mind of the spectator audience in the shortest duration in a subtle, yet irresistible, way. This influence is technically called '*Kāntā-sammita upadeśa*' – similar to the persuasive advice of the beloved, and it moulds the behaviour, character, personality, actions, traits, value standards, culture and language usage, etiquette and behavioural patterns of individuals as well as of society. The *Vāstu* of the entertainment hall, therefore, should be so powerful as to promote healthy development of these aspects and deter negative aspects.

The *Vāstu* of the entertainment hall should be so selected that it brings healthy entertainment to the mind and not cause excitement only to lead one to an evil path.

According to the traditional concepts, the theatre, technically called the *Nāṭyaraṅga*, and the act of entertainment (*nāṭya-prayoga*) are closely comparable to the Vedic sacrifice. The sage Bharata calls Nāṭya Śāstra as the Fifth Veda (*pañcama-veda*), which has been extracted from the four Vedas; the act of entertainment (*nāṭya*) is called a sacrifice (*yajña*). The divinity is infused into every act of entertainment. The goals of life (*puruṣārtha*) are integrated into the act of entertainment hall. Thus, the removal of vulgarity and downfall on the path of entertainment are arrested. The deterrent on production and performance of vulgar entertainment in public to cater to the baser needs of the audience are thus introduced in the section of *Vāstu*. The responses of the inner soul and sensitivity of the mind for nobler aspects of life are points of consideration here. Imagine your own experience and inner feelings if you were to see an obscene movie in a temple complex! This is the influence attributable to *Vāstu* clearly.

अभिनवगुप्त के अनुसार
मत्तवारणी की दो स्थितियां

(१) समचतुरस्त्र मत्तवारणी

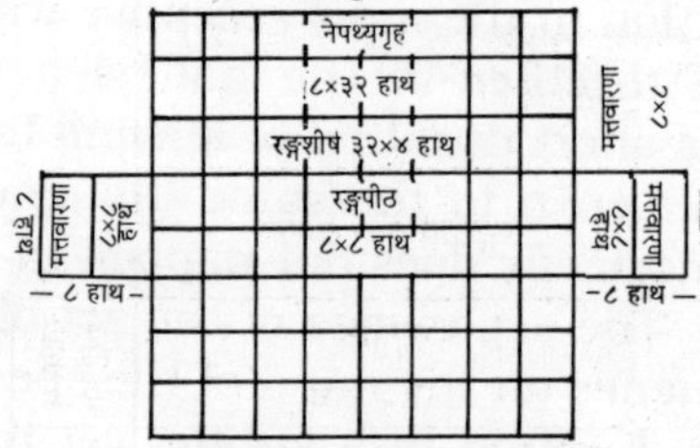

'अष्ट हस्त विस्तीरा समचतुरस्त्रामत्तवारणीभवति'

(२) आयताकार मत्तवारणी

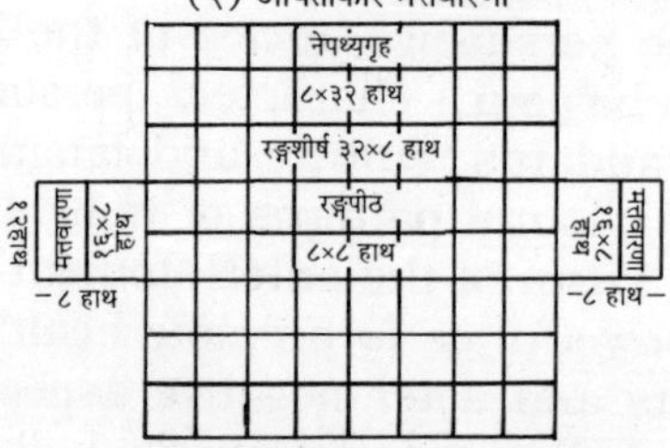

आयामस्तु प्रमाणमितियेवर्दान्त तेषांमते दैर्घ्यदिष्ट-हस्ता
विस्ताराच्छोडशाहस्ताइस्येवविकृष्टतामत्तवारण्या भवति

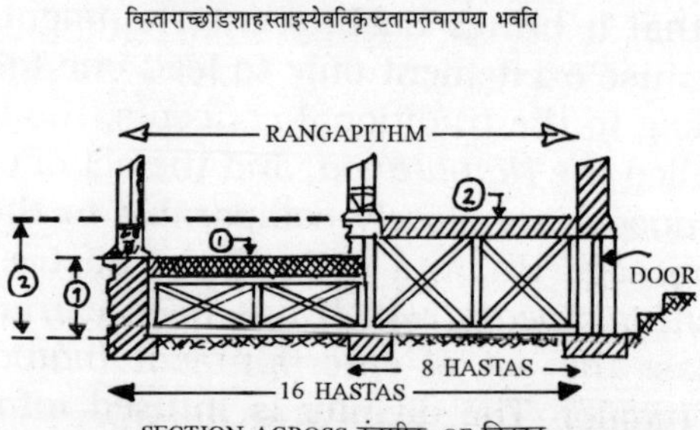

SECTION ACROSS रङ्गपीठ OF विकृष्ट

(१) समचतुरस्र मत्तवारणी

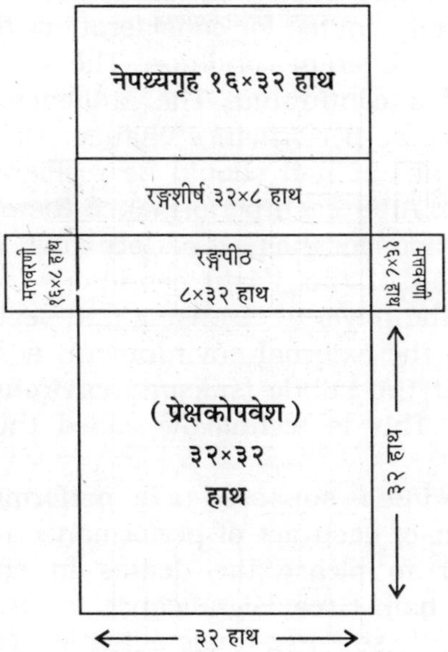

रङ्गशीर्ष मे षड्दारुक की प्रथम स्थिति

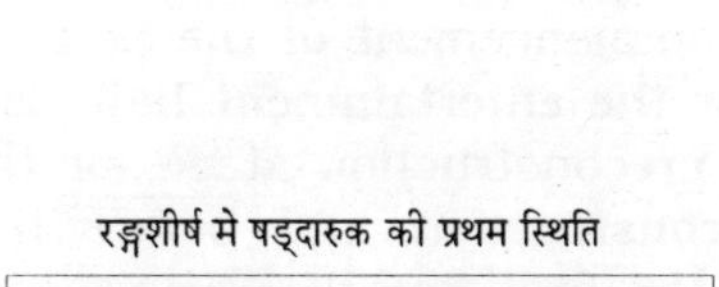

रङ्गशीर्ष में षडदारुक की द्वितीय स्थिति

रङ्गशीर्ष में षड्दारुक की तृतीय स्थिति

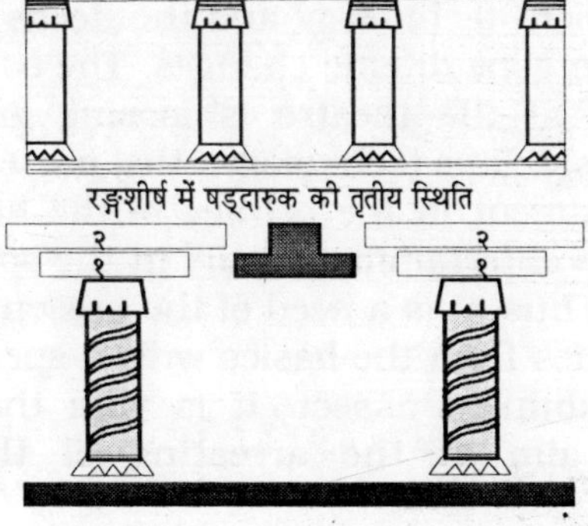

Unlike places like a house, temple and business centre wherein one primary activity in relation to a set of people can be reasonably limited for consideration, the entertainment hall has a different condition. The situation here is dynamic. It is a continuum. The audience change; the performers and the performance change. Thus, the *Vāstu* of the entertainment hall should be resilient enough for this dynamism. After each performance there is a need to reset the conditions for the next performance. (Shall we call this the upkeep of the *Vāstu* conditions and power of *Vāstu!*) While the physical cleansing and seating arrangements refer to the external environment, a different procedure to reset the subtle (*sukṣma*) environment is also recommended. This is technically called the *Nāndī*, the prelude.

This act of *Nāndī* is supposed to be performed before the commencement of each act of performance for entertainment in order to please the deities in charge of the entertainment hall. Great significance is attached to the performance of these *Pūrva-raṅga* activities, i.e., acts prior to the actual commencement of the performance.

The *Vāstu* for the entertainment halls is considered in two parts: the preconstruction stage for the auditorium, and the post-construction and before the use of the auditorium for the first time.

One can make a study of the religious performances prescribed for the *Natyagṛha* and the *Gṛha-vāstu* as a matter of importance and notice the subtle differences like the three days' stay, the sacrifice, the bali, etc.

As times have changed the constructional technology, the entertainment technology and the needs of the society also have undergone drastic changes. The concept of mass entertainment at the theatre is loosing ground on the onslaught of satellite technology; the present concept is mass entertainment in the privacy of the house. But the function of the entertainment halls in the society also has not changed. Thus, it is a need of the present hour to take up *Vāstu* studies from the basics with a specific reference to the entertainment aspect. It is vital that this study should also aim at the arresting of the trends of entertainment degenerating into cheap excitement instead of enlightenment and education. This calls for a dedicated research type of study, afresh, as the present *Vāstu* practitioners seem to extend the *Gṛha-Vāstu* concepts beyond the purview of its limits, not giving due importance to the purpose aspect of *Vāstu*. The other dimension of this is that in house-*Vāstu*, specific considerations for the entertainment hall also should be considered appropriately keeping the present needs in mind. In closing, I wish to mention that other traditional disciplines of *Arthaśāstra* and *Kāmaśāstra* make references to the planning of such entertainment halls for masses (as a part of the town planning) and the planning of the palace for a king. The study of the existing palaces and historical entertainment halls will yield valuable clues for the tradition of *Vāstu* prevalent in ancient India.

Vāstu Śāstra and Ancient Temples (With Special Reference to Temples in Karnataka)

*M.N. Prabhakar**

The etymology of the word '*Vāstu*' is as follows:

वसन्ति प्राणिनोऽत्रेति वास्तुपदव्युत्पत्तिः।
vasanti prāṇino'treti vāstupadavyutpattiḥ /

This is explained in the *Mayamata* in two stages:

अमर्त्याश्चैव मर्त्याश्च यत्र यत्र वसन्ति हि तद् वस्त्विति मतम्।
amartyāś caiva martyāś ca yatra yatra vasanti hi tad vastv iti matam /

'The place where the immortals and mortals live is called *Vāstu* (वास्तु), i.e., the dwelling site'; and

प्रासादादीनि वास्तूनि वस्तुत्वाद् वस्तुसंश्रयात् ।
prāsādādīni vāstūni vastutvād vastusaṁśrayāt /

'The dwelling is the structure proper erected above the dwelling site, hence called *Vāstu* (वास्तु).'

Thus, the word '*Vāstu*' includes both the dwelling and the dwelling site.

The word '*Śilpa*' is defined as follows:

'शील् समाधौ' इति धातोः मनस्समाधानकारकं वस्तुजातमिति।
'śil samādhau' iti dhātoḥ manassamādhānakārakaṁ vastujātam iti /

* Deputy Manager, State Bank of Mysore, Fort Area, K.R. Road, Bangalore.

Prāsāda, pratimā, ārāma, gṛha, vāpī, etc., and their construction are included under *Śilpa Śāstra,* according to ancient seers:

प्रासादप्रतिमारामगृहवाप्यादिसंस्कृतिः।
कथिता यत्र तच्छिल्प शास्त्रमुक्तं महर्षिभिः॥
prāsādapratimārāmagṛhavāpyādisaṁskṛtiḥ /
kathitā yatra tac chilpaśāstram uktaṁ maharṣibhiḥ //

Prāsāda and its construction is dealt with in architecture, and *Pratimā* is the study of iconography. The word '*Śilpa*' is often used synonymously with sculptural studies, but it has a different meaning altogether. *Śāstra* and *Śilpa* are the two faces of the same coin; the former represents theory and the latter refers to the practice or technique. This is evident in Bharata's *Nāṭyaśāstra*:

सर्वशास्त्रार्थसम्पन्नं सर्वशिल्पप्रवर्तकम्।
नाट्याख्यं पञ्चमं वेदं सेतिहासं करोम्यहम्॥
sarvaśāstrārthasampannaṁ sarvaśilpapravartakam /
nāṭyākhyaṁ pañcamaṁ vedaṁ setihāsaṁ karomy-aham //

Temple studies generally include both architecture and sculpture. An inscription of *Kamalanārāyaṇa Basadi* at Degave refers to *Prāsāda-lakṣaṇa* and *Pratimā-lakṣaṇa.* These two were probably popular texts during the 11th and the 12th centuries A.D. in Karnataka.

Though *Vāstu* means all types of constructions, including palaces, public buildings, halls, tanks, etc., the majority of surviving structures of ancient days are temples. Hence *Vāstu-śilpa* generally means the study of temple architectures. '*Devālaya Vāstu*' is the appropriate word to indicate temple and its architecture. It partly includes sculpture as iconographic details also form part of temple construction.

Study of temple architecture began as early as in 1828 A.D. First it was by a native scholar Ramzaz who served the British Government as a native judge in Bangalore. His work, *An Essay on the Architecture of the*

Hindus, was posthumously published in the year 1937 A.D. His approach to the subject was with the help of *Vāstu* texts. He has explained the methodology adopted by him. He had to collect the texts, read, collate and comprehend the terms and phraseology of contemporary architectural science. He had to collaborate with the existing edifices. He took the assistance of artists and philologists. His final task was to interpret the result in the scientific and technical language of the West. James Fergusson was the next scholar who made a comprehensive approach towards the architecture of India. He neither used the *Vāstu* texts nor visited the temples in person. According to him, chisels of the sculptors are more to be twisted than the pens of the scholars. The assistance he received in understanding the texts was not encouraging. Stella Kramritch attempted on the 'Hindu Temple' based on the available *Vāstu* texts. Though it is a massive work on the subject, she failed to create a new vision for fresher studies.

A systematic study of temples essentially include origin and evolution of temple structures, differentiation of traditions and styles, ornamentation and its archaic types, etc. Any hypothetical study without clearcut vision in these aspects will certainly be incomplete.

The majority of *Vāstu* texts are often sectarian in their presentation dubbed with theological aspects. Study of one or two texts will not yield expected result at a stretch. A comprehensive look observing essential characteristic features from various texts may pave the way for a systematic study. This paper is an attempt in that direction, selecting some primary aspects with relevant references picked from Karnataka.

Man is seen living under the rock shelters and in caves, when traced back to the down of civilization or even to the much earlier period. It fulfilled the basic necessity of shelter. When he started believing the existence of God, he often housed his favourite gods and goddesses in the same cave structures. Thus, cave temples came into existence.

Cave temples are of two types: natural and manmade.

Pañca Pāṇḍava Liṅgas at Candravalli near Chitradurga are rock sheltered. Gavi Gaṅgādhareśvara temple at Sivagange near Tamkar is under a huge rock with door frame and pillared *Maṇḍapa* structure added during Hoysala times. Hiḍambeśvara, Phālguneśvara, Sampige Siddheśvara were under rock shelters earlier. Temple constructions were added later on. The *Badami* caves were made are dated to sixth century A.D., according to the inscriptional evidence. *Vāstu* texts have no reference to cave structures, but they speak about independent structures.

"*Prapā*" is the simplest, elementary, independent structure, according to *Vāstu* texts, which fulfils the basic necessity of shelter. The Kāmikāgama identifies it as follows: आच्छादितं प्रपा नाम प्रस्तरं चात्र मण्डप: *(Ācchāditaṁ prapā nāma prastaraṁ cātra maṇḍapaḥ)*. *Prapā* is that which has its top covered. The etymology of the word indicates the protection or shelter it provides. 'पा रक्षणे' *(Pā rakṣaṇe)*. The word is also defined as "प्रपिबन्त्यस्यां प्रपा" *(Prapibanty asyāṁ prapā)*. It refers to the place which provides water for drinking. It is often noticed in Kannada inscriptions. It is used synonymously with the word *Aravaṭṭige*, a roadside shelter which provides rest for short period and water for drinking. The word *Aravaṭṭige* is derived from the Sanskrit word *Ārdrapaṭṭikā*. The word *Prapā* appears together with the word *'Pānīyaśālikā'* in the *Nāmaliṅgānuśāsana*: प्रपा पानीयशालिका *(Prapā pānīyaśālikā)*. M.M. Ganapati Sastry adds in his notes "प्रपा द्वयर्थ: पानीयशालायाम्" *(Prapā dvyarthaḥ pānīyaśālāyām)*, thereby indicating the next stage of *Prapā* as *Pānīyaśāla*. The structure of *Prapā* is described in the *Mānasāra* as:

अधिष्ठानं विना कुर्याज्जन्मादि प्रस्तरान्तकम्।
अथवा पादवंशं च संयुक्तं तत् प्रपाङ्गकम्॥
adhiṣṭhānaṁ vinā kuryāj janmādi prastarāntakam /
athavā pādavaṁśaṁ ca saṁyuktaṁ tat prapāṅgakam//

Prapā is also known as *Prapāṅga*. It is without *Adhiṣṭhāna*. It is raised above the foundation. The topmost member of the foundation is *Homa*. *Khātapada* or

Homastambhas are pegged in the *Homa* structure. These pillars may be wooden or of bamboo with thatched coconut leaves stretched to cover the top. The whole structure may be made out of stone. Thus the description available is about the structure that provides shelter. Some scholars are of the opinion that the word *Prapā* used to mean Aravaṭṭige or *Ārdrapaṭṭikā* is a later concept.

Northern school of *Vāstu* texts describe *Catuṣka,* which shows closer affinity to *Prapā. Catuṣka* is four pillared: चतुष्कं च चतु:स्तंभै: (*Catuṣkaṁ ca catuḥstambhaiḥ*). It may be an independent structure also. It stands in between *Prapā* and *Maṇḍapa. Catuṣka* gained importance when it occupied central portion in structures, especially *Sabhā,* which will be described later. *Catuṣka* may be opened or closed. When closed it is covered by *Bhitti* on all the sides. The *Maṇḍapa* structure that is seen in *Puṣkariṇī* in *Mahākūṭa,* the *Nandi Maṇḍapa* in *Jyotirliṅga* group of temples at Aihole are to be identified as *Catuṣka.* Though these structures are generally called *Maṇḍapas,* they are *Catuṣkas,* the early phase in the development of structures; the *Prastara* above the pillars is not fully evolved.

Maṇḍapa is next to *Catuṣka.* The *Mayamata* defines it as: मण्डं सुभूषणं तं पातीति मण्डपमिष्यते (*Maṇḍaṁ subhūṣaṇaṁ taṁ pātīti maṇḍapam iṣyate*). *Maṇḍapa* is that which protects the decoration. While describing *Maṇḍapa* the basic aspect of *Vāstu,* i.e. providing shelter or protection to living beings is lost as it protects decoration. The structure of *Maṇḍapa* is known as *Trivarga. Adhiṣṭhāna, Pada* and *Prastara* are the three elevational parts noticed:

पंक्तित्रयसमायुक्तं कलास्तम्भसमन्वितम्।
अधिष्ठानादि मञ्चाख्यं वर्गत्रयसमन्वितम्॥
paṅktitrayasamāyuktaṁ kalāstambhasamanvitam/
adhiṣṭhānādi mañcākhyaṁ vargatrayasamanvitam //

This explanation of the text is supported by the fact that *Rauravāgama* lays emphasis upon the decorated aspect of the *Maṇḍapa,* i.e. *Kalāstambha.* Hence the role of pillars is known as the main feature of the *Maṇḍapa* structure. Protection of decorative aspect means, protection of decorative pillars of the *Maṇḍapa*.

The growth and development of *Maṇḍapa* structure, further, is in two directions, vertical and horizontal. The same is known as *Ūrdhva-krama* and *Tiryak-krama*, respectively. In the *Ūrdhvakrama*, *Caturvarga* structure is known as *Lupākāra*, *Pañcavarga* is *Sabhā* and *Ṣaḍvarga* is *Vimāna*. The details regarding ancient *Lupā* and *Sabhā* structures are irretrievably lost and presently available features are also scattered. By virtue of the textual explanation *Lupā* is identified as *Caturvarga*. The *Ajitāgama* explains *Sabhā* as *Pañcavarga*, but the description is totally lost.

Adhiṣṭhāna, *Pada*, *Śikhara* and *Stūpī* are the four elevational parts of *Lupā* structure. The *Kaśyapaśilpa*, while explaining *Ekabhūmi-vimāna* describes *Sarvakāmika* variety with *Caturvarga*. It is peculiarly included instead of *Ṣaḍvarga* form:

उत्तुङ्गे सप्तभागे तु व्योमांशं धरातलम्।
पक्षांशं पादतुङ्गं तु शिखरोच्चं गुणांशकम्।
स्तूप्युत्सेधं तथैकांशमेतत् स्यात् सर्वकामिकम्॥

uttuṅge saptabhāge tu vyomāṁśaṁ dharātalam /
pakṣāṁśaṁ pādatuṅgaṁ tu śikharoccaṁ guṇāṁśakam/
stūpyutsedhaṁ tathaikāṁśam etat syāt sarvakāmikam //

Lupā temples have sloppy roof which is the *Śikhara* portion. They are found in western coastal area. Such temples with modern terminology are built even today in Kerala region. The *Śikhara* portion is mostly made of wooden structure.

Sabhā is known as *Pañcavarga* structure according to southern texts wherein the description is not available. Northern texts like the *Aparājita-pṛcchā* and the *Samarāṅgaṇa-sūtradhāra*, however, have descriptions of *Sabhā*. Before the temples took a definite shape, public buildings were utilised to house gods and goddesses, and *Sabhā* is one such structure which is evident from Ladhkhan structure of Aihole. This temple has stood as a landmark in Karnataka in the origin and development of temple structure.

The word *Sabhā* may be traced to the Vedic days. It refers to a body of learned, who assisted in local administration: सभा च मा समितिश्चावतां प्रजापतेर्दुहितरौ संविधाने (*Sabhā ca mā samitiś cāvatāṁ prajāpater duhitarau saṁvidhāne*). *Sabhā* and *Samiti* are symbolically represented as daughters of Prajāpati, according to the *Atharvaveda* (7.12.1). The word *Sabhā* is derived as follows: सम्यक् भातीति सभा (*Samyak bhātīti sabhā*). 'भा' means 'to shine', and *Sabhā* refers to the shining body. The *Pāraskara Gṛhyasūtra* explains it as सह धर्मेण सद्भिर्वा भातीति सभा (*Saha dharmeṇa sadbhirvā bhātīti sabhā*). Maintenance of *Dharma* was the main role of *Sabhā*. The word that was used earlier to mean body of elders and learned was later on applied to the place where they used to assemble to discuss. Thus, the place, building or structure came to be known as *Sabhā*. These elders and learned scholars were called as *Mahājanas* according to the *Samarāṅgaṇasūtradhāra*. It links *Mahājanas* with *Sabhā*: छन्नं भवेन्महाजनस्य स्थानं सभा या कथिता शाला (*Channaṁ bhavenmahājanasya sthānaṁ sabhā yā kathitā śālā*). Two inscriptions found in the temple of Ladhkhan at Aihole mention Āryapura 500, a group of selected learneds to whom donations are made according to inscriptions. These *Āryapura* 500 are believed to be *Mahājanas* of Aihole. These inscriptions are assigned to the 8th century A.D.

The structure of *Sabha* as explained in the *Aparājitapṛcchā* is as follows:

चतुरस्रीकृते क्षेत्रे द्विरष्टपदभाजिते।
मध्यमपदचतुष्केण चतुष्कोऽलिन्द शेषतः॥
नन्दा नाम समाख्याता सर्वकामफलप्रदा।
चतुष्के भद्रविस्तारा एको भागश्च निर्गमः॥

caturasrīkṛte kṣetre dviraṣṭapadabhājite /
madhyamapadacatuṣkeṇa catuṣko'linda śeṣataḥ //
nandā nāma samākhyātā sarvakāmaphalapradā /
catuṣke bhadravistārā eko bhāgaś ca nirgamaḥ //

Catuṣka occupies the central portion of *Sabhā*. It is surrounded by *Alinda*. It will have a *Nirgama* entrance on one side.

Ladhkhan temple is a larger structure with four massive pillars in the middle to form a *Catuṣka*. It is surrounded by *Alinda* in two stages. The pillars of outer *Alinda* are smaller than those of the inner *Alinda*. The sloppy roof extends over the *Alinda* structure. The outer pillars are inter-connected by *Bhitti-pālaka* or *Jālandra*. *Kuḍya-stambhas* are seen at the corner. *Mukhamaṇḍapa* with *Kakṣāsana* is seen in front which provides entrance through *Sopāna* or steps.

Vimāna is known as *Ṣaḍvarga* structure and the southern texts describe the temples as Ṣaḍvarga Devālaya. The *Samūrtārcanādhikaraṇa* explains the same, thus:

विमानानां च सर्वेषां सामान्यमिदमुच्यते।
अधिष्ठान पादवर्गः प्रस्तरग्रीवकादपि।
शिखरं स्तूपिका चेति षड्वर्गः परिकीर्तितः॥

vimānānāṁ ca sarveṣāṁ sāmānyam idam ucyate / adhiṣṭhānaṁ pādavargaḥ prastaragrīvakād api / sikharaṁ stūpikā ceti ṣaḍvargaḥ parikīrtitaḥ //

The word '*Vimāna*' is applied to mean *Śikhara* and above portion of the temple by some scholars. However, it is evident from the above that it refers to the structure from bottom to top in *Ṣaḍvarga* structures.

The southern texts usually refer to *Garbhagṛha* as *Vimāna*, whereas the northern texts identify them as a *Prāsāda*. Several scholars name them as southern *Vimāna* and northern *Prāsāda*, respectively. *Vimāna* is pyramidical and *Prāsāda* is curvilinear in outline. The *Ṣaḍvargas* of the *Vimāna* are *Adhiṣṭhāna*, *Pāda*, *Prastara*, *Kaṇṭha*, *Śikhara* and *Stūpi*. A simple *Vimāna* structure with *Adhiṣṭhāna*, *Bhitti*, *Prastara*, *Kaṇṭha* and *Śikhara* is seen beside Ravalphadi cave at Aihole. It is in a very crude form. The date of the structure is uncertain. However, *Ṣaḍvarga* forms excluding *Stūpi* may be traced from this very simple structure.

Ṣaḍvarga Vimāna is further developed into *Dvitala* and *Tritala Vimāna* adding *Pāda* and *Prastara* for each *Tala* or *Bhūmi*. The *Mānasāra* restricts the number of *Bhūmis* to twelve: एकभूमिविमानादि रविभूम्यवसानकम् (*Ekabhūmivimānādi ravibhūmyavasānakam*). The *Kāmikāgama* and the *Kāśyapaśilpa* extend them upto sixteen: एकादि षोडशान्त भूमीनां क्रम उच्यते (*Ekādi ṣoḍaṣāntaṁ bhūmīnāṁ krama ucyate*). The *Kāmikāgama* explains another *Aṣṭavarga* structure with *Masūraka, Jaṅghā, Kapota, Śikhara, Kaṇṭha* (Galā), *Āmalasāra, Kumbha* and *Śūla* as its elevational parts:

मूलं मसूरकं जङ्घा कपोतं शिखरं गलम्।
ऊर्ध्वं चामलसारेणाष्टवर्गः कुम्भशूलयुक् ॥
mūlaṁ masūrakaṁ jaṅghā kapotaṁ śikharaṁ galam /
ūrdhvaṁ cāmalasāreṇāṣṭavargaḥ kumbhaśulayuk //

Aṣṭavarga described above are of a northern structure, i.e., a curvilinear *Śikhara*. The *Kāmikāgama*, though a text of the southern school, has given the details of the northern structure. It may be inferred from this that the text was compiled when the northern school was still in its infant stage, and had not developed its other styles or variants. There are several curvilinear *Śikhara* models at Aihole, *Mahākūṭa* and *Pattadakal*. Tarabasappanagudi, Huccappayyuna Malla, Aihole, *Saṅgameśvara, Pāpanātha* and Kashi *Viśveśvara* temples at Pattadakal are important curvilinear *Śikhara* forms in Karnataka. The earliest representative of this model is *Paraśurāmeśvara* temple at Bhuvaneshvar. Based on the location, it was known as *Kaliṅga* style. Temples of Karnataka succeed this structure and hence are known to belong to *Kaliṅga* style with regional variations.

Kolalu inscription of Ballary district mentions four different temple styles: *Nāgara, Drāviḍa, Vesara* and *Kaliṅga*. The inscription is assigned to the 12th century A.D. on the basis of paleographic evidence. These styles existed during the reign of Badami *Cālukyas*. *Kaliṅga* style has already been noticed.

The other three styles belong to southern school represented by several structures during the same period of Badami Cālukyas. Mahakūṭeśvara and Mallikārjuna temples at Mahākūṭa belong to Drāviḍa style with hexogonal

Śikhara. Virūpākṣa and *Vijayeśvara* temples of Pattadakal have square *Śikhara*, hence called *Nāgara* style. *Mallikārjuna* temple of Pattadakal is a unique representative of Vesara style with circular *Śikhara*. These structures mark a stage in the study of temples, where they have attained a definite shape in *Ūrdhvakrama*.

Development of structures in horizontal direction or *Tiryakkrama* has not moved in a straight line and hence its assumptions are from different angles, unlike formation of *Ṣaḍvarga* in *Ūrdhvakrama*. These explanations and hypothetical pictures presented, though based on textual knowledge, still requires sanction from *Vāstu-śāstras* for the order in which they have been described.

To begin with, the four types of *Maṇḍapa* structures that are added to *Garbha Gṛha*, one by one, is explained:

मुखमण्डपमादौ तु प्रतिमामण्डपं तथा।
स्नापानार्थं तृतीयं तु नृत्यार्थं च चतुष्टयम्॥
mukhamaṇḍapamādau tu pratimāmaṇḍapaṁ tathā /
snāpanārthaṁ tṛtīyaṁ tu nṛtyārthaṁ ca catuṣṭayam //

The first annexed structure is *Mukhamaṇḍapa*; it is also known as *Antarāla* or *Ardhamaṇḍapa*, when it is surrounded by further structures:

कारयेदन्तरालं वा मध्ये मण्डपसद्मनोः।
kārayed antaralaṁ vā madhye maṇḍapasadmanoḥ /

Next is *Pratimā-maṇḍapa*; it is also named as *Navaraṅga* or *Navakhaṇḍa*. It is usually with nine *Aṅgaṇas* and sixteen pillars:

नवाङ्गैः नवरङ्ग नाट्यार्थं नृत्यमण्डपम् ।
navaṅgaiḥ navaraṅgaṁ nātyarthaṁ nṛtyamaṇḍapam /

Navaraṅga will have a raised platform in the middle and side-*Aṅgaṇas* are often utilised to house *Parivāra-devatās* and hence called *Pratimāmaṇḍapa*.

Though the *Kāśyapaśilpa* speaks of *Snapana-maṇḍapa*, it is conspicuously absent in several temples. Hence *Navaraṅga* is immediately followed *Nāṭya-maṇḍapa* or *Nāṭyaśālā*. *Navaraṅga* and *Nāṭyaśālā* will have entrance from east, adding *Mukhamaṇḍapa* structure to it.

Mukhamaṇḍapas are sometimes added to its North and South portions also depending upon size of the temple. These are the common features of *Tiryakkrama*.

Now, the growth and developmental aspects may briefly be analysed step by step under the following captions: *Garbhagṛha, Ekālinda, Alinda / Ekaśāla,* and *Dviśāla*.

(a) *Garbhagṛha: Garbhagṛha* itself fulfils the purpose of a temple. The annexures are only supplementary in nature and their presence is not out of necessity. The temple may be without annexures also. The *Padmasaṁhitā* explains the temple structure as one built like a chariot: आरभेत स्थपतिभिस्साकं रथकृदालयम् (*Ārabheta sthapatibhis sākaṁ rathakṛdālayam*). *Ratha* consists of a single cell which represents *Garbhagṛha* to house the sacred idol, i.e., Carabera, surmounted by lofty *Śikhara* like structure. A simple curvilinear structure situated in front of Hucchappayya Matha at Aihole is another example. A *catuṣka* with the top covered when used for the purpose of a temple serves as *Garbhagṛha;* this structure is known as '*Dhruva*' when no annexures are added to it.

(b) *Ekālinda:* The structure that was noticed earlier beside Ravalphade cave at Aihole had *Garbhagṛha* with four pillared porch or Mukhamaṇḍapa. There is also another flat-roofed sanctuary with an adjoining four-pillared porch in the same location. Scholars have identified similar structures from the Gupta period. These are known as Ekālinda-racanā. The porch or *Mukhamaṇḍapa* represents *Ekālinda*. Similar structures are also seen at *Mahākūṭa* with curvilinear *Śikhara*. *Saṅgameśvara* temple structure is with a *Garbhagṛha* and a porch. The porch is provided with Kakṣāsana. The *Mānasollāsa* has described four types of *Ekālinda-racanā* of which *Purvālinda* is of common occurrence:

ध्रुवं हीनमलिन्देन पूर्वालिन्दं तु धान्यकम् ।
जयं स्याद्दक्षिणालिन्दं पश्चालिन्दं खरं भवेत् ।
दुर्मुखं चोत्तरालिन्दमेकालिन्दं चतुर्गृहम् ॥

dhruvaṁ hīnam alindena pūrvālindam tu dhānyakam /
jayaṁ syād dakṣiṇālindaṁ paścālindaṁ kharaṁ bhavet /
durmukhaṁ cottarālindam ekālindaṁ caturgṛham //

(c) *Alinda/Ekaśāla:* When *Alinda* is situated on all the four sides it is known as 'Vijaya': सर्वतोऽलिन्द संयुक्तं विजयं गेहमुत्तमम् (*Sarvato'lindasaṁyuktaṁ vijayaṁ geham uttman*). Such a temple structure is a rare occurrence. However, presence of *Alinda* on the four sides leads to formation of *Parikrama* or *Paribhrama*. *Devakoṣṭhas* are also seen in this space: अलिन्देन परिक्षिप्ता ससीमा देवकोष्ठकम् (*Alindena parikṣiptā sasīmā devakoṣṭhakaṁ*). Ekaśāla consists of a *Catuṣka* in the middle portion surrounded by *Alinda* and a *Mukhamaṇḍapa* in front. This is almost a *Sabhā* structure. *Sabhā* is a general term technically adopted by *Vāstu* to mean specific public place. *Ekaśāla* structure when adopted to a temple, the central *Catuṣka* is covered by *Bhitti* and a door-frame fixed in the east. *Alinda* is also covered by *Bhitti* or *Jālaka* on the three sides, adding *Catuṣka* to form *Mukhamaṇḍapa* in the east. *Mukhamaṇḍapa* is also provided with *Bhitti* or *Kakṣāsana*.

(d) *Dviśāla:* In *Dviśāla* structures two *Ekaśālas* are added one in front and the other on the rear side. The rear side *Catuṣka* will be a closed structure with *Garbhagṛha* shifted to this portion. The central *Catuṣka* remains with *Alinda* to form *Navaraṅga*. The front *Catuṣka* will be the usual entrance to the temple. Temple number 9 at Aihole is a typical *Dviśāla* structure from the groundplan itself.

There are several other temple structures which are evolved from *Sabhā* or *Śālā* structures. One such example is *Gaudaragude* at Aihole. This has been developed by reduction of *Alinda* space sidewards as well as in the back portion:

पुरतः पृष्ठतः पार्श्वे यदि वालिन्दवर्जिता।
गृहे न शस्यते शाला देवागारे तु शस्यते॥
purataḥ pṛṣṭhataḥ pārśve yadi vālindavarjitā /
gṛhe na śasyate śālā devāgāre tu śasyate //

Study of ancient temples may otherwise be grouped in three phases, viz., origin and development of structures, differentiation of traditions and styles, and ornamentation. These phases may be broadly marked periodwise also. The first phase ends in the middle of Badami Calukyan period; the second phase stands upto the beginning of Hoysala period; and the last phase stays with the Vijayanagar period. An accurate chronological micro-treatment is very difficult as often builders repeat features which are no longer current in the chain of evolution.

This is a broader perception developed from the study of *Vāstu Śāstras* in respect of the development of temple structure.

Basics of Temple Interiors

*Ganapathi Kadirappa**

In the modern world of today, knowledge of Science and *Nāstika ·āda* is increasing rapidly. At the same time, the construction of temples, religious associations, *Pīṭhas* or centres of spiritual teachings, and of astrology are also growing, as modern science can provide man only with physical comfort and not spiritual happiness. More and more people are getting interested in the scriptures and philosophy as they are struggling for the achievement of spiritual happiness and peace.

Is *Vāstu Śāstra* necessary for the construction of Temples? I have studied the matter deeply and found the following points. There is a close relationship between the planers and idols according to ancient Hindu tradition. Planet (*graha*) means that which receives. Idol (*vigraha*) means that which transmits power that has been received from *Graha*. According to Hindu Astrology, the nine planets rule the eight directions. It is proved that each idol, which receives power from its concerned planet radiates only the concerned directional power. The combined power of the idol in the eight directions is called *Akhilāṇḍeswarī* or *Ādi-parā-śakti*.

The shape of the *Ādi-parā-śakti* is that of an elliptical atom or *dīrghāṇḍa-vṛtta*. The shape of each idol, as ruler of a particular direction, is that of one sub-atom. The rectangle and square in geometry have an important place in *Vāstu Śāstra*. The atom-shaped ellipse can be inscribed in a rectangle. So the rectangle is the form of *Aṣṭa-padma* or Octagonal lotus, and the sign of the power of eight directions. The square is the form of sub-atom, in the

* Kotaburuju Village, Via., Peapully, Dhone Taluq-51822. Kurnool Dt., Andhra Pradesh.

Octagonal lotus, or *aṣṭa-dala-padma* and it is the sign of power of one direction. As per the above theory, it is proved that the house-site (*gṛha-āyāma*) which is the shape of the complete Octagonal lotus and the sign of an atom, should be in the form of a rectangle. The temple site (*devālaya-āyāma*) which is the shape of only a petal of the Octagon and the sign of only a sub-atom should be in the form of a square. Site area or *Āyāma* means the house-site or temple-site which is correctly marked as per the mariner's compass. Both the sanctum sanctorum of the temple, and the Maṇḍapa constructed before it, should be in the shape of squares. Then only does the temple completely radiate the sub-atom power of that direction.

I shall discuss about the area of a temple to be constructed anywhere. The average height of a man is six feet. So the sanctum sanctorum should be in the shape of a square, inner length and breadth of which is six feet. The width of the wall of the sanctum sanctorum must be two feet each only, and it should be the same on all the four sides. When the width of the wall is two feet the outer measurements of the sanctum sanctorum would be 10 x 10 feet. Wherever a temple is constructed, the construction of a *Maṇḍapa* before the sanctum sanctorum is a must. If not so constructed, we are not following the temple architecture.

Now let us discuss about the correct inside measurements of a *Maṇḍapa*. The sun's rays fall for a period of six hours on each directional wall of any building. The sanctum sanctorum that we construct faces towards one direction only. If a direction or a side of a square is divided into four equal parts, only the middle two equal parts face the main direction. The other one-fourth equal parts on the either side become non-directional points. In the light of the above rules, the inner length and breadth of the *Maṇḍapa* should be twice the outer length and breadth of the sanctum sanctorum. For example, if the outer side of the sanctum sanctorum is 10 feet, the inner side of the *Maṇḍapa* should be 20 feet.

From the mid-point of the face side of the sanctum sanctorum extend 10 feet on either side to make in the inner side of the *Maṇḍapa*. Then the sanctum sanctorum faces the middle direction in the complete temple direction. The whole temple, i.e. the sanctum sanctorum and the Maṇḍapa, should be constructed in the correct direction using magnetic compass. If the temple is constructed exactly as per the above measurements, the Sun's rays fall for six hours only in the *Maṇḍapa*.

To understand this formula scientifically, let us take an example. *Śrī Vīrāñjaṇeya Swāmī Temple* is constructed in the southern direction. Make a small circular hole in the middle of the roof of the *Maṇḍapa*. You can observe the Sun's rays falling in the *Maṇḍapa* for six hours from 9-00 a.m. to 3-00 p.m. only on the day, when the Sun rises at 6 a.m. and sets at 6 p.m. This is not possible when the temple is not constructed in the correct direction. If the temple is constructed in the correct direction you can observe that on the above day the Sun's rays come through the hole an fall at the foot of the Western wall in the *Maṇḍapa* exactly at 9-00 a.m. Gradually it moves and reaches the South-West corner point, the South or Middle point, the South-East corner point of the sanctum sanctorum and the foot of the East wall of the *Maṇḍapa* exactly at 10.30 a.m.; 12-00 noon; 1.30 p.m. and 3-00 p.m., respectively. Exactly at 12-00 noon all the rays fall only in the *Maṇḍapa* of the temple.

The idol of 6 feet height should be installed in the middle of the sanctun sanctorum. If the height of the idol is less, the pedestal should be raised sufficiently to obtain this height. The *Dhvaja Stambha* should be perpendicular and directly opposite the idol. The base of the idol and the *Dhvaja* should be of equal height. At the same height as the middle point between the eyebrows of the idol, there should be carved on the *Dhvaja* three vertical marks or the middle point between the eyebrows of a bowing man. A line making an angle of 22.5° with the normal sight line of the idol should cut exactly the top of the *Dhvaja*. Thus, the height of *Dhvaja* is fixed. A hole should be made in the roof of the *Maṇḍapa* where the line of the above angle touches the roof. The middle point between the eyebrows of the idol, the hole in the roof and the top of the *Dhvaja* should be in the same line. The above angel line when extended should reach the top of the *Kalaśa* the *Gali-Gopuram*. Thus, the *Gali-Gopuram* should be constructed at a convenient distance. As the earth axis makes an angle of 22½° with the Sun, the small hole, the top of the *Dhvaja* and the top of the *Gali-Gopuram* should be in a line making an angle of 22½° with the normal sight line of the idol for the correct powerful radiation of the directional power.

The idol of God enjoys sixteen phases completely when

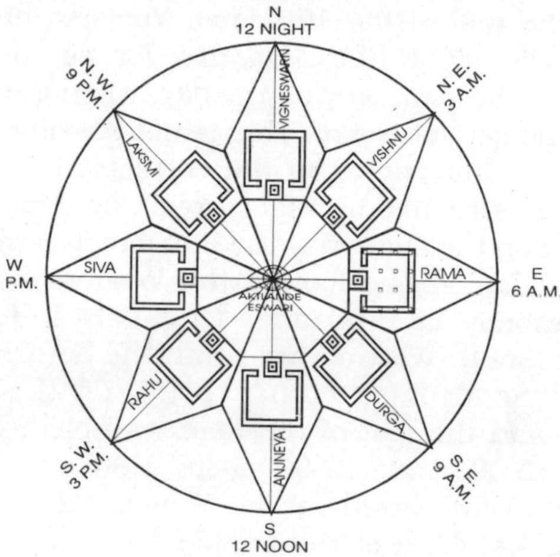

the temple is constructed in the right direction. So the idols should be installed exactly towards the middle point of the concerned direction. Even if the idol is installed to the left side (ascending direction) of the mid-point of the concerned direction, nothing happens. But is the idol is installed to the right side of the mid-point (descending direction) of the concerned direction, the installation is completely useless and the idol has no power at all. In the former situation the Sun's directional power reaches the middle point, between the eye-brows of the idol, which relates its power on the *Prāsādam*. In the latter situation (in the descending direction) even if the Sun's directional power reaches the mid-point between the eye-brows of the idol, it is of no use as the idol does not radiate its power on the Prasadam. So all the houses and temples should be constructed in the correct direction by using the magnetic compass.

The architects complete 50% of the construction of the temples as detailed above. The remaining 50% of the work should be completed by the astrologers, by fixing the auspicious time for laying the foundation for the construction of the temple and for the installation of the idol. If the auspicious time is not correctly calculated, the construction faces many obstacles. The donors of the temple face financial troubles and accidents. The devotees do not visit the temple regularly. God in the temple does not get the daily worshipping. In course of time, the temple will be abandoned. So, houses and temples are properly constructed only be efficient and learned astrologers and architects.

You may, please, refer to the standard sketch given herein. One form of God (or Goddess) is the lord of each

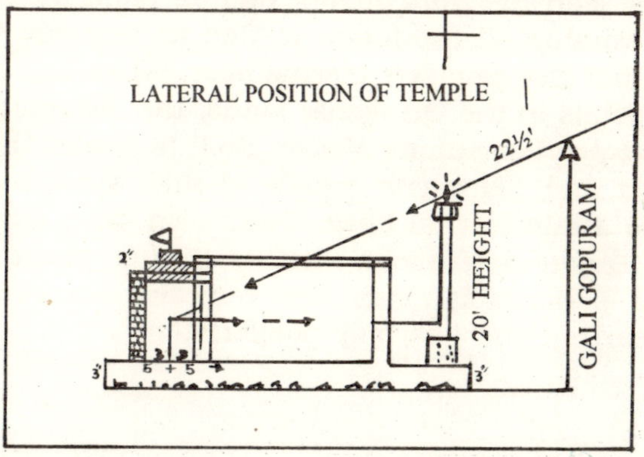

petal in the Octagonal Lotus. It is proved that the measurements of the sanctum sanctorum and *Maṇḍapam* should be as stated above. As shown in the sketch all of the temple should be constructed in one place. In this temple complex, people of *Vaiṣṇava* sect worship their favourable form of God: (1) Śrī Rāma; (2) Śrī Veṅkaṭācalapati and Sun, the lords of Eastern direction;

(3) Śrī Vīrāñjaneya and Aṅgāraka, the lords of the Southern direction; (4) Śrī Mahālakṣmī and the Moon, the rulers of the North-West direction; (5) Śeṣaśayana, (6) Śrīmannārāyaṇa; and (7) Śrī Kṛṣṇa Paramātmā and Ketu and Jupiter, the lords of the North-Eastern direction. These deities are worshipped in the fixed timings and the people receive *Prasādam* and thus evoke the blessings of the concerned lords. People worship (8) Kanaka Durgā and Venus, rulers of the South-East direction; (9) Five-headed Black Cobra called *Karkoṭaka* and *Rāhu*, lords of the South-West direction; (10) Lord *Śiva* and Saturn, lords of the Western direction; (11) Lord Vināyaka, Vīrabhadra and Mercury, lords of Northern direction, through '*Dāna, Dharma, Abhiṣeka* and *Homa*', and thus please the evil effects of these lords. Thus, finally, they evoke the blessings of '*Ādi Parāśakti*' and enjoy earthly and heavenly comforts. Contrary to this the Śaiva sect people do the reverse of the above act and enjoy earthly and heavenly comforts. *Hari* and *Hara* are one and the same. A *Rāja Yogi* has to worship all the forms of God as any one form of God cannot give complete eternal bliss. When he conquers all the petals in the Octagonal Lotus, the *Jīva* enters into *Akhilāṇḍeśvarī* or attains *Mokṣa*. So it is proved that both *Vaiṣṇava* and *Śaiva* cult people should worship all the forms to attain eternal bliss. One's own birth Ascendant (*Janma Lagna*) determines whether *Śiva* or *Viṣṇu* is suitable for performing *pūjas* and remedies accordingly to attain earthly and heavenly comforts.

Some Research Notes on Vāstu

Bramha Ganapathi Kadirappa

Arvana in Vāstu

Vāstu Śāstra is part and parcel of ancient astrological science. It is not a separate branch. The construction of a village (village plan) or the house must, therefore, be studied in relation to Astrology or in relation to the movements of the Sun and other planets.

Some modern-day scholars have come out with strange theories saying that *Grāma-arvana* (village plan) or *Gṛha-arvana* need not be observed. But this is not supported by *Vāstu* principles. Ancient books of *Vāstu* are authentic. The theories enunciated in them are true and applicable for all times. The validity of theories can be verified with actual experience. Stray isolated cases of experience should not form the basis of new theories.

Grāma-arvana (Plan of Village)

Mark a road latitudinally from the East to the West (*rāja-vīthi*) and mark another road from the North to the South longitudinally (*uparājavīthi*). The roads intersect each other and we get four parts of the village. The four parts are traditionally allotted to the four *Varṇaṣ—Brāhmaṇa, Kśatriya, Vaiśya* and *Sūdra*. The *Brāhmaṇa* division is allotted to *Ācāryas*, artists and men of intellectual calling. The *Kśatriya* division is meant for political leaders, government employees and such other men in general. In the *Vaiśya* division live the merchants, industrialists and other business men. The *Sūdra* division is meant for unskilled labourers in agriculture and industry. If men construct their houses in their allotted divisions, according to their professions, they can live in harmony and peace. This *Grāma Arvanam* is scientific and conducive to the well-being and development of all classes of men. But some scholars have missed the significance of *Grāma Arvana* and their ignorance affirm that no purpose is served by *Grāma Arvana.*

Gṛha-arvana

Business shops should be arranged in the *Rąja-vīthī.* Some shops will face each other; some facing South and other facing North. Residential streets should run parallel to the *Upa-rāja-vīthī,* from North to South, with a distance of 132 feet. Half of this length, i.e., upto 66 feet, will have house plots, which will face East and other houses will face West. The width of these plots will be 33 feet. Thus, the streets will stretch from the North to the South and the houses will face the East and the West in every street.

The direction of the house of person is decided by the first letter of his name. There are 12 *Rāśis,* out of which Meṣa, Karkaṭaka, Siṁha, Vṛscika, Dhanus and Mīna are opposite to the other six *Rāśis,* viz., Tulā, Makara, Kumbha, Vṛsabha, Mithuna and Kanyą. The lords of the first six Rāśis are Mars, Moon, Sun and Jupiter belong to *Guru Varga* and they are friendly to one another. They ąre lords of the 1st, 5th and 9th houses. Similarly, the lords of the other *Rāśis* are Venus, Saturn and Mercury. These three planets are friendly to one another. They are known as Sani Varga planets not only in the Zodiac but also in the *Aṣta-dik Cakra.*

The Sun is the lord of the East. So those who are born in Guru Varga should live in houses facing East (*pūrva-siṁha-dvāra*).

Saturn is the lord of the West. Those who are born in *Śani Varga Lagna* should live in houses facing West (*paścima-siṁha-dvāra*).

I feel the East facing and the West facing doors are alone called *Siṁha-dvāras,* because they are in the path of Sun. The North facing and the South facing doors are not Siṁha-dvaras. These are only side doors (*pārśva-dvāra*).

The lord of the East direction is the Sun, and the lord of the South is Mars. These two planets are friends. So

East *Siṁha-dvāra* house must have the side door on South and also some open place in the South. The lord of the West is Saturn and the lord of North is Mercury. These two planets are friends. So the West *Siṁha-dvara* house must have the side door in the North and also some open space.

For business shops, those who are born in *Guru Varga Lagnas* should have South facing shops and those born in *Śani Varga Lagnas* should have North facing shops. If they do not follow this arrangement, and if their shops are in contrary directions, the good planetary results will be reduced by 50%, the bad effects will be aggravated by about 50%. This is the reason why our ancient scholars added *Gṛha-arvana* to *Vāstu* texts.

Gṛha-āyāma

Multiply the length of the house with the width and divide it by 8 (length × width ÷ 8). If the remainder is 1 = *Dhvajāyāma*, 3 = *Siṁhāyāma*, 5 = *Vṛṣabhāyāma*, 7 = *Gajāyāma*; and other remainders 2, 4, 6, 8 are not good. Thus, with the other multiplications and divisions we get *Dhana, Ṛṇa, Vara, Tithi, Nakṣatra, Karaṇa, Yoga* and *Āyus*, called *Nava Varga*.

Modern *Vāstu pundits*, with no knowledge of astrology, say that there is no need for *Nava Varga, Ekādaśa Varga* and *Ṣodaśa Varga*, because the *Āya-sādhana* measures are different like Yard (36"), *Hasta* (24") and foot (12"), and these measures changed with a change of kings and rulers. So, they argue that this theory is not acceptable.

I reject both the traditional and modern methods of Āyāma. I have introduced a new method according to the Solar path. We construct an East facing house on *Bhumadhya Rekhā* with the height of 12 feet from the floor, because the average height of man is 6 feet; so we take double this measure and correct the house with compass for the correct direction. We must construct the roof at the height of 12 feet and put a hole in the centre of the roof. From the hole (*gavākṣa*) of the roof, the solar rays enter the house on September 22nd, when the Sun will be on the *Bhūmadhya Rekhā* on that day at 12 O'clock (according to L.M.T.). We must observe where the solar rays fall and drive a plug or nail where the solar rays fall on the floor.

On June 22nd when the Sun will be on the *Karkaṭaka Rekhā*, on that day at 12 O' clock (L.M.T.) observe where the solar rays fall, and drive a plug on the floor where the solar rays fall. If we measure the space between the two plugs we get 10 feet distance from the South wall. On December 22nd the Sun will be on the *Makara Rekhā*. On that day at 12 O' clock (L.M.T.) observe where the solar rays fall and drive a plug in. We measure from the plug on September 22nd and we get 10 feet of space at the North wall; we get 20 feet distance from the June 22nd plug to December 22nd plug. According to this the Sun moves 20 feet wide in a 12 feet height house in a year. This is the width of the East or West facing the house. Also, the Sun moves double (40 feet) this distance from East to West. So the solar rays enter and touch the whole house within a year. This is called *Krānti-vṛttam* or *Dikcakram* and jointly called *Āyapramāṇam*.

(1) According to the height of the house or the height of the hole (*gavākṣa*) the length and width also increases or decreases. For example, take a theatre whose internal height is 30 feet. So its length will be 12 : 40 : : 30 : x. 12x = 1200 and (x) = length = 1200 ÷ 12 = 100 feet. The width will be 12 : 20 : : 30 : x. 12x = 600 and (x) = width = 600 ÷ 12 = 50 feet. So if the height is 30 feet, length and width will be 100 and 50 feet.

(2) According to the distance from the *Bhūmadhya Rekhā*, the length of the solar rays will decrease or increase. In the house measuring 40 x 20 x 12 on the latitude of 15° 30' N, on the date of December 22nd, the solar rays fall in the house at 10 feet distance from the centre of the house and touch the edge of the North wall. On June 22nd when the Sun is on the *Karkaṭaka Rekhā*, the solar rays fall in the house only 3'-5" distance from the centre of the house and do not touch the South wall. Like this, for every North latitude the length of the solar rays decreases.

We should construct equal length house when all the houses will be of equal length and there will be no

Vīthīsūla. There is no problem of authorised measures. There is no problem of short and long house. There is no bend of *Vīthī* or street.

Deciding Simhadvāra and Bad Results of North-East (Aiśānya) and North-West (Vāyavya) Dvaras

(1) The Entrance door (*Dvāra*) will be exactly in the centre point of the temple's width. (2) The door will be on the right side (*ucca*) from the centre point for the houses (facing East and West). (3) The door will be on the left of the centre point to the cattle sheds. By so placing these doors, the *Doṣa* of walking on the *Vāstu-puruṣa-nābhi* (*Śrī-cakra Sthāpana* place) will be eliminated. For the cattle shed the *Doṣa* of walking under Vennugadi (under the beam) will be eliminated.

Modern *Vāstu pundits* do not seem to know what the length of the direction and length of the "*Mūla*" or corner mean or imply. They put the door in the North-East (*aiśānya*) for the East facing house. But this door will give bad results as it is to the left of the East facing house and is not Ucca Sthana. The South-East (*āgneya*) will be in excess on the right side. The Agneya is the female or *Strī-yajamānya* direction. So there will be the ladies of the house that will dominate. Female issues will be born. If the door is in the North-East, the space said to be for God will be spoiled. So the divine power will be reduced. Male issues will not be born.

If the door be in the South-West for a West facing house, men's domination will increase. Ladies will be neglected. Doors in the *Mūla* (North-East or South-West) are also not desirable. The main door of the house is like the mouth of the man. Suppose the mouth is placed on the cheek, instead of in the front centre of the face. Will it not cause much inconvenience? The toilet and bathrooms must not be in the North-East or the South-East for the East facing house. Toilet and bathrooms must not be in the South-West or North-West for the West facing house. They give ill-health and unhappy life. The excretory (*mala-mūtra*) organs are in the back portion or the lower portion of our body. Similarly, the toilets and bathrooms must be in the South-West (i.e. in *Rāhu*'s place and the place of poison) for a East facing house and in the North-East (i.e. *Ketu*'s place and place of poison) for a West facing house. The drainage must be at the back portion of every house.

Dvāra-saṁkhyā-nirṇaya (Deciding the Number of Doors)

There are three kinds of doors: (1) East facing door and West facing door; these two doors are called *Siṁhadvāras*. (2) South facing door and North facing door; these two doors are called side doors or *Pārśvadvāras*. (3) Internal doors which connect one room to another in the house; these are called *Sandhidvāras*.

The doors which face the same direction or are in the same line (though there may be some hundred doors) must be considered as only one door. If there is a door to the East and another door to the South they are called two doors. So, *Sari-saṁkhyā-dvāra* means two directional doors, but not even number like 2, 4, 6, 8, 10.